Karl Merz

Music and Culture

Comprising a Number of Lectures and Essays

Karl Merz

Music and Culture
Comprising a Number of Lectures and Essays

ISBN/EAN: 9783744750912

Printed in Europe, USA, Canada, Australia, Japan

Cover: Foto ©Thomas Meinert / pixelio.de

More available books at **www.hansebooks.com**

MUSIC AND CULTURE.

COMPRISING A

NUMBER OF LECTURES AND ESSAYS.

BY

KARL MERZ, Mus. D.

PHILADELPHIA:
THEODORE PRESSER,
1712 Chestnut Street.

SANDUSKY, O: CHARLES H. MERZ, M.D.

PREFACE.

The history of this volume is told in the Introduction. It was the privilege of the editor on many occasions to participate in the labors of the author, and it has been his aim to follow out his ideas as closely as possible. He has closely followed the manuscript, and has spared no pains to render the work worthy of its author and its subject.

It is hoped, therefore, that this book, which possesses a filial as well as an individual interest for him, may prove an acceptable memento of its loved author.

CHARLES H. MERZ, M. D.

Sandusky, O.

INTRODUCTION.

In handing to the reading world the heirloom left by a departed friend, the editor will surely be pardoned for endeavoring to inspire the reader with a little of the love and deference which the departed one received at all hands while he lived.

Not as an opinion, but as a fact, which many of the best musicians of this country will cheerfully corroborate, it may be said that—

Karl Merz was one of the most learned, scholarly musicians of this country;

Karl Merz was as a teacher almost unparalleled in inspiring his pupils with the beauty and *dignity* of his art;

Karl Merz was one of the most lovable of men, idolized by his pupils and friends, uncommonly well respected as a citizen, and highly esteemed for his multiform and profound knowledge.

The essays collected here were written at different times, originally for the purpose of being read to the students of Wooster University, where he occupied the chair of the music department. A few of them appeared in some of our few serious music papers and attracted such general attention, that their author was frequently urged to publish them in book form; but his retiring, modest disposition shrank from publicity, and so he always refused the publication, adding: "My wife and children may publish them when I am dead!" Alas! that now, all too soon, the time for publication had to come; that the feeling of gratification at the sight of the book has to mingle with the tears of sorrow and regret for the lost friend!

And yet—in the face of the irrevocable, unfathomable decree of Providence, it is a consolation to the author's friends to read his papers again, to spread their contents of truth and beauty and to thus widen the public appreciation of a truly noble, capable and good man.

But aside from all which personal relations may prompt the editor to say in regard to these essays, the fact will be readily admitted by the reader, that they form a *most valuable* and *eminently useful* contribution to musico-æsthetic literature. Especially the student of music will find in them a source of correct and necessary information, as well as a gentle guide towards an earnest and ideal conception of music, of its ethics, nature and mission on earth. But also the unmusical reader will not put the book out of his hands without confessing to himself to have profited by it.

Dr. Merz was, as mentioned before, a man of multiform knowledge, but besides, he was also an earnest and profound thinker—far too profound not to have fully outgrown such mental perversions as religious skepticism, and it is on this point that the essays will prove most beneficial; a sound religious sentiment, free from denominational barriers, prevails in his essays, which at the same time reveal the author's wonderful gift of making his abstract knowledge practically useful and applicable for the student.

It can really not be praised too much that Dr. Merz, for one, escaped the disastrous tendency of modern science (or rather, of the erroneous and frivolous interpretation of its wonderful disclosures); that Dr. Merz, for one, avoided the widespread mistake of allowing his scientific researches and their results to destroy his idealism. With keen, unerring judgment, he kept the founts and elements of art and science separate, assigning spheres of equal proportions to both healthy emotion and cold reasoning. How forcibly he impressed his powerful convictions on these subjects upon his hearers, the reader will now witness; certain it is, that every particle of truth in the following pages was earnestly sought for and arrived at by a path of love, of true love to God and to his fellow beings; and love—though said to be blind—errs seldom in matters relative to sentiment, the guiding principle in art.

CONSTANTIN STERNBERG.
JOHANNES WOLFRAM.

TABLE OF CONTENTS.

CHAPTER I.
Genius, ... 9–21

CHAPTER II.
Success in Professional Life, ... 22–32

CHAPTER III.
Schopenhauer's Musical Philosophy, ... 33–44

CHAPTER IV.
Music of Nature, ... 45–58

CHAPTER V.
Head and Heart, ... 59–72

CHAPTER VI.
Sanctity of Music, ... 73–88

CHAPTER VII.
Church Music, ... 89–108

CHAPTER VIII.
Hints to Pupils, ... 109–110

CHAPTER IX.
Philosophy of the Beautiful, ... 111–120

CHAPTER X.
A Plea for Music, ... 121–131

CHAPTER XI.
Value of Musical Education, ... 132–144

CHAPTER XII.
Memory, ... 145–156

CHAPTER XIII.
Woman in Music, ... 157–167

CHAPTER XIV.
Harmony, ... 168–175

CHAPTER XV.
Imagination, ... 176–186

CHAPTER XVI.
Expression, ... 187–192

CHAPTER XVII.
Maxims, ... 193–206

GENIUS.

> Time, place and action, may, without pains, be wrought,
> But genius must be born, and never can be taught.
> —DRYDEN. *"Epis. to Congreve," Line* 59.

The Latin word *genius*, signifies the divine nature which is innate in all human beings. According to Webster, the word means that peculiar structure of mind with which each individual is endowed, but especially mental superiority and uncommon intellectual power. Great philosophers differ in their metaphysical definition of this word, while little philosophers use it with a freedom that is alarming. Thus we find that he who dabbles in everything, but does nothing well, is by many called a genius. Let a young man be able to play a few tunes upon each of the several horns of a brass band, and immediately he is called a genius. I believe it was Josh Billings, that country-store philosopher, who said, that "a genius is a person who thinks he knows everything, but who in reality knows nothing, except how to spill 'vittles' on his clothes." But why multiply quotations? "Sensibility," says a writer, "is that power, which distinguishes man from the animal, and predominating sensibility is Genius." Says James Russell Lowell, "Talent is that which is in a man's possession, Genius is that in whose possession a man is." Being endowed with unusual mental powers, the man of genius is a higher sort of a being. According to some, this term should only be applied to persons engaged in art pursuits; the human mind, however, is gifted in many ways, and the definition of the word as meaning predominating sensibility, includes all the various directions in which the mind may show forth its superiority.

Before saying anything about the characteristics of Genius, a distinction should be made between Genius and Talent. Talent is often mistaken for Genius; yes, men of talent frequently aim to pass themselves off as men of genius. What, then, is the difference? Genius is a *creative* power, using this word in a finite sense. Talent, on the other hand, is an *imitative* power, and inasmuch as men rarely become great by imitating others, men of talent but seldom acquire universal reputation. Genius originates; it substitutes the new for the old; hence it is revolutionary, radical and aggressive. Talent merely imitates. Only that which is already in existence can be imitated, hence Talent reproduces and perpetuates the old. Talent must, therefore, be regarded as conservative. Genius makes its own laws; it boldly oversteps those rules which have hitherto fettered the human mind. Talent, however, follows in the wake of Genius and patiently submits to those rules which Genius dictates. Talent learns art rules from books,

Genius reads them within himself. "Talent," says a scholar, "is a bird fastened to a string, Genius is the bird unfettered." Genius dares to do what Talent would be severely criticised for doing. Beethoven was once approached by a young man with the request that he would examine one of the young student's compositions. The master made a few corrections but was soon reminded of the fact that he in a like manner had overstepped the rules. Beethoven smiled and said: "I may do so, but you dare not."

Genius is rare, and its scarcity makes it precious. Talent is abundant, and its abundance makes it common. It is the scarcity of the finer metals that gives them their value, and it is the abundance of paper money which depreciates it. All men are more or less gifted, hence Talent is not much esteemed, while Genius always has been, and always will be, an object of human admiration. And, while speaking of our admiration for Genius, let me say, that the less we see of men of genius, the greater they appear to us. Thus, it is said, "the king, whom a nation reveres, is but a common mortal in the eyes of his valet, who sees him every day."

Talent can be brightened to an astonishingly high degree, but Talent can never be converted into Genius, no more than silver can be changed into gold. Talent toils and gains knowledge through labor and study, while Genius sees things as if by intuition, and, says a writer, "it takes in at a glance the true relations between men and things." Yet Genius is not perfect. It often goes to excess, and seeks its ideals in wrong directions. Unbridled, misdirected, Genius leads to deformity and insanity.

In his relations with the world, the man of genius is *objective*, that is, he looks out into the world and perceives things as they are—he sees what escapes the notice of plainer mortals; hence, Genius draws pleasures from objects which thousands fail to notice, and, on the other hand, he suffers from causes which would not affect others. The average man, however, is *subjective*, that is, he merely sees the world as it appears to him—he views everything through the lens of his own affections or prejudices. All situations are colored by his own feelings, and he is ever ready to put his own short-sighted interpretation upon his neighbor's actions. Men of genius, therefore, have refused to recognize their fellow-creatures as men; hence, we learn that Diogenes walked about the streets in broad daylight carrying a lantern, searching for men. Of course, there is a great diversity of talent, and some are far above others in nobility of character, as well as in learning.

It is an old saying that "the world is a stage, and all the men and women merely players." Says a humorist: "In youth, they usually play 'Romeo and Juliet,' but when farther advanced in years they occasionally perform the 'Tempest.'" As a rule, men of genius occupy the auditorium (says a philosopher), looking calmly at the scrambling and fussing of the actors.

It has been said that the average man views the world through the lens of self, hence, he is generally suspicious; at least, he is vigilant in his intercourse with others. Yes, the average man is almost always bent upon selfish projects. Half of his life is spent in gaining wealth, and the other half, it is said, is employed in studying how to keep or how to enjoy it. The genius, on the other hand, regards his physical existence as secondary to his mental life. Physical wants are often an annoyance to him. He is generally of very little value in business affairs; he is ignorant of the ways of acquiring wealth, hence, he generally remains poor. Schopenhauer says: "Genius is about as useless in the affairs of life, as a telescope would be in an opera house." Originality of thought is the golden path that leads Genius into his kingdom, and, inasmuch as he seeks wisdom wherewith to benefit the human family, it must be said of him that he is the *thinker*, while the average man is the *worker* in the human bee-hive. The latter produces material wealth, and, although he aims to produce exclusively for himself, he nevertheless produces for the masses. Thus we see men attend to the affairs of self; but the constant attention to self is apt to make one selfish, and selfishness is always littleness of character. Men of genius, on the other hand, as a rule, are always self-sacrificing; they are humane; they live and die for a cause, and herein Genius is always great. The average man can never produce those works of art which Genius produces, no matter how he applies himself, no matter who teaches him. Lacking, as he does, that high degree of sensibility which distinguishes Genius, he fails to receive those impressions which Genius alone can receive; how, then, can he give expression to the lofty inspirations of the man of genius? Art and literature are the principal domains in which Genius feels at home; in them he delights to revel. In art, Genius searches for the beautiful, for art is the bodily representation of the beautiful. All that is beautiful and perfect must be concentrated in the Deity, hence, the artist, in his work, strives to give us a portion of the Infinite, a glimpse of the Deity itself. To lead us to this source of perfection is the high, and the *only* true, mission of art.

When Genius conceives of a work of art, he carries it with him in his mind and affections. It has been said, "Genius does not take pencil in hand and say, now I will write a symphony, nor does he prepare colors and say, now I will paint a Madonna." *No!* something precedes all this! The ideas spring up in the artist's mind as buds spring forth on trees and bushes, and as these gradually develop so the art-work is perfected to a good degree ere the artist begins to write or paint. It may be said that no artist is, in the real sense of the word, a free, voluntary creator, while in another he is. He cannot tell why and how the ideas develop themselves within him. Says a writer, we know not whether we think thoughts ourselves, or whether they are thought within us; whether we create them, or whether we merely discover them. We feel the power of the mind within us, but cannot describe its operations. Dante said: "I am one of those poets who, if love breathes on them, writes it down, and that just as it was felt by the inner man."

When the artist has conceived a design for a new work, there is no rest for him until he has carried it out in tones, in colors, in marble, or in words. He models and remodels it, until it conforms to his ideal of the beautiful. If this ideal is low, so will be his art-work; if it be pure and sublime, the art-work will be pure and great. The production of an art-work is to the artist the greatest pleasure possible, for the privation of which no earthly possession can compensate. This pleasure rewards Genius for the many privations incident to his career.

When the artist is at work, he often sits still, as if dead to the world without. It requires great mental concentration to produce an art-work; its production has been compared to the shedding of a skin. But if the production of an art-work requires great mental concentration, the same is required of him who aims to reproduce it. To enter into the spirit of a piece of music is not an easy task; the average pupil sinks under the strain; he cannot endure it long, hence many fail in their appreciation of the masters. Observe how the artist infuses himself into his art-work. He impresses upon it his heart's noblest emotions, he fashions it after his best thought; therefore, he who studies a work of art comes into close contact with the artist's thoughts and emotions, and their influence will either be for good or for evil, just as the artist's conceptions were good or evil. Many believe that the arts have an influence only so far as they produce pleasurable sensations, but such is not the fact.

There are many who compose, many who paint or make verses, yet their work is but as brass, when compared with the gold that comes out of the workshop of Genius. But who would discourage the manufacture of brass? It is a most useful article in the world's workshop. So the work of our amateurs and of men of talent is not to be despised in the history of art and literature. While many amateurs use music merely as a plaything, as an accomplishment, or as a means of livelihood, Genius is always unselfish in the use of the arts; he aims not so much at personal aggrandizement as at the advancement of his fellow creatures. The person who seeks self first and alone, in art, is like he who unites with the church for mercenary reasons. He who is unselfish in his art pursuits, is the art disciple. Herein consists the highest aim and position of artists, and it is their only true relation to art.

The more a people are given to the pursuits of material things, the less will they be able to enter into the spirit of true art. Thousands look at a picture or hear a grand piece of music, but in the language of the Bible, "they have eyes and see not, they have ears and hear not." As the body develops, so the mind must grow. The taste for the beautiful must be cultivated, else we shall not enjoy it. The pleasures of the mind alone are enduring, for they come from the Eternal and they lead to the Eternal. He, therefore, whose pleasures consist merely in bodily gratification, is yet near the brute; he has no abiding place in the temple of art. Genius needs culture. Horace said "that neither diligence without genius, nor genius without education will produce anything thorough. Men of genius must study the works of Genius. However, when the education of Genius is completed, he asserts his own independence, and boldly steps forth into those domains where no human footprints are seen. Talent, on the other hand, continues to walk in the path which has been pointed out to it. The man of talent reads in order to gather knowledge; Genius reads oftener in order to stimulate his mind. Talent gathers information as water is gathered in cisterns; the mind of Genius, however, is like a well, it supplies itself. Men of talent become great scholars, immense storehouses of learning, but men of genius are preëminently thinkers.

Says Holmes: "*One*-story intellects, *two*-story intellects, *three*-story intellects. All fact collectors, who have no aim beyond their facts, are one-story men. Two-story men compare, reason, generalize, using the labors of the fact collectors as well as their own. Three-story men idealize, imagine, predict; their best illuminations come from above, through the skylight. They are the men of genius. On the sea of thought men of talent are as coast travelers, while the minds of the common people are as skiffs that can safely cross a stream if the water be calm. The mind of Genius, however, is as the majestic steamer, which, well equipped with compass and instruments, steers out upon the open sea."

Genius lives in a world of his own, a world into which the average man never can enter. There are millions that have no idea of its existence, while millions more have but a faint glimmer of it, like that from a far distant luminary. He wanders in gardens full of roses; he sleeps in bowers strewn with the richest flowers; he rests on banks covered with the softest moss; he drinks of the coolest fountains; the birds sing sweetest to him; the atmosphere which he breathes is rich and balmy, and he is surrounded by creatures of his own fancy, too lovely to describe. This is the dream-land of Genius, wherein the muses and graces wait upon him and carry him on their hands. Is it, then, a wonder that he loves to roam there? Alas! how great is his bewilderment and suffering when he is forced to attend to the affairs of the world? How great his agony when he feels the rough stones and the stings of the thistles which *our* hardened feet have long since ceased to regard? How helpless is Genius when he has to deal with the cunning men of the business world; how sad to see him enslaved by designing men, who rob him of his honest toil? Schopenhauer compares genius, under such circumstances, to a vase which is being used for culinary purposes.

When the troubles of life pursue him, Genius seeks his dream-land, and there he bemoans the realities of his existence, and with his utterances he touches our hearts until the tears begin to flow. On the other hand, when in his dream-land, Genius often forgets the everyday world, with its worriments, and he often bursts out in strains of joy, which shed sunshine into the darkest of lives and the gloomiest of hearts. There is another class of dreamers; those who build castles in the air, or those who see forms in the clouds above; but such dreamers never realize the pictures of their fancies. Geniuses are dreamers, but not all dreamers are men of genius.

The man of genius generally concentrates his entire self upon one subject, hence the intensity of his woes or joys. In changing his attention from one subject to another, his hilarity may therefore suddenly be changed into deep sorrow, and *vice versâ*. This explains the changeableness of the moods of men of genius. One moment they are driven to despair, and the next they act like children. Cardinal Richelieu would play leap-frog with the little ones. But, then, read the biographies of our great men, and you will no doubt find many illustrations of this statement.

It is a well known fact that men of genius are full of eccentricities. Aristotle has said, "that no distinguished genius is free from madness." Pope says:—

> "Great wits to madness
> Sure are near allied,
> And thin partitions
> Do their bounds divide."

How often men of genius are denounced as "cranks," while the "cranks" are regarded as wise men. Columbus was called a fool, while Joan D'Arc was considered inspired.

Men of genius are instruments used by God wherewith to improve mankind. They are always revolutionizers in some departments of the human household.

The masses, however, do not like to be disturbed in their accustomed mode of doing things, and he who attempts to introduce new ways is denounced as a meddler. Hence the antagonism between men of genius and the masses.

As capital and labor are needlessly antagonistic, so are the principles of beautifying and utilizing the earth. Both ought to coöperate, both are necessary for the world's economy. Business men usually have very little regard for men of genius, because of their apparent uselessness in the affairs of this world. They are often denounced because they produce no material wealth and because they are poor managers at home. But these (dollar and cent) critics overlook the fact, that the works of genius are the wealth of the mind. And surely the mind must also be fed in order that it may grow. If men of genius do not build railroads, they build those roads which lead to refinement and culture, in a word, to mental progress.

It is not the bread we eat, nor the clothes we wear, that makes us better—nay —next to the word of God, it is the truth as revealed in art, in the sciences, in literature, that penetrates men's souls. Hence next to the word of God literature and art are the best civilizers and refiners of men. Genius and art in their purest essence are humanity, and humanity is a large part of religion. How sad, however, when Genius leaves the paths of truth, and produces works that are antagonistic to pure morality, or when perchance he denies his God. It is, though, more generally the would-be genius that errs in this direction. Bacon said that, "a little philosophy inclineth man's mind to atheism, but depth of philosophy bringeth men's mind about religion." Alas, how often young men attempt to pass themselves off as profound thinkers, by denying their God, or by scoffing at religion. When Genius leaves the paths of truth, his words become a shower of fire, which consumes men's peace and happiness. A certain writer has said that every genius is a child, and every child, in a measure, is a genius. Study the life of Mozart, who was a child until his death, but who was a giant in his art. Most of our art geniuses were children in many things.

Genius searches after the truth—the truth is a portion of the Eternal. Genius embodies the beautiful—the beautiful also is the Eternal, for God is the embodiment of the beautiful. Again the Eternal is love—truth therefore is love—the beautiful is love—art is love—religion is love—children are love; genius, truth, art, religion, children, all are akin, all draw breath from the same source, that divine atmosphere, where love reigns supreme. Art and religion, therefore, are akin, and the true artist should love and revere the source of all that is beautiful.

The common man views life from a personal standpoint; it begins and ends with him, except it be in his love for his children, and even herein men are often extremely selfish. It is the aim of the average man to live in comfort and ease. Genius however, so to speak, forgets life's pleasures. Seeing the human family in ignorance, he feels the impulse to bring about reform. Loving his art, he knows no higher delight than to serve it. In turning over history's page we learn that those who have carried forward the work of reform were carried onward on the wave of conviction, which bids defiance to prisons, scaffolds and faggots. It is the divine spark which takes away the fear of man. But what if Genius dies bearing testimony to the truth, let us remember, that though his body moulders in the grave his soul marches on. Men of genius are as beacon-lights in the storms of life, they help the cause of human freedom and progress, and when looking around upon the misery of the human family, let us thank God, that he gave us these lights to help us on our way. There is a constant mental and social evolution taking place. Generation after generation becomes better and wiser. Governments become more liberal, sciences shed more light, the press as well as the pulpit are becoming more powerful, and all this we owe to the influences of great minds that lead us on.

Genius is never servile. He is the true nobleman of the human family. He is always conscious, more or less, of his powers as well as of his high mission. Hence he demands recognition. This self-consciousness of superiority even manifested itself in one of those unfortunates who had lost his reasoning powers. An insane genius having been asked by a visitor what brought him to the asylum, gravely pointed to his head and said: "What never will bring you here, sir: too much brain, too much brain." There never lived a genius, but felt that the opinions of the coming generations must conform to his own. While the man of talent sees the faults of his times, he generally utilizes them; Genius, however, sees what the world will be fifty years hence, and this is the goal toward which he labors. This is the difference between statesmen and politicians—the one advances humanity, he lives and dies for his country, he foresees its future; the other lives only for the present, he aims to advance himself. Genius is always in the advance of his times. He is the lofty mountain peak which first receives the rays of the rising sun, while there is yet darkness in the valley below, where the common people dwell. As the eagle soars high toward the source of light, while the little birds make their nests in hedges near the ground, so genius in the flight of his imagination is above the common people. And as little as our bare eye can count the strokes of the eagle's wings, when it appears only as a mere spot before the clouds, so little can the average man count and comprehend the beatings of the wild-throbbing heart of the genius. The man of talent usually is appreciated by his contemporaries, because they understand him; the man of genius, however, will not be generally appreciated until mother earth has received him into her bosom. Inasmuch as he lives for the coming generations, his own has but little sympathy with him, hence men of genius are often allowed to die in neglect and want, while coming generations erect monuments in their honor. Colton says, "the drafts which Genius draws upon posterity, although they may not always be honored as soon as they are due, are sure to be paid with compound interest in the end." Posterity honors them, travelers visit their graves, towns dispute over the honor of calling them their own. Men of genius make cities famous, and guides point out the places where they lived, toiled and died. Henry Giles was correct when he said that the great battle of Lepanto was famous, merely because Cervantes fought in it as a private soldier. Yes, the very chastisement which Genius inflicts upon enemies makes them immortal, unenviable immortality though this be! Yes, immortality in a sense seems to be inscribed upon everything Genius touches.

As a social being, Genius is a peculiar mortal. He is generally his own best company. He is never alone, except when surrounded by much fashionable company. He may then, again, be compared with the eagle, who has descended from his heavenward flight, and now sits upon a low tree, surrounded by small birds. Though they cannot harm him, their incessant twitter annoys him. Many men of genius were but poor conversationalists. Thus Cicero says that Scipio was never more alone than when alone. Tasso's conversation was neither gay nor brilliant. Dante was either taciturn or satirical. Milton was unsociable. Chaucer's silence was more agreeable than his conversation. Ben. Jonson used to sit silent in company. Of Goldsmith it is said, that he wrote like an angel, but talked like a poor Poll. Longfellow says that "Genius is often dull and inert in society, as a blazing meteor when it descends to the earth is only a stone." Schopenhauer remarks, "that a genius among common people is like one who enters the ball-room for the purpose of dancing but finds only lame people there." It has been asserted that silence and constant seriousness are unmistakable characteristics of genius, in short, that a laughing person cannot be a genius. This I consider false. Human life presents much that is comic and ludicrous, and, as Genius is a close observer, it is not reasonable to expect him to be serious under all circumstances. And no one dare say that men of genius do not laugh; the fact is merely that in promiscuous company they are unsocial. Among their equals they are generally found to be good laughers and talkers. "God gave the power of laughing to man alone," says a writer. The animal that lacks sensibility never laughs. "The gravest creature to look at," says Kellgreene, "is an ox," yet no one would claim that the gravity of an ox indicates learning. Silence is often used as a mask to cover stupidity, yet such owls are often credited with much learning.

In his habits, Genius is generally disorderly, for he is too much occupied with the operations of his mind to pay attention to the condition of things around him. The older Dumas used to tell his son that he would never become a great man, and assigned as his reason the son's orderly habits. Said he, derisively, "he has twelve pairs of boots, and they stand side by side in his bed-room, as straight as if they were being drilled." I would, however, not have you understand me to say that a lack of the sense of order is an infallible sign of genius. While there is an apparent disorder in the dress and household affairs of men of genius, there is strict order in their mental activity.

I will whisper in your ears, ladies, that men of genius do not always prove to be good husbands—they are often neglectful of those gallant little attentions to their wives which distinguish good husbands. Being poor managers, their wives are generally forced to assume the reins, and for this reason they are often called shrews. While many men of genius have written sensible articles about women and married life; while they have laid down good sensible rules for selecting a wife, they have not infrequently missed the mark, and married regular viragos. Many instances of unfortunate marriages might be cited, from Socrates down to Shakespeare, Milton, Byron, Haydn, Dickens and others, but this subject had better be dropped.

Men of genius usually are very absent-minded, and it is natural that they should be, for they are more or less always absorbed in thought. Many amusing stories may be told to prove this.

It is true, as has been said, that there never was a philosopher who could endure the toothache patiently. Men of genius are bundles of nerves, and for this reason they shrink from pain. When suffering awaits them, they seem to be unable to reason themselves into a brave endurance of the same. Thus Peele is believed to have died because he was unable to bear an operation which a less sensitive man might readily have endured. Yet, while we must record a Demosthenes who deserted his colors, and excused himself by saying that "He who turns and runs away may live to fight another day," we might also give many instances of heroic bravery exhibited by men of genius.

The sensitiveness of men of genius, especially of musicians, is proverbial. Artists, actors, orators, painters, poets, are almost morbidly sensitive to public criticism. Approbation is of more value to them than money, for if they fail in their mental efforts they fail in everything; hence, they are often troubled with fear when stepping before the public. Thus, it is said of Cicero that he had a bad night before his great speech at Murena. Plutarch says that Cicero not only lacked courage in arms, but also in his efforts at speaking. He began timidly, in many cases never ceasing to tremble, even when he came thoroughly into the current of his speeches. But then there are many guilty of the same weakness, whom no one would suspect of genius. It may well be said that many artists and authors suffered death, almost, because of unjust criticism. Schiller said that no genius comes to a good end, by which he means that men of great mental gifts usually suffer much. Was not Homer a beggar, and Torrence a slave? Was not Tasso poor, and did not Cervantes die of hunger? Bacon led a life of distress; Spencer died in want, and Mozart had not enough to prevent his being buried in a pauper's grave. Yes, often the grim messenger of death takes away our great men early, for it is said that he loves a shining mark.

It is a common belief that Genuis works best in youth. A distinguished physician says that the period from thirty to forty is the golden period for brain-labor, while that from forty to sixty he calls the silver period. There are, however, many instances on record, where great works were accomplished by men of advanced years. While Mozart, Raphael, Schubert and others produced their great works in youth, while some of the world's great generals had built up and destroyed empires before they were much advanced in years, we must not lose sight of the fact that Homer produced his best works in old age; Xenophon wrote when ninety-two years old; Æschylus wrote his greatest works three years before his death, when he was sixty-six years of age; Sophocles wrote his "*Œdipus*" in his ninety-sixth year; Phidias produced great works in his seventy-sixth year; Michael Angelo painted his celebrated "Judgment" between his sixtieth and sixty-seventh years; Gluck wrote his "Iphegenia" in his sixty-fifth year; Haydn wrote the "Creation" in his sixty-third, and Goethe produced his "Faust" in the fifty-seventh year of his life. But these are illustrations enough.

Artists must picture and express passions, and in order to do this effectively they must have felt those passions. Thus it happens often that their nervous systems suffer, and in order to build up the wasting powers, they will resort to stimulating drink. I do not believe, however, in the theory advanced by some, that men work best under the influence of strong drink. There may be those who are so accustomed to the use of wine, that their minds cannot work without the aid of stimulants, a condition in which our celebrated Webster is said to have been. Let me say most emphatically that if drunkards rise to eminence, they do so in spite of their habits, not because of them. It is an error to teach that the moral law is not as binding upon great men, as it is upon lesser mortals.

As heavenly bodies have their satellites, so men of genius have theirs. These hang on the outskirts of intellectual circles, and being unable to enter their magic bounds, they imitate those within, and as a rule they imitate their vices first. Let us cover the frailties of our great men with the mantle of charity, remembering, that the greater the power of perception of wrong, the greater also is its sting.

Those whom we admire we also imagine as perfect in form. Men of genius, however, often were insignificant in their appearance, yes, many were deformed, or suffered from maladies. Milton, Homer, Bach and Händel were blind, Beethoven was deaf, Weber and Byron both suffered from physical deformities. These sufferers were often extremely sensitive about their ailings, yet when touched by the warmth of humor they sometimes made fun of each other's weaknesses. Talleyrand was lame, Madame de Stael was cross-eyed. Said the latter, on one occasion, "Monsieur, how is that poor leg of yours," to which the statesman sarcastically replied : "Crooked as you see it." Who can imagine a Hannibal, an Alexander, an Achilles or a Hector as small, yet many geniuses were very frail in form. Voltaire was puny, Pope was small, Tom Moore was likewise, Milton was only of moderate size, Napoleon was not commanding in person, Wagner did not reach much over five feet.

While the mind of Genius is quick to work, it often needs peculiar surroundings, in order that it may become active. Spontini the composer preferred to work in a dark room; Cimoraso preferred noise around him, when he wrote; Haydn always put on the ring Frederick the Great gave him, before he went to his desk, and when his ideas ceased to flow, he resorted to his rosary. Mozart wrote down many ideas while playing billiards. Beethoven communed much with nature; he moved frequently, believing at one time that he could write best on the north side of the street, and then preferring the south side. Mendelssohn, the refined, stimulated his mind by walking in gardens, as if he gathered his ideas from flowers. It is said of Halevy that he was partial to the sound of boiling water. Verdi reads Ossian's poems and then writes, while Wagner dressed himself in the costumes of the characters of which he was writing. But enough.

Kant, the great German philosopher, said that just as the powers of genius display themselves differently in individuals, so they differ among nations. Thus the Germans strike the root, Italians, the crown of the tree, the Frenchman the blossom and the Englishman the fruit. The greater the degree of culture of a people, the greater also is the number of geniuses which that people produces; the greater however the love for financial and mercantile speculation, the smaller will be the number of geniuses.

Some men of genius have been great in more than one art or science. Thus, Michael Angelo was a painter, an architect, and a musician. It was he who made those beautiful bronze doors, of which it is said, that they are grand enough to be the gates of Heaven. By the side of him stands Leonardi Da Vinci, the architect, the sculptor, the painter, the musician, the poet, the scientist, and the mathematician. Such geniuses, however, are, among the world's gifted men, what the Kohinoor is among diamonds.

It has been asserted that the powers of genius are the product of circumstances; others claim that they are the product of education. There would not be a Napoleon in history if the French Revolution had not broken out. What would our Grant, and Sherman, and Lincoln have been without the civil war? Let us, however, bear in mind, that men are made for occasions, not occasions for men. When great works are to be done, God also provides the men to do them. Yet there are many instances on record, where men assumed their God-appointed duties with hesitating steps and fainting hearts. Schopenhauer says that Genius comes at irregular times, and follows his own course, like a comet, yet he always comes when needed, and he always finds the path of his career unobstructed. Henry Giles says that Genius is always born in the right age of history, the proper spot on earth waits for him and receives him. For all, it is at least reasonable to believe, that throughout history many great minds failed to shine, just as there are many diamonds which have not yet been found, and never will come to light.

But is genius the product of education? Geniuses are as rare as are the high peaks in mountainous countries; there are few of them. It is the secret desire of all men, more or less, to have their names inscribed on history's page. If genius, then, is attainable by education, why have so few secured the coveted prize? If genius can be produced by education, then education has indeed failed most effectually. "Good will and earnest determination are of great aid in matters of morals, and in study," says a philosopher, but in art pursuits, the *will* itself is helpless. When speaking of the lives of our intellectual princes, they are described to us as having been thoughtless, lazy boys, who regarded but little their teachers' instructions. They had, however, a capacity for work, and if they failed to apply themselves, the fault usually lay with the teacher and his system, and not with the boy and his powers. The fact that these boys became men of fame has produced the impression that Genius does *not* work, that he need not labor like other men. This is a false notion. Men of genius always were hard workers; they are not only profound thinkers, but quite frequently they are excellent scholars; they are, as a rule, hard students—but after their own methods and with their own purposes. When old enough, they defy the yoke of tutelage and walk out boldly into paths of their own. Who would assert that a Shakespeare, a Milton, a Raphael, a Michael Angelo, a Dante, a Goethe, a Schiller, a Beethoven, a Mozart, a Luther, a Napoleon, a Bismarck, a Franklin, a Webster, a Clay, and many others, were made in the school-room what they finally proved to be. From whom did these men obtain their superior powers? Where did they light the torches which have burned throughout centuries? They were illuminated by the spark divine which comes only from the fire divine. Genius is a gift which is laid by the side of the little babe, and whosoever has not received it at his birth, need never expect to receive it in later years, no matter how superior his educational advantages may be. Genius is a gift, education and learning are acquirements, and it will be easily proven that the inborn qualities are stronger than those that are acquired.

Swift says: "When a genius appears, you may know him by this sign, that generally the dunces are in a confederacy against him." "If you have the power of genius," says Jean Jacques Rousseau, "you will know genius; if you have it not, you will never know it. Does a grand piece of music cause the tears to flow? Does it cause your nerves to vibrate? If so, you have a spark of genius; but," adds the philosopher, "if you remain cold, do not even inquire about the workings of genius." Be careful, however, that you are not deceived by the false article. There were false prophets, and there are false geniuses. Such men, of course, must assume and imitate the eccentricities of genius in order to appear like it; for the power of thought and the flight of imagination of men of genius no one can assume or imitate. The donkey may put on the lion's skin, yet when he opens his mouth we all will know him to be a donkey. A great Grecian philosopher, who was remarkable for the negligence of his dress, met a young seeker of fame with a robe full of holes. The philosopher stepped up to him and reprovingly said: "Friend, out of the holes of your cloak looks your vanity." Be not deceived by the holes in men's clothes; do not judge by outward signs. As iron is drawn toward the magnet, so will you feel the power of Genius when you come in contact with it, be it through his works or through personal intercourse. Says Bulwer: "Fine natures are like fine poems; a glance at the first two lines suffices for a guess into the beauty that waits for you, if you read on."

An old legend says, that while the gods were distributing the possessions of this earth, giving to the king the throne, to the merchant the seas, to the soldier the weapons, to the priests the temple, to the hunter the woods, to the farmer the soil, etc., Genius was out wandering, dreaming, and feasting his eyes on the beauties of nature. When at last he came in, everything had been given away, and there was nothing left for him. But the gods took pity on him, and in order to compensate him for his losses, they bade him welcome upon Parnassus Hill, whenever he desired to come, and gave him the freedom to go in and out among the gods.

The light of genius is given to but few, so that it may shine all the brighter on the road of human progress. According to physicians, talent is often inherited, but genius is rarely ever transmitted to posterity. It is a gift, not an inheritance. Men may be their fathers' sons, or their sons' fathers, but seldom are father and son alike famous. If genius is a gift, has not the giver the right to bestow it upon whomsoever he chooses? And thus we find that the poor lad Burns has the gift bestowed upon him, by the side of the sons of kings and lords. Genius is, by birth, the true nobleman of the human family. Neither cross nor stars can increase his dignity. Putting a ribbon or an order on his breast is as ridiculous as it would be to daub colors on the face of a statue, or to hang a cloak on a finely cut piece of marble. Being thus highy favored, his powers for good or evil are so much the greater, and so likewise is his responsibility.

Though we may not be geniuses we are nevertheless the fellow-beings of these great men, and this thought should inspire us. Let us study their lives and their works, for by communing with them, we become more and more like unto them. Who can sum up all the good that has been done throughout the world and throughout all ages, by the works of men of genius, by art and literature?

When viewing the highest mountains of the earth or when diving down into the lowest mines, when exploring the ice-bound regions of the North Pole, or when wandering through the woods and along the immense rivers of the hot zones with their variety of scenery and wild animals, when measuring the Falls of Niagara, or when viewing Vesuvius in convulsive action, one may well cry out in the Bible language, "Great and marvelous are Thy works, oh Lord God Almighty." But there is something far greater than these wonders of nature, and that is the mind of man. Though electricity travels quickly, there is something that travels more rapidly, and that is human thought. How sad it is that while men climb the highest mountains, while they dive into seas and rivers, while they spend years in the ice-bound regions of the North, or waste away under the tropic sun of the South, and all this for the sake of scientific investigation, they do so little to fathom their own hearts or to study their own minds. Truly did Pope say: "Know Thyself; the proper study for mankind is man." Though the mountains and the seas are great, the one shall tumble in, and the other shall dry up, but your souls and mine shall live forever. Oh blessed immortality, in which we shall be near the great geniuses that ever lived on earth, when we shall comprehend the mysterious connection between mind and matter, when we shall forever be near the source of love and light, and all that is good and beautiful, when we shall be near the great Genius above, whose works here are so grand in their perfection. Are there any who seek an additional evidence of the existence of a God? Let Genius, let the mind of man be this evidence, for God did not manifest himself half so well in the greatest mountains or the mightiest seas of the globe, as he manifested himself in the creation of the genius of man.

SUCCESS IN PROFESSIONAL LIFE.

An Address delivered before the Graduating Class of the Medical Department of Wooster University, Cleveland, Ohio.

My ignorance of your most noble science forestalls all attempts on my part to say anything in connection with it that might prove of benefit to you. I might have endeavored to interest you in the health influences of music, its effects upon the nervous system, upon our emotions and through them upon our thoughts, but I preferred not to undertake this subject, interesting as it is, because I have but recently published some articles with reference to it. Neither would it be appropriate to speak here of the beauties and growth of the art which I have studied and taught for many years. There is, however, one subject, which is, or which at least ought to be of mutual interest, namely, that of a *successful professional* life. My address, therefore, shall simply express some practical advice to you, how to live and how to act in life, and I hope that what I say will not be spoken altogether in vain. You are about to take one of the most serious steps in your lives. The first half, that of preparation, has at last come to an end, and you are now ready to enter the busy world, for better or for worse; let us sincerely hope for the former. Life is a most serious reality, so is your profession one of seriousness, and necessarily my remarks must partake of the same character.

It is the aim and ambition of every thinking man to make life a success, that is, to make it useful and pleasant. Many men have spent useful lives, but they were far from being pleasant, and so one finds men everywhere who endeavor to spend their lives pleasantly without making them useful. The former class challenges our respect, the latter deserves our pity. There is no happiness in life without usefulness, and this is the one cardinal truth I wish you always to keep before your minds. I take it for granted that you mean to be useful, for your profession points to a life of usefulness of the noblest kind; but look to your right and left, and see the many lawyers, doctors, preachers and teachers who have started out in life with honest intentions and with the brightest of prospects for usefulness, but who finally failed in life's work. How many are there whose professional lives are unpleasant to themselves as well as to those with whom they come in contact? This is often owing to wrong ideas of life, to a lack of knowledge of human nature. Having started wrong, having, perhaps, had no friend to warn or to guide them, they went on and on, until they became pessimists, leading lives of bitterness and torment. How much good might such men have accomplished had they known how to safely steer their youthful crafts while passing through the breakers near the shore. But by some neglect or mistake on the part of teachers, parents or themselves, they sprung a leak somewhere, and after having once passed out upon the high seas, it was impossible to return or to repair the damage. Says a writer, our sins will be punished in the world to come, but for the acts of our own stupidity, for our lack of judgment, for many errors of teachers and parents, we must pay the penalty here on earth. Close observation is necessary for correct judgment, and he who would be happy in life, as far as mortal man may be happy, must be a close observer of men and situations. The reason men bump their heads and stub their toes, is because they fail to look where they step, because they fail to see what is before them.

You will have to deal with men and women of all grades and classes, you will meet them in their worst moods and conditions, and it behooves you, more than men of other professions, to study human character. Would you be masters of the situation, you must know those with whom you have dealings; more than that, you must thoroughly know yourselves. Weigh and scrutinize carefully men's characters, study their mental and moral make-up, as well as their bodily condition, for thus only will you become successful physicians.

"This world is a mirror," says Lichtenstein; "if a donkey looks into it, you cannot expect to see the face of an apostle or that of a physician looking out of it." This world will be to you exactly as you see it, as you meet it and fashion it. If your views are correct you will be able to steer clear of much trouble, thereby putting you on the vantage ground in making life useful. The avoidance of trouble is a species of happiness; it is a sort of negative happiness that may be made to spread over a greater portion of our lives than the actual enjoyment of social pleasures and creature comforts will reach. If your views of life are false, trouble is sure to ring your office bell at all hours, day and night. Talk not to me of luck, good or bad. That which some men bemoan as bad luck is simply bad management—a lack of good sound sense and tact. Each of you has it in his power to make life useful and happy, provided you understand life and its issues and have the will to do your full duty. Many men with diplomas and high-class grades have had to succumb to men of lesser ability and lower standing simply because they lacked worldly wisdom. He who lacks this precious gift is helpless, in spite of friends and wealth.

It is of the utmost importance that you start right, for if you take the wrong track, you will find it a difficult task in later years to switch off. Doubtless, during the first few weeks or months of your medical career, you will have plenty of time for self-study; but be assured of this fact, that whether you have work to do, or whether you are simply waiting to be called out, the world-lessons will begin at once and continue until some other doctor will say of you: "He is dead; bury him out of sight."

You must possess very superior powers if you expect to impregnate the world with one new idea. In other words, if you aspire to give the world new lessons. You must be made of rare stuff if you would instruct your professional brethren and lead them onward. Rather be prepared to be led and to submit to many conditions which in your judgment are wrong. The world is a hard pupil, and so is it a hard teacher. It knocks ideas into men's heads if they are taken willingly, and it causes us to suffer if we stubbornly hold fast to false principles and notions. I would not, however, have you understand me to say that you should conform to the world in all things. It is not safe, nor is it always right, to be on the popular side. It is, however, prudent and wise at all times to be moderate in speech. Bear in mind that you are not called upon on all occasions to correct what you think is wrong in this world of ours. Would you meet with tolerant treatment, be tolerant to others. But if you feel it to be your duty to contradict public opinion, if you feel called upon to gainsay and to expose error, let me beseech you to examine well the timber of your platform; next, see to it that you stand solidly upon it, keep your temper, and if you finally must lock horns with public opinion, do so with earnestness. My experience, however, is, that it is best to keep out of public disputations, for he that is overcome by your argument rarely ever forgives you for having defeated him, while if you yourself are defeated, you are apt to experience a great deal of useless irritation. Unless truth or a great principle is at stake, meddle not with loud-mouthed talkers; let them alone. Strive to know your powers well, so that you may not overrate them in any contest. Never undertake that which is beyond them, but use every means to strengthen, to increase your powers, and in a silent way to deepen and widen your influence.

The man that is not honest to himself cannot be honest to others. This is an old saying. Of course, you are honest to others and to yourselves, and in this light of honesty I desire to ask you now, What is your aim in practicing medicine? If you aim, in the main, at wealth, you are on the wrong road, and you had better turn off at once. But if you desire to aid mankind, if you see before yourselves a world in suffering, and aim to help it through your professional skill, if you desire to improve the condition of the human family as far as lies within your professional power, then, indeed, are you to be congratulated, for you are the right men in the right places, and I bid you God-speed, for this track is safe and clear to the end of the road. Of course, you must live, you must earn money, and no one says you should not, but this I do say, that the man who lives and labors for money exclusively, who sees his sole reward in earthly gains, is, so far as I can judge, not worthy of the name of a healer or a physician.

Be men of honor and integrity, of soberness and moderation in all things. Guard your personal and professional good names with jealous care, for henceforth you cannot separate the two. The physician whose good name is even tainted, cannot expect to be called into respectable homes, either on professional or social grounds. Were I a physician, nothing would sting and wound my pride quicker than to feel that while, as a physician, I am sought, as a man I am only tolerated or even detested. First see to character, for without it neither wealth nor reputation will give you any comfort. Doubtless, in time you will be confronted by many temptations, but bear in mind that yielding to wrong is like putting chains around you; it is like hanging a millstone around your neck. You may carry it for a while, but the load is sure to sink you in the end. Let me beg of you to keep your consciences clean, for Shakespeare said that conscience makes cowards of us, or something to that effect. No doubt many secrets, professional and domestic, will be revealed to you. Keep these sacredly within your breasts, like men of honor and sterling integrity. The talking doctor is in constant danger of being led into trouble by inquisitive people. Parade not your cases nor your cures before the public; let others speak well of you. Rather say too little, for fear you might say too much. It is still better to say nothing, for if you have not as yet learned the disposition of society gossips, you will discover to your own sorrow that they are not great lovers of truth. Each, desiring to make the news more effective and startling, will add something to it, until truth has become a hideous lie.

Talent is a gift which all of us possess, genius is bestowed upon but few. It is gratifying to rise and have one's name mentioned honorably, but for all it must be regarded as a truism, that a day well spent is better than years of honorable distinction. Honors alone make no man happy. It is pleasant enough to have enough of this world's goods to be relieved of the uncertainties of life, but wealth alone makes no man happy. Only that which a man is, says a philosopher, makes him truly happy, not what he has. It is better you should be worthy of honors, and not have them meted out to you, than to secure them upon false grounds. Neither honors nor wealth will make you truly useful, but character and sound learning are great powers in themselves, they are the true levers of usefulness. Not what the world says of you constitutes true greatness, but what you are in the sight of God. The consciousness of true inward merit makes any man strong, deception makes him weak.

Soberness and frugality also are necessary for your success. A physician should be a sober-minded man, he should be a model man. Would you trust a druggist given to drunken spells with the filling of an important prescription? If not, how can you expect the public to trust a physician guilty of such wrongs? Machinists, engineers, even common laborers, are discharged if found guilty of drunkenness. What right has a physician to indulge in this vice when we entrust him with health and life, our two greatest earthly possessions? Be it far from me to suspect you of evil habits; my object is simply to warn you in time, so that you may start out on the right track, for it is a tremendous task for an habitual drunkard to switch off from the road that leads to destruction. Be temperate in all things; in working and seeking pleasures, in eating as well as in speaking. Trust not too much to your powers of endurance; keep an eye on your own health. A poor, but a healthy doctor is a happier man than a sick king. A healthy doctor is an inspiring spectacle; a sick doctor is a doubly distressing object to behold. Be also temperate in your desire for wealth. Property is desirable, as has been already stated; on the other hand, its possession entails much care, and the desire to become rich may become as strong a passion as is the desire for intoxicating drink. Beware of it. Every thinking man considers it his duty to lay enough aside during the years of activity to support himself in old age. Your knowledge and skill is as a bond from which you cut away every year so many coupons. But remember that there comes a time when there are no more coupons for you to cut away. It is a national failing of ours to trust the young, and to shove aside the aged, denouncing them as "old fogies." In Europe, aged physicians are sought first, because of their great experience and superior skill. In America, we often prefer to trust the young and inexperienced, believing them to have newer ideas and perhaps clearer heads. A greater mistake never was made. You may derive advantages from this error, but remember that you are also sure to suffer from it in the long run. Be saving then.

Beware, however, of that second American vice, that of striving to accumulate fortune quickly, regardless of the means used. To acquire wealth is not your mission; your aim should be higher, for by the side of the minister of the gospel, who aims to cure men's souls, and by the side of the teacher, who strives to dispel ignorance and error, your calling is one of the noblest, for you are called upon to cure those ills that make men miserable and prevent them from being useful and happy. Only a useful professional life will make you happy.

Many men fail in life because of a lack of politeness and cheerfulness. It is your duty to be polite, but true politeness cannot be put on or off at pleasure; it must be a part of our natures in order that it may pass for the genuine article. Said a philosopher, "politeness is a coin of no intrinsic value;" how foolish then to be stingy with it. Yet there are men so proud and close-fisted that they cannot afford to be polite to others, for fear they bestow more than they receive. Politeness is a grace that recommends us in the eyes of others; it puts people mutually at their ease. Cultivate it then, and exercise it toward all, even toward those who belong to a different medical school. It is wisdom to be polite, for many a physician has lost patronage because of a lack of civility. With politeness cultivate cheerfulness. A cheerful doctor is as a ray of sunlight in a gloomy room. No one likes the grumbling, growling doctor about the house, if, indeed, it can be said at any time we really like to see a doctor enter our homes. Cheerfulness betokens a contented, calm frame of mind; it indicates inward repose, which begets confidence and restfulness in your patient, while the fretful, nervous doctor produces exactly the opposite effects. Physicians need to cultivate much cheerfulness, for they see much of the misery of life, and despite their best efforts to alleviate it, unjust criticism is sure to be meted out to them. Cheerfulness and health go hand in hand; a cheerful doctor, therefore, means a healthy doctor. A growling, ill-natured doctor is sick somewhere, and one feels like saying to him, first cure yourself before you attempt to cure others.

A cheerful sick room is as essential as a clean and well-ventilated sick room. Cheer brightens things. I believe in seriousness and earnestness, but I have often observed that sick rooms are made unnecessarily gloomy by alluding to the uncertainty of life and the certainty of death. Be watchful in this particular, else your medicine as well as your own cheerfulness is sure to be counteracted. Probably the hours a young physician spends during the first months of his professional career will be lonely and trying in the extreme, and there is danger that disappointment and gloom may make a permanent impression upon his character. Keep bright; be hopeful, and remember that all beginning is difficult. Remember that others have traveled the same road before you and succeeded.

There is another enemy calculated to destroy cheerfulness, and this is too great sensitiveness. Take no bad meaning out of every incidental expression and apply it to yourselves. If you do, you will be constantly in hot water. A noble-hearted minister, while speaking on the subject of sensitiveness, told the following incident: He had unexpectedly been called away, and for this reason could not prepare a sermon for Sunday morning. He selected, therefore, an old one which he had preached some three years previously, hoping that no one would remember it. His conscience, however, smote him, and after the services were over he remained in the pulpit for fear some one would speak to him about the old sermon. At the door, however, stood the choir-leader, who was evidently waiting to see his pastor, and as there was no escape, he arose and came to the door. Seeing an expression of dissatisfaction in the musician's face, he asked for the cause. "I might as well have stayed at home to-day," was the quick reply. This went to the minister's heart like an arrow, and he quickly sought his home. He could not eat, neither would slumber come to his eyes. The choir-leader's words were ringing in his ears like a sentence from the bench. At last he made up his mind to see the musician, and while in a store next day he met him. "What did you mean by that expression yesterday?" asked the preacher. "Why, did you not notice," said the offended musician, "how poorly the choir sang?" A breath of relief escaped the minister's lips, and he made up his mind to two things: first, not to preach an old sermon again; second, not to be too sensitive and suspicious.

Said a city physician: "More than once I felt miserable because I saw another physician's carriage before the house of a family who used to call upon me. At last I found out that he called next door, but had tied his horse before my patron's house because there was a good hitching post." How many useless sorrows we suffer because we are too sensitive, because we come too quickly to conclusions! Do not take trouble at interest; jump not hastily at conclusions. Be faithful in the discharge of duty, and let the rest take care of itself. Public opinion is not always correct, but you may put it down as a rule that no man can afford to defy it. Set not your happiness upon it, else you will be tossed about like a chip in an eddy. If you are the right kind of men, you need not feel the public pulse every week or every day in order to find out whether its beatings are favorable to you or not. I am by no means a pessimist, but I make free to say, that this world indulges much in selfishness, in slander, and deceitfulness, and that a great deal of narrow-minded prejudice prevails in all strata of society. Add to this an immense amount of ignorance prevailing as yet, like cobwebs in an old building, and you will get a correct estimate of public opinion and public criticism. The public tongue is like a wasp: it delights to sting because it is its nature to do so. Whatever you do, let not the sting raise a blister, for in the public eye this betokens a bad condition of blood, and is regarded as a sure indication of guilt. Keep calm, hold your own tongues when the public tongue wags, but if you must speak, be first sure that you use the right words.

A conceited man is a harmless sort of a creature. He hurts no one. Like a little balloon, he bobs up and down, inflicting no injury whatsoever, no matter how hard he hits us. All conceited people are cordially disliked, because conceit presupposes ignorance on our part. To try to make us believe that you measure six feet when we know that you measure but five and a half, is provokingly impudent. To step on the scales with pockets full of stones, says Schopenhauer, and then ask us to believe that you weigh heavy, puts us in the light of ignorance, as if we were too stupid to see your own cunning. Be assured, young gentlemen, your brain must be filled with something. If there is no solid learning, there is usually air to fill the empty space. What a blessing it is that hollow heads do not pain us as hollow teeth? If it were not so we would see a great deal of suffering. It is the world's disposition to ridicule the conceited man, and while it is not generous to do so, many delight in putting a pin into the air-pillow on which the conceited one rests so contentedly. This operation is usually painful, nor is there any medicine to be found that will relieve such suffering. Leave all conceits, if you have any, right here, and if you are free from them guard against this folly with an ever-watchful eye. Always endeavor to see yourselves as others see you, and this again means self-examination, which has been commended to you at the very outset of my remarks.

Many people seek their happiness in social pleasures. Allow me to repeat a lesson already given you, namely, that there is greater happiness found in the art of avoiding trouble. This was one of Aristotle's lessons, and if he was a heathen he was a wise man. Pleasures are often mere mirages, at best they give no satisfaction, for after they have been enjoyed, there arises a desire for other and still greater gratification. Not all our desires can be fulfilled, and the disappointment arising from this is apt to produce discontent. He who asks the least of life but gives most to it, he is the happiest man. All real social and bodily pleasures fill but a very limited period of our lives, while the pleasures arising from a quiet life, free from troubles, may be enjoyed every hour and day. The art of avoiding trouble, therefore, is a pleasure-giving faculty, and I ask you earnestly to seek more of this negative joy than that which may be called positive. Troubles must and will come to you, as they have come to us of riper years. You cannot escape them, for this is a part of the philosophy and economy of this world. Your and my Saviour was a man of sorrow and of grief, and we all must follow in His footsteps, willingly or unwillingly. Maybe you imagine that you have already tasted much of life's cares. Perhaps you have, but in the course of years you will discover the fact that up to this period you were merely playing soldier. Perhaps you have had a good deal of target practice, while on one or two occasions you may have smelt gunpowder in a little skirmish. Now, however, the bugles are calling you into battle array, you are about to fall into line; soon the duties of life will weigh upon you, and I hope that you may accept your positions with a spirit of contentment and discharge the duties of your lives with fidelity. I hope that you may constantly improve, so that when men in high places pass away, you may be fit to take their positions. Move slowly. Oaks require many years of growth ; pumpkin-vines spread over an acre lot inside of three months. Make no greater demands upon the world than you are entitled to make, and in order to know what is due you, in order to know what you may expect and what you can do, I am compelled once more to put before you the selfsame lesson—*study yourselves.*

Men must have rest, but there are those who think they must be *idle* in order to have rest. Idleness is not leisure, said Benjamin Franklin. There is rest in a change of occupation, hence, men who have correct views of life are ever active. There is too much to be done in the little span of time granted us here on earth to waste hours in what the Italians fondly call *dolce far niente*—sweet idleness. Many people, when looking over the day that is passed, are compelled to say, in the language of Horace Mann : " Lost, yesterday, somewhere between sunrise and sunset, two golden hours, each set with sixty diamond minutes. No reward offered, for they are gone forever." Says a German philosopher, "To-morrow is not to-day," and unless you have done the duty of to-day, unless you have done something for your own progress and for that of the world, you have lived it in vain. Multiply your working years with 365 and notice how few your working days are. Work then, work every hour, whether you are paid for it or not, for your reward is sure to come.

Reserve not your energies for the future, when you expect to do great things, but exercise them every day, so that when the time for great deeds does come, your strength will be developed. Many dream of greatness, and aim at it as if they had to kill a nine-headed hydra ere they could be called famous; but true greatness is the result of an honest discharge of one's daily duties. You will never rise in the world without doing your daily work well. The devil does not walk about with hoofs and horns in order to tempt us. No; he generally comes to us with fancy pictures, working upon our imaginations, thereby leading us from the path of duty. The young mind loves to dwell upon the brightness of the future, and while doing so is neglectful of present duty. Beware, however, of all such fancy pictures, for the future is apt to be deceiving. It often presents itself like a lovely landscape, when viewed from afar, but when we come near to it we find hard roads, burning sands, with thorns and thistles growing among the flowers. Enjoy every day's work, enjoy every mile of your life's journey, for then only will you be able to say in advanced years that you have spent happy lives.

Have you thought of the fact that physicians are often called upon to confront death? It is a most serious duty to accompany a soul to the brink of that river which divides the known from the unknown. You may not be Christians, but you cannot at such a time escape the question, Is this all of life? Can you close your eyes to the fact that an hour will strike for you, when some other physician will say, he is dead, where shall he be buried? You may deny everything, but the fact that you must die is the greatest certainty that awaits you. What is your idea of the great beyond? Will you be able to say a kind and cheering word to a hopeless, dying person, if circumstances require you to do so? What opportunities for doing good you have constantly before you, and what a beautiful picture it is to see the healer of the body point the patient also to the Healer of the Soul.

There is one more point I must speak upon. Be progressive, young gentlemen, be studious. I know many physicians who never look into a book except they are called upon to attend a serious case of illness. As to medical journals, they never seem to think of such things. Let me advise you to read wherever and whenever you can. This world is like a huge army, and your medical profession is as a division of it. The command is to advance, and if you keep in line you must straighten up, carry your musket and keep your powder dry. Keep step with advancing forces, else you will soon be among the stragglers, and then you must fight like bushwhackers. Be honest soldiers, who occupy a place in the front. Unless you read and keep up with the world, you will be regarded as antiquated specimens of medical ignorance, and the first wide-awake and progressive man that comes into your town will overshadow you and take your patronage from you.

As men accumulate great wealth by first laying up little sums, so men become learned by storing away every day a few lessons. In the end you shall be rich in mind, and before you are aware of your own superiority, others will see it and select you for honorable positions. Would you rise in your profession, let me advise you to be studious. Wait not for a great discovery or for a great surgical operation that shall lift you suddenly to the highest honors, but gather knowledge every day, so that when the time for your discovery and investigation may come, you will be prepared and possess the necessary mental force. A lazy, idling doctor bears the stamp of a worthless man. He may have a fine span of horses, he may live in an elegant house, but he will be regarded as a poor apology for a doctor. He started out with scanty rations in his knapsack, and during the many years of practice he has added nothing to his original pork and hard tack. In all probability he was a deficient student when he received his diploma, and the little knowledge which he then possessed he failed to keep bright. He will be denounced, and justly so, as an ignoramus, and only ignoramuses will employ him.

I have seen doctors in small country towns, for there they usually are objects of observation, that had more time than they knew what to do with. The studious doctor never has too much of this precious article. The one is found everywhere except at the post of duty, the other is always there. Such doctors are constantly in search of amusement and diversion, hence they are found in all manner of places and company. If nothing better offers itself, they loaf in stores or in taverns. This brings them into doubtful company, it lowers them to the level of the ignorant and uncultivated, and before they are aware of it, their status is fixed in public opinion. To switch off from a track like this is indeed a difficult task. The studious doctor has no time to waste, he makes his calls and then returns to his books. Imagine not that the world is blind or indifferent to your doings, and that the public eye will not scrutinize your conduct. Intelligent people watch physicians, they notice how they spend their time, they notice, when passing their offices, whether they are studying or whether they are sitting idly in their chairs with their feet on the table. The intelligent will observe whether the doctors have books in hand, or whether they while their time away playing checkers. Without being aware of the fact, a stamp of some sort will be put upon you by the public; see to it that this stamp represents a good character. Be studious, start on the right track, no matter where your lot may fall. Invest not every dollar in lands or in houses, nor in horses, but buy yourselves good books, for these will be among your best friends.

The man who reads and stores his mind with knowledge is his own best company. The one that does not read becomes an idle talker; he lets himself down and loses the respect of people of culture. The richer your mind becomes the happier you will be in your professional work; the greater will be the pleasure of acquiring knowledge. Its possession alone makes you independent. Never overlook the fact that character and learning are the keys which open to you the doors of the best society.

Have a literary and also an art existence. By no means confine your reading entirely to your own profession. Read, however, only good books; waste no time upon novels. It is a sad sight to see people chew up husks when there is so much good sweet corn ready to be consumed. If you can study other languages, do so; for thereby you increase your own powers tenfold. Good reading, genuine art-culture, are admirable means to brush off that brusqueness and apparent roughness of manners one notices so often in country physicians. Through reading you learn to know life, and through it you will be better fitted to read men's characters. Only what you KNOW is your own, not what you HAVE. Make the most of yourselves, for so will you make the most for yourselves and for mankind.

I have endeavored to show you that in order to be successful in life you must be manly men, you must be sober and intelligent, studious and progressive men, you must know human nature, you must be prudent in act and speech, and you must love and labor for the advancement of your profession. On the other hand, there are many men who call themselves successful because they have acquired much wealth. Their reasoning is based on the theory that some superiority is better than none, and thus they make wealth a substitute for mental and moral superiority, which is beyond their reach. Seek not your success in that direction. For the sake of the love you bear to your chosen profession, aim to honor and to elevate it by being the right sort of men. In entering upon the duties before you, borrow courage and inspiration from the many illustrious men that have adorned the history of your profession. No matter what the difficulties may be that present themselves, no matter what privations or criticisms you may be called upon to endure, live as men that have chosen an honorable profession. Hold fast to your calling; blame it not for your own blunders, but honor and defend it, practice and improve it, to the best of your ability. Give your whole soul to your work; love it, for love must be the propelling power in your calling, as it is in that of the minister, teacher, and the artist. Labor unceasingly, labor earnestly, and then wait patiently for public recognition. You may become great, but, be assured, you must work hard and wait long for it. Thousands have entered the medical profession before you, thousands will enter it after you; but the bulk of these are standing down in the valley. Very few have reached the summit of the mountain. Are you willing to remain at the foot of the hill of fame, or are you ambitious to rise? No matter what your powers may be, endeavor to rise, at least as high as you can. But bear in mind that true happiness is only found in the act of rising, not so much in being elevated above others. Many imagine that there is great satisfaction in standing high in one's profession. Such, no doubt, is the case, but a high position brings also great responsibilities, and the higher one rises on a mountain the colder becomes the atmosphere. The satisfaction of standing high diminishes in the same ratio as one rises, for the higher you ascend the greater becomes also your view of the immensity of the fields which have not as yet been explored. Thus, the higher a man rises the better he appreciates his own deficiency, and it will therefore be generally found true that the scholar is humble. On the other hand, he has a perfect right to feel his own worth, when viewing the common people before and behind him on the streets.

My prescription is made out, and it remains to be seen whether you will have it filled and whether you will use it in life. Every doctor likes to see his medicine taken; so do I in this case. I may never see you in life again, but I part from you feeling satisfied that to the best of my ability, I have improved the little time granted me to direct you into the right path. No doubt all that has been said is old, but the old truths, the plain truths, must be repeated to every rising generation. They are plain old maxims, but for all that, they are often difficult to remember and still more difficult to follow. Your teachers know from experience how often they have repeated the first lessons of medicine, and yet they will again be called upon next term to reiterate them. But no one would say that the lessons themselves are the worse for it.

Take, then, my prescription, with my best wishes for your success. Fill it out in life, and take a dose whenever needed. It is patent medicine, though perfectly free from quackery. It is medicine patented to make you happy and healthy in soul, mind and body. Let me recommend you the following words uttered by a great and good man, as your life's motto or as your professional text. Said he: "I expect to pass through this world but once; if, therefore, there is a good thing I can do to any fellow human being, let me do it now, for I shall not pass this way again." To which I will add: if there is a good thing to do toward helping any good cause along, do it to-day, for you will never live to-day over again. May God richly bless you and, through you, your profession and mankind. This is my parting wish.

SCHOPENHAUER'S MUSICAL PHILOSOPHY.

Germany is preëminently the land of music, and in a like sense it is the land of metaphysics. Strange to say, among the many philosophers that Germany has produced, few have dealt successfully with the subject of music. Even Kant, the founder of an art-philosophy, regarded music merely as a pleasant play of the emotions; "but," says Hand, "he failed to make out whether a mere sensuous impression or the effect of a discernment of form prevailed in that play." Kant denied what every student of art now acknowledges, namely, that music is a language of the emotions and a means of awakening æsthetical ideas. According to Richard Wagner, only one philosopher has fully understood and correctly set forth the high position of this art. In his little book, entitled, "Beethoven," he says : " Schopenhauer was the first to recognize and designate with philosophical clearness the position of music with reference to the other fine arts, in that he awards to it a nature entirely different from that of the plastic or poetic arts." This decided testimony in favor of Schopenhauer's musical philosophy is all the stronger in view of the fact that Schopenhauer was by no means a follower of Wagner. Yet, at first sight, it would seem as if the two men were musical antipodes; for Schopenhauer speaks favorably of Rossini's music, which, in its character, its construction and tendency, is as far from Wagner's ideas of musical art as the east is from the west.

Music cannot be made the medium of a special theology or of a code of ethics; we, as musical students, have therefore nothing directly to do with Schopenhauer's peculiar theories. Still, as his philosophy of music is closely connected with his theory of the will, we must make you acquainted with it.

When reviewing this philosopher's theories we must judge of him in the light of his own times and surroundings. The convulsion in society produced by the French Revolution, and the bitter Napoleonic wars which followed, could not fail to make its impression upon such a mind as that of Schopenhauer. Religious skepticism prevailed everywhere among the learned as well as among the masses. True religion was scarcely found anywhere. After the years of warfare had at last ended, the masses gave themselves over to pleasure seeking. The various governments of Europe did all they could to turn the people's attention from the affairs of state and public morality. Every conceivable amusement was provided for the masses, and it was at that time that Rossini, with his sensuous operas, prevailed everywhere, overshadowing even a man so great as Beethoven, and that in the very city of Vienna, where Beethoven dwelt almost as an exile. It was at this time that Strauss and Lanner, the dance-kings, appeared on the arena, furnishing their charming new dances for ball-rooms.

While the people were thus made drunk with pleasures, the affairs of state being in the hands of reactionists of the worst kind, all thinking men cherished secret sorrow at the existing state of things. But what they cherished as their own grief, was the common grief of the best men of the nation. It was produced by that political and moral mildew which was setting upon the minds of the people, and this grief is called in German, the Weltschmerz, or the grief of the world.

Beethoven gives expression to the "*Weltschmerz*" in many of his matchless works, but Schopenhauer is the true representative of this idea, and he carried his state of dissatisfaction to such a degree, that he became a pessimist of the very first water. There runs throughout his writings a vein of despair that shocks one, and the reader is often chilled and even frightened at the terrible coldness with which he destroys and dispels all those fond illusions and pictures of fancy to which the human mind often resorts and clings as a relief. As Schopenhauer took a deep interest in sacred Hindoo literature, one meets quite frequently in his writings a peculiar Oriental cast, a sort of Buddhistic spirit, which here and there lends a peculiar coloring to his essays. Then the attentive reader cannot fail to discover, also, Schopenhauer's peculiar views about women, which almost causes one to believe that he lived a few centuries ago. But enough of these preliminary remarks.

Schopenhauer was born in Danzig, Germany, in the year 1788. His father was a rich merchant; his mother was the well-known authoress of novels, Johanna Schopenhauer. A literary vein seems to have run in the larger portion of the Schopenhauer family, for the daughter, Schopenhauer's only sister Adele, also was a novelist. When Danzig was ceded to Prussia in 1793, the family being anti-Prussian in political sentiment, moved, at considerable loss of property, to Hamburg. The elder Schopenhauer was a very intelligent man. He was fond of reading, but still more so of traveling, and he made frequent and prolonged visits to England and France. These visits to foreign countries made young Schopenhauer a good linguist, for he spoke and wrote both English and French quite fluently. He was also well versed in the ancient languages, both in Latin and Greek, and wrote dissertations in the former language. While the father had many excellent points of character, he had also some great weaknesses, and these the son not only inherited, but they became intensified in him. One of these failings was a decided morbidness of temperament, which sometimes seemed to overwhelm him. His mother evidently had no special affection for her husband, and sought pleasure in society and travel, which separated her much from her family. Young Schopenhauer, being the only son, was designed by his father for the counting-house; but the son persistently rebelled against all mercantile employment. Mild forms of correction were employed, but these were of no avail, and at last the choice was left between a regular college education and a trip through Europe. Although young Schopenhauer was eager to learn, he chose the latter, and in 1803 the family started for England and Scotland, where they remained for a considerable time. During this period our young philosopher was placed in a boarding-school at Wimbledon, near London, and it was here that he acquired a thorough knowledge of English, which he often displays in his writings. But what is far worse and much to be deplored, is the fact that in this boarding-school he took a cordial dislike to English formality, and especially to the English clergy and English ideas of religion. He is most unsparing when the opportunity offers itself to speak of the clergy of the Church of England, and he himself says that a great deal of that bitterness which he feels toward religion in general and the ministry in particular is chargeable to the clergyman who presided over the Wimbledon school.

After leaving England, the family visited Switzerland and then returned home. But scarcely had they been settled again in the old home when the father died. Prompted by a sense of reverence for his parent's wishes, the son now entered the counting-house; but the desire for higher knowledge at last became irresistible, and, impelled by his thirst for learning, he finally entered the University of Göttingen, where he studied history and natural sciences, two studies, he says, which in his later work proved very helpful to him. Here he became acquainted with Schultze, who aided him with his sound advice. When referring to his metaphysical studies, Schultze counseled Schopenhauer to read Kant and Plato first, and cautioned him under no circumstances to read any other philosopher, especially not Aristotle and Spinoza, until he had thoroughly digested the two first-named authors. In 1811 he went to Berlin, drawn thither by Fichte, but after hearing a few lectures from that philosopher he felt disappointed and turned from him. In 1813 he endeavored to secure the Doctor's degree at the University in Berlin, but the war with France being then at its height, he was prevented from making the attempt. He finally, however, took the degree at Jena and then turned toward Weimar, the literary Mecca of Germany, where he was favored with Goethe's friendship. It was here, also, that he met the oriental scholar, Meyer, who caused Schopenhauer to interest himself in the holy writings of East India, which, as has already been stated, gives some of his essays such a strange cast. During the period from 1814–18 he lived quietly in Dresden, and while there he wrote his famous treatise on "Sight and Colors." About this time he also wrote his most famous work: "The World as the Will and its Representation." In 1818 he visited Rome, and then returned to Berlin, where he connected himself with the University as a lecturer. But he was soon drawn a second time to Italy, where he remained until 1825. He again settled in the Prussian capital, but the approach of the cholera drove him a second time from that city, and this caused him to finally settle in Frankfort-on-the-Main, where he spent his life. He was fortunately situated, for his father had left him ample means. He was, therefore, not compelled to labor for his support; he had command of his own time, was independent of the powers that ruled, and could afford to say exactly what he thought and felt. He was never slow to express his opinions, and did so, regardless of people or place.

He now gave himself exclusively to metaphysical studies, and wrote diligently. His first work, "The World as the Will and its Representation," failed to be recognized, and was left totally unnoticed; this was to him a source of great mortification. Not until 1836, when he published a little pamphlet, entitled "The Will in Nature," in which he set forth his philosophy in the most concise form, did his writings attract any attention whatsoever. In 1839 one of his theses was crowned by the Norwegian Academy of Science. In 1851 he wrote his best work, entitled "Parerga and Para-li-pomena," a series of short essays on metaphysical subjects, which are very fine specimens of writing.

Schopenhauer lived for thirty years in Frankfort, and was known there as the Misanthropic Sage. On lonely walks he was always accompanied by his poodle, to which he was much attached. In fact, it is said of him that he spent more time in the company of his dog than in that of man. It is the opinion of those who lived nearest to our philosopher that his sad experiences in his dealings with men, and his antipathy to his mother, made him the pessimist he was, but that at heart he was kind, especially toward the suffering. He felt much sympathy for those who had to battle with the adversities of life, and in his philosophy he advises us *not* to become angry at the meanness of men, but rather to pity them on this account, and to regard them as fellow-sufferers. Says he : "When you meet a human being, try not at once to settle his mental and moral value, nor endeavor to fix his inherent degree of dignity, neither attempt to fathom his mind or to settle the absurdities of many of his views. The first would lead to hatred, the second to contempt ; but rather regard your neighbor from the standpoint of suffering ; see him in his perplexing anxieties, in his vain strivings, in his unsuccessful endeavors to secure peace and quiet, in his needs and wants, in his ailings of body and mind, and you will be forced to regard him as your kinsman. Instead of indulging in hatred and feelings of contempt you will then arouse sympathy, *that* sympathy which is love, and (says this pessimistic Schopenhauer, who is regarded as totally devoid of all regard for religion), it is this love which the Gospel teaches." As far then as this basis is concerned he stands on religious ground. But let us follow him a few steps further. Says he, "If you have cast a glance at the meanness of man, and are ready to become exasperated over it, endeavor to awaken sentiments of sympathy by looking at the suffering you see everywhere among the children of men. And if this again alarms you, turn your eye upon the corruption of human nature, and thus will you establish a healthy equilibrium in your mind. Then will you learn that there is eternal justice and that this world is judgment." Schopenhauer was a firm believer in the doctrine of total depravity in man, even in infants. He recognized the need of a change of heart, but in the use of means we differ with him, as we shall presently see.

Schopenhauer turned away from all society, from all active participation in those aspirations which agitate the human family; but for all he was a diligent reader of the European press ; he often took its statements to illustrate and to prove his teachings. That he and his mother could not agree is a sad fact, yet there were good causes for it. She delighted to live in a whirlpool of social pleasures, and wrote weak novels. She saw the world only from the standpoint of enjoyment, while he was a deep thinker, a philosopher who saw the world only in the light of suffering. He believed in Aristotle's idea, that the avoidance of trouble, which he calls a negative sort of happiness, is far more desirable than all the pleasures which society offers. He was a profound scholar, a misanthrope, a pessimist, while his mother was one of the worst optimists. In one of her letters she said to him, "your lamentations over this stupid world and the misery of mankind, give me bad nights and evil dreams." Another reason why Schopenhauer felt bitterly toward his mother was her neglect of his father's memory.

There was a great gulf, so to speak, between the two, and so mother and son went their own ways. They had apparently nothing in common but their names. If I should be forced to take sides between the two, I would stand with Schopenhauer, for his ideas of the human family in all its corruption, his ideas of the evil propensities of human nature, correspond most nearly with my experience.

But let us drop the curtain upon this sad picture. I merely raised it in order to show you that the strongest men often find it impossible, by their own strength, to swim against the current of circumstances. Philosophy always has had a clear perception of the disturbed condition in the human heart, but philosophy never found the true remedy. This the Gospel alone supplies. Schopenhauer was well read in ancient as well as in modern literature. His best ideas, he says, came from Kant, Plato, and the sacred writings of East India. He always was serious; he could not bear to see anything abused, neither man nor beast, literature nor art, religion nor philosophy. He hated all cliques, all unmanly means to oppose those that think differently; he despised the socialistic ideas of modern times, as these developed themselves during the revolutionary days of '48 and '49; in short, he was completely at outs with his own times, and with many of the men that held the wheels of government or that fashioned public thought. Despite his exclusiveness, many great men came to Frankfort to make his acquaintance, and not a few remained with him in order to study his philosophy, or to listen to his interesting conversations. This made the last years of his life more pleasant and himself more social. By nature he was an aristocrat; in his teachings and conversations he was an autocrat. He denounced many of those who taught philosophy in the Universities of Germany as mere *Sophists*, and upon the whole, he called them a most sorrowful crew. Hegel he regarded as the arch-humbug. Even Kant he accuses of veiling his ignorance at times by using language that is difficult to understand. Yet it must be said of him that he held Kant in the very highest esteem, and he often pronounced him the clearest thinker of modern times. Schopenhauer despised obscurity in anything, and so he was also a despiser of all duplicity in the use of language. When he speaks he always aims at a point; he never sets off mere fire-crackers, or Roman-candles. He always uses hard shot that hits, though from a Christian standpoint he often shoots at a wrong target. If he uses the knife he cuts to the bone, and what he says he utters regardless of the opinions of others. He displays the utmost faith in the correctness of his own theories, and predicts that in the future, when men shall judge with more freedom, when philosophy shall be less under the influence of those in authority, his philosophy will be accepted as the only correct one. What if such a man had been a Christian, a teacher of sound theology. His writings are sometimes difficult to understand, partly because he uses technical terms with special meanings attached to them that must be learned by much close reading of his theories. Moreover, he often writes in lengthy and intricate sentences, but after studying these, his ideas always stand out clearly. No matter how we may dislike many of these ideas, and no matter how much we may deplore the fact that they were not turned into the right channel, we must give them credit for fearlessness, for candor, and for freedom from all school-cant. The fundamental ideas of his philosophy are these: The will of man is the real [thing in this world, all else is mere representation. This will, of which Schopenhauer speaks, is not what in common language is meant by the absolute free power of action, but implies, in the philosopher's mind, the essence of all things, the all-pervading power manifesting itself everywhere. This will stands separate from the faculty of reasoning; it is the thing in itself, in which the created world and the Creator meet. From this standpoint man becomes the act, the true manifestation of the will. The will, which lies at the foundation of all representations and appearances, develops into a succession of ideas. From the animal downward, the will is void of cognition and ideas; it is a mere blind force, an unconscious seeking and fleeing. It is active in plant life, in animal life, until in man it manifests itself through the nerve power and the brain, thereby reaching its highest state of self-consciousness. The will comes first, it is the greatest factor, and the intellect stands second to it. According to Schopenhauer's theories, the intellect is a tool in the hands of the will, if I may be permitted to use this expression. The will always manifests itself through motives. In the animal the intellect is subordinate to the will. The animal knows and follows only the laws of self-preservation. Prompted by instinct it seeks food and shelter. Among the *common people*, that factory-ware of society, as Schopenhauer calls them, the will has no higher aims and wants than self-gratification. With them the will is the master and the brain the servant, but when the man becomes educated, when he reaches a high state of culture, the brain begins to rule and gradually subdues the will. In genius, which is the highest type of sensibility and intellectuality, the mind becomes the supreme ruler. The intellect is so completely absorbed and so intensely interested in the clear perception of things, that the will is, as it were, put into chains; the mind emancipates itself from the will and its powers, and it is then, and not until then, that the mind learns to see things in their true light; that is, the mind sees things no longer in the light of mere usefulness and productivity—but simply for their own sakes. This is the pleasurable, æsthetic contemplation of which Schopenhauer speaks so much, and of which I will say more in another place. This æsthetic contemplation affords us, however, only temporary relief; it suppresses the will-power only for a brief period of time, for the renewed activity of the will forces upon us new wants, and thus prevents us from enjoying permanent rest. The will desires to have and to live, but, as life is inseparably connected with suffering, the will, if gratified, must necessarily lead to suffering. The more the will is suppressed, the more effectually it is denied, the better and purer man becomes, until finally in sanctification, by turning from life, he realizes in himself a complete deathness toward this world, and a cheerful resignation to its conditions, which gives him the much sought for relief. Thus we see how our philosopher sees through self-negation that which, according to the teachings of the Bible, can only be found in a cheerful resignation to the will of God, and in accepting the plan of salvation. But, continues the philosopher, that which appears only in single instances among the pure, the good, and the sanctified—that is, the perfect denial of the will—would, if it were reached by all, lead to the destruction of mankind; as we now know it, it would be the end of that world which represents the will. For this new order of things, however, we lack all conception, says our author, and to us it is, therefore, equal to nothing. On the other hand, we must bear in mind the fact that our world *is nothing* in the eyes of those who have denied the will, and who have come to realize its tendency.

At one time Schopenhauer's philosophical theories seemed to reach the masses of Germany, but they have lost much of their popularity. In the land of Locke and Bacon he became known in 1853, through an article which appeared in the *Westminster Review*, and it is claimed that the attention which was bestowed upon him by the English press tended largely to make him known among his own countrymen.

Schopenhauer died in Frankfort on the 21st of September, 1860, at the age of 72. His housekeeper found him one morning, after breakfast, lifeless in his chair. He left a portion of his estate to the Invalides of the Prussian army, who fought against the Socialists and Liberals in the revolution of '48 and '49. He allowed nothing to be put upon his tombstone but the bare name, *Arthur Schopenhauer*.

Perhaps some may think, that inasmuch as we are concerned only in Schopenhauer's musical theories, I have paid too much attention to his life and philosophy; but you will presently see that, in order to understand this latter, the facts given you are necessary as a basis. His life-story might have been omitted, but I know that there are many among you who would be interested in it. So let us now retrace our steps in order that we may properly get a clear understanding of the real subject in hand.

Kant, in his "Critique of Pure Reason," says, that he has proven the absolute impenetrability of the essence of things by human knowledge. In order to see objects, we can only behold them in time, in space and in their mutual relations to cause and effect. We cannot, therefore, go beyond the appearance of things, and there must always be something unknown, namely, that which exists independent of the appearance, independent of time, space and causality. This Kant calls the "thing in itself," and as we cannot grasp it, this thing in itself is called the X of the universe. Schopenhauer steps in and says that the will is that which represents this X, and he claims that by this solution he has given positiveness and consciousness to the metaphysical world. The will pervades all things, hence, we become identified with all things, and there is, therefore, no longer a mystery which we cannot solve. It is true, all things must be seen through time, space and causality, but there is one exception, and this exception is man. We are conscious of a vital power in ourselves, and this power is the will; it is ever present, ever active, it makes itself forever felt, it is the *thing* of our being. This recognition of self Schopenhauer regards as the only metaphysical knowledge, in the proper sense of the word. Looking at the world we see a repetition of ourselves, and that on a gigantic scale. There can be no other substratum, says he, in the universe than the will in its various stages of consciousness. There is, therefore, a spirit of unity in the created world, and this makes us a part of the whole, it fills up the chasm that divides the mental and material forces, and enables us to glance fearlessly at the struggling and suffering of mankind. The history of the world, says Schopenhauer, is but a struggle of the will to become conscious, and this consciousness is reached in man. Will and interminable desire are the essence of all beings. Everywhere we see the will struggling for an existence; whatever obstructs its path is resisted;

species devour species; race contends against race; even mother earth is seething in its interior with fires, ready to burst forth at any time. Thus we see the will devour its own children. The author points to the apparent cruelty of nature and tells us it is the nature of the will. But is there no escape from this torment? Even if we could agree with Schopenhauer in all he said, here we have reached the parting point for good. While it is my belief that all these evils can only be remedied by regeneration in Christ, Schopenhauer points out two ways for us in which we may escape from the torment of the will. One of these is *self-denial*, as has already been shown, that is, the subjection of the will by the aid of the brain. The misery of the will is mirrored in the brain, and through its aid the will is enabled to subdue its desires. This leads to the deadening of our desires, and this is what *Christianity* teaches or points to. Schopenhauer by no means hesitates to point in this direction, for he sees the greatest ideal of happiness in the strictest order of the Catholic Church, the Trappists, an order which forbids its members even the privilege of speaking, and which demands most complete self-denial. In fact, Trappists live in a tomb where deathly silence reigns.

There are, however, other means, says Schopenhauer, of temporarily emerging from this struggling and suffering, these ever-continued wants of the will, and these means are the arts which lead to pure reflection and temporary peace. I have, in a previous part of my lecture, referred to that pleasurable æsthetic contemplation of which Schopenhauer says so much. Allow me now to explain. When viewing objects in art or nature, the artist beholds them without desire or without the action of the will. He divests things of their accidental surroundings; he sees the real essence of the things, that is, the idea which lies beyond time, space and causality. The mind is completely absorbed, and the will is, for the time being, silenced. He who thus enjoys art is in a will-less state, he feels not its wants. This, no doubt, is the true enjoyment of art. It is the divine character of the beautiful, inherent in every true work of art, that lifts us out of our every-day existence, that ennobles our thoughts and emotions. The beautiful can have but one source, it can be concentrated in but one being, and this is none other than God. True art therefore brings us in contact with the Divine idea, and in this sense all true art must be sacred. Pure art impressions, therefore, must be good, and for the time being they gently whisper peace to our souls. This æsthetic contemplation, however, affords us only temporary relief, it suppresses the will for a brief period only. This temporary state of elevation, together with the mental culture brought about by true art studies, shows the benign influence of the beautiful when we take it into our hearts. Schopenhauer says it is the aim of all the arts to express the true essence of things; and this expression of the essence of things brings me to the ultimate object of my lecture, namely, the philosophy of music.

Schopenhauer starts out by saying that Music stands alone; that it is separated from all the other arts. Being neither an imitation of anything created, nor a repetition of anything seen, not even a repetition of *ideas* of objects, it must, nevertheless, be analogous to the other arts; it *must* stand in the same relations to the world as the representation stands to the real thing, as the copy stands to the original. These relations, however, *must* be very intimate, true and correct, for music is readily understood and most deeply felt by all men. The question which now presents itself is this: Wherein consists the peculiar relation of music to the world; wherein is it distinguished from the other arts? In answer, the philosopher says it is the object of the arts to lead to the cognition of ideas through the representation of objects. They all represent the will, but only through ideas, through objects. Music, on the other hand, needs no objects, it represents the will itself; hence, it is direct in its operations, and, as the will is the same everywhere, music is easily understood and felt by all nations. Music, therefore, represents the real thing, the thing itself, not a mere appearance. The other arts only speak of the shadow; music speaks of the real substance, for it represents the will. For this reason it can be said that music could exist without this world; yes, the world might be called embodied music, and, continues he, were we able to give a perfect and satisfactory explanation of music, we would also have the true philosophy of the world itself. Music is the melody, and the world is the text to the same. In the lower tones of harmony we recognize inorganic nature; in the voices lying between bass and soprano we see the successive creations, while the upper voices represent the higher organic law and life. In the melody which leads the whole we recognize man. There is a limit to the depth of sound beyond which no tone can be heard, which is analogous to the fact that matter must have form in order that it may be perceptible. The four voices, bass, tenor alto and soprano, represent the mineral, vegetable, animal kingdoms, and, finally, man himself. The bass, like a crude mass, moves but slowly, while the higher voices move quicker; yet not one of them has a full meaning without the melody, which leads all, which imparts ideas and sentiments, and which expresses the will, the striving of man. The melody tells the most secret emotions of the heart, and reveals every desire of the human will, hence, it is called the language of emotions. Wagner's admiration for Schopenhauer's musical theories is mainly based upon a few leading principles, one of which is the assigning to music a separate and higher position from the other arts; for Wagner has abolished melody, at least in that sense in which Schopenhauer refers to it. This will be plain when I refer to the fact that he points to Rossini as the master of melody. Every musical student at all conversant with Wagner's ideas of art, knows how low is his estimate of the Italian maestro and his art work.

Our existence in life, says the philosopher, is a continued alternating of desires and gratifications. The will is forever wanting, and it strives continually to gratify its wants. We really know but two states while in the body, the state of want and the state of satisfaction; the conditions of desire and gratification. Analogous to this, music has but two leading chords, from which all others are derived. These are the tonic chord and the dominant chord of the seventh. The first is a chord of rest and calmness, the second is a chord of unrest, of longing and striving. Music is a continued succession of these two chords, and in this is represented our never-ceasing desires as followed by gratification. Thus, the composer reveals the innermost condition of our souls, he speaks the greatest truth, and speaks it in a language which reason comprehends not, but a language which is understood alike by men the world over. This art of disclosing all the secret desires of the will through the agency of tone, is the work of a genius, who, in producing music, does not labor so much with a purpose or with the understanding, but by inspiration, which puts him in a state of clairvoyance, as it were. The simple idea of reasoning in the act of composing music is fruitless. Like a somnambulist, the composer gives himself over to uttering revelations without reasoning about what he does. He speaks or writes of that which, in a state of wakefulness, he has no idea. Hence, it may be said that in the musician the artist is more effectually separated from the man itself than among other artists. Hence, also, it is that the act of composing music is looked upon as more mysterious than is that of painting, cutting marble or writing poetry. This is a second principle which Wagner endorses. In his little book entitled "Beethoven," he says that "through the effect of music upon us our vision is depotentialized in such a way that even with open eyes we no longer see intensively. And, in fact, it is only in this state that we immediately belong to the musician's world. From this world, which otherwise we have no means of portraying, the musician, by the disposition of his tones in a certain measure, spreads a net for us; or, again, he besprinkles our perceptive faculties with the miracle-working drops of his sounds in such a manner that they are incapacitated, as if by magic, for the reception of any impressions other than those of our own inner world."

In another place, when speaking of the clairvoyant state in which the composer writes, the same author says: "Only one state can surpass his own, that of the saint; and that especially because it is enduring and incapable of being clouded, while on the other hand, the enrapturing clairvoyance of the musician alternates with a continued returning state of individual consciousness, which must be thought only the more miserable in proportion as the inspired state elevates him higher above all limits of individuality. For this reason, *i. e.*, the sufferings with which he must pay for the state of inspiration in which he enraptures us so inexpressibly, the musician may well appear to us as worthier of reverence than other artists, indeed, as almost possessing a claim to our veneration. For his art, in fact, sustains the same relations to the complex of the other arts that religion does to the church."

Now let us return to our two chords, those of rest and unrest. Quick succession from want to gratification, says Schopenhauer, produces pleasure. So melodies and harmonies with quick successions from the dominant to the tonic are cheerful and please us at once. Being sprightly and easily understood, they gratify the uncultivated, those in whom the will rules supreme as yet. While melodies of a slow character, melodies with complicated harmonies which fail to step quickly from the dominant into the tonic, produce slow gratification; hence, they are sad, they deny or curb the will, and for this reason fail to please those who lack musical culture. Mazzini says that this is preëminently the nature of German music, that it is too elegiac in its character. In short, it may be said that there is, according to the Italian writer, too much of the "Weltschmerz" in it.

A melody which never leaves the original key fails to interest us; it represents neither want nor gratification, it is therefore unlike life, it is lifeless. Man does not stand isolated, but is related to and connected with the lower beings, and these again are connected with beings of still lower grades; so melody is only perfect in harmony, which enables it to make more powerful impressions. Music that speaks less of want and more of gratification, music with light melodies and simple harmonies, bespeaks only light emotions.

Music is a living language, it is a universal language, it pictures and expresses every shade of sentiment, and does so far more powerfully than does the language of words. Yet, when it portrays joy, sorrow or love, it does not depict any particular joy, sorrow or love, but it gives us simply these states of mind in general. In this particular direction music reveals to us the quintessence of life itself, and the heart, therefore, understands this language and its emotions without seeking to know the motives that produced them. But, inasmuch as our thinking faculties do not like to remain idle while the imagination is active, we clothe music with the word, we have accompanied it with action; and this leads us to song, the oratorio and the opera. Though music does give us the quintessence of life itself, it never can picture situations or events; hence, programme music is against the spirit of the art. When men, therefore, imitate things, scenes and situations, they reduce music to the level of the other arts, for then music ceases to address the heart and attempts to speak to the head, the reason and intellect. Music of the heart touches us; music of the head fails to reach us in the same degree of intensity. Music, when it appears to us as a far-off paradise, is so easily felt, yet so difficult to comprehend, because it reveals to us our inner natures. Says Schopenhauer, good music tells us what we are or what we might be. It gives us a picture of life full of love and void of its sorrows. It is the best commentator on our lives; hence, when listening to a symphony, continues he, we feel as if the secrets of our hearts had been told us, it seems as if our lives were passing before us, without being able to say wherein consists the connection between music and these lives. Hence, music is the lock and key to our memories and our affections. When listening to a grand piece of music we are transplanted into a world of sentiment, into the land of imagination. Our emotions are aroused and we forget, as it were, the real world without, with all its griefs and sorrows, and we exist for the time being in a world without sorrow. This reminds one forcibly of the theory of preëxistence so often alluded to by the ancient Greek writers, when speculating about the effect of the beautiful. Good music, continues the philosopher, expresses pure emotions, and for this reason it will eventually pass around the world and remain true forever. Poor music also expresses human sentiments but poorly; and for this reason it is bound to die before it goes very far. It comes not from the heart, hence it fails to go to the heart, and for this reason it lacks true life and must pass away.

It has already been stated, that music does not express ideas, but affects the soul directly, intensifying and purifying our emotions. From the close relations sustained by music to all things, and especially to our souls, it follows that, if words, scenes, or actions are accompanied with suitable music, it acts as the best commentator. No art operates upon man so directly and so deeply as music, and that for the reason, that none of the other arts permit us to look so deep into the true condition of the things of this world as music does.

When comparing the productive artist with the reproductive one, Schopenhauer says, that the power of composing outweighs that of executing. A good musical composition imperfectly performed gives us greater pleasure than does the best performance of a bad composition. A bad drama, on the other hand, if well played, gives more satisfaction than a good one but poorly performed. Much more might be added concerning our philosopher's theories, but time forbids.

Schopenhauer, no doubt, was a profound thinker who uttered many true words concerning music, but he advances also ideas to which I cannot subscribe. One of his objectionable theories is, that he ascribes to music those powers which thinking men accord only to religion. We all think highly of music; we love the art, and delight to know that by common consent it is called the "Divine Art;" but it is not designed to supplant religion.

We all believe in the existence of misery and suffering, in the depravity of human nature; we believe in the need of a change of heart, of a relief from suffering. But your teacher utterly disavows the idea that music, despite its refining and soothing influences, can accomplish what God alone can do, that is, change man's heart and cause him to look for a perfect peace in the beyond. With this faith firmly fixed in our hearts, we detract nothing from either art or artist; nay, we are all the better enabled to accept, to enjoy, and to use music as one of the richest and best gifts God ever gave to man. With this faith firmly rooted in our minds and hearts, we can read Schopenhauer, accept that which is good, and reject that which is false. I have felt it to be my duty to make you acquainted with this philosopher's theories, because as future teachers of music, you should know something about them. Rousseau has already said that musicians read too little, and it may well be added, that many of them think too little. The cause of musical culture is fast advancing in this country, and the time is near at hand, yes, it is now, when teachers of music are expected to be more than skillful players and singers. The world demands that they shall be well-read men and women, capable of thinking independently about their art.

MUSIC OF NATURE.

When speaking of the music of nature, the word music is not used in an art-sense, for art-music is not found in nature. It would be degrading to man to intimate that he learned music from birds, or that he caught it from the whispering winds, for the same hand that fashioned the bird also implanted in our breasts the love of song. It cannot, however, be denied that the voices of nature have exercised a decided influence upon the development of the art. While all intelligences can hear the sounds of nature, not every one hears music in them. These sounds never become music unless our own heart-strings vibrate with them. When we listen to music, be it that of art or that of nature, our imagination must aid us; we must have song in our hearts, else we hear nothing but sounds.

Complete silence, like complete darkness, is unendurable; our nature revolts against it. God's earth is one of motion, therefore one of sound. The earth whirls onward at great speed, and is it reasonable to suppose that it moves silently? Even light vibrates and produces sound, and is not the universe full of *it?* The noise which the heavenly bodies are supposed to produce is called the music of the spheres. For over 3000 years the idea of a celestial music has engaged the human mind. It is this sort of music the Psalmist must allude to when he says: "The heavens declare the glory of God." Imagine the heavenly bodies speeding their way through the universe, making sounds like peals of mighty organs, while myriads of beings shout Hallelujah in honor of Him who made all things. It does not follow because we cannot hear this music that it does not exist. If we could strengthen our hearing as we do our eyesight, what wondrous sounds we would hear. But let us leave the heavens and visit mother earth, whose sounds we do hear.

Doubtless, you all have heard of the strange sounds which the statue of Memnon produces at sunrise. On the island of Ceylon there is heard what the natives call the Devil's music, so terrible at times that the people become frightened. In Thibet there are heard noises which seem to call strangers by their names. On the waters of the Orinoco there are heard trumpet sounds, which the people call the voices of the holy trumpets, while near its shore stands a rock which, at sunset, produces tones deep and solemn, like those of an organ. On the Isle of Bourbon are trees the leaves of which sing. On the battle-field of Marathon there are heard noises at night which remind one of the march of an army. It is said that Miltiades is still passing nightly over the plains where he won his victory. In a cave in Finland there are heard from time to time the most horrible sounds, as if produced by wild animals. A cavern in Hungary emits sounds that resemble the firing of pistols. Strange noises are heard in oriental countries, and even in this country, which are produced by the shifting of sand. There is a certain kind of rock found in China, which, when rubbed with the fingers, produces sounds like those of a trumpet. In France there are found rocks which produce whole chords when struck with the palm of the hand.

The sounds produced by the avalanches as they come down mountain sides are described as something bordering on the terrible, while those who have visited Vesuvius when about to be active, describe the sounds produced by the seething mass as altogether fearful. There lived near my home a person known all over Germany as the wild hunter. The story goes, that this hunter, who was a rich baron, murdered his family, and being unable to find rest for his troubled conscience, donated his mansion to the Catholic Church, by whom it was afterward turned into a monastery. It was within the walls of that old building that I lived for three years. The owner, Baron Roddenstein, moved into two castles standing a few miles east of my home. It is said that to this day the unfortunate man wanders from one castle to the other, and those who are courageous enough to approach may hear the shouts of men, the barking of dogs, the rattling of wagons, etc. It is the popular belief that whenever these sounds are heard, war is to follow between Germany and some other nation. What it is that produces these noises is not known, but there is no doubt that heat and electricity are the forces to which many of them are attributable. The discovery has lately been made that the air, under process of heating by the rays of the sun, emits sounds. Several French savants, in order to investigate this fact, ascended in a balloon at early morning and remained up until after sunrise. While thus above the clouds they heard beautiful musical sounds, as if produced by a gigantic Æolian harp.

If the land has its strange voices, the mighty deep is not less remarkable on that account. Sailors claim that the sea is full of fairies and spirits that produce these strange noises. On the coast of the North Sea there are heard sounds which seem to come from a person in great distress. On the Gulf of Mexico one hears mysterious sounds, which some say come from singing fishes, while others ascribe them to the waters rushing through coral caves. Near Land's End, in England, there are heard sounds which the fishermen attribute to spirits of the deep. These noises are no doubt produced by the rocks on the Cornish coast. On the Ægean Sea there are heard tones which resemble chords struck by a guitar. They arise from the waves washing upon loose stones. The drops of water falling within the Fingal's Cave produce a most pleasing effect to the poetic mind, and Mendelssohn could not resist the temptation to introduce their lovely chime in his overture to the Hebrides.

The echo is one of nature's mocking instruments. The Hebrews call it the laughter of the voice. The ancients believed it to be a nymph, who, having been deceived by her lover, was turned into a tear, and nothing was left her but the voice with which she replies to the passions. An echo in England repeats everything three tones lower. Another repeats a word seven times in day and twenty times at night. An echo in Russia repeats one word one hundred times, while another in Algiers does so one thousand times. If we, like the echo, must repeat what we have heard, let us, like *it*, be at least truthful, if we cannot be charitable.

Humboldt, in his "Views of Nature," describes a scene near the Orinoco river. Having stopped with his party near the edge of one of those impenetrable woods so plentiful in South America, they hung up their hammocks, surrounded their camp with fire, in order to protect themselves against the attacks of wild animals. They rested undisturbed, except by the snoring of the Delphines in the river, and by the approach of alligators, who raised their heads in order to see the strangers. At eleven o'clock, however, there was heard such a noise in the woods that all sleep was at an end. The strangest and wildest mixture of sounds reached their ears. The jaguar, the tiger, and Brazilian lion were out on a hunt. Their roars resounded in the woods; their basses were accompanied by the tenors of the larger and smaller monkeys, while the parrots and pheasants, with their loud screams, made up the sopranos and altos. At one time they screamed together, then they howled alternately. Presently a tiger's voice was heard in the tree-tops, while the whole monkey family affrighted, fled with screams and snarls. This, in turn, alarmed the birds, who shrieked with terror and fled. But, hark! a jaguar has caught a wild pig, and while the poor animal screams in the death agony, the successful hunter growls loudly to keep his jealous companions away. Thus, the whole animal creation seemed wild and terror-stricken. But, to heighten the effect, a violent storm set in; lightning flashed, the thunder roared, the wind howled, bending the palms, and breaking off limbs of trees with terrific crashes. Thus, it may be said that all creation was in a terrible turmoil. This is one of nature's wildest concerts, of which we happily know nothing. The storm king is a mighty sovereign; he rides over hills and mountains; he sweeps through valleys and along rivers; he tries everything to make his voice heard; he uses trees like so many harps, and their limbs like so many strings; he whistles on reeds and howls in caverns, and when he lays hands upon the thousands of instruments in his way, there are heard shrieks and wailings, while lightnings illumine his way, and the thunder, like a huge drum, beats time to his terrible march. What a spectacle when the elements rage, when the rain comes down in torrents, when the wind breaks off the limbs of trees, as an excited harpist snaps the strings of his instrument, and when the earth seems to be shaken to its very centre?

The sea is the mightiest organ among nature's musical instruments. Even when still its vastness impresses us, and the mighty waters lie, like nature's largest child, in a cradle, gently rocking itself. When the tide comes in the little waves that come on shore seem to say, "Step back, or I wet your feet," and they come just near enough to cause you to fear that they will do so, when suddenly, with laughter, they recede, as if they had merely tried to frighten you. Listen! Hear the laughter, the incessant chatter of the bubbling ripples. Behold the beautiful bright sunlight shining upon them, reflecting the rays like sparkling diamonds, while the pebbles and sand beneath form a rich background. Verily the best artist fails when attempting to paint such a scene.

The calm sea talks gently, but when the storms rage you hear the sea moan and sing, then its slumbering powers are aroused, and the waters rush through caverns, producing sounds like the deep murmurings of an earthquake. Wildly the waves dash against the rocks, turning into foam and spray, yelling and screaming, and falling back in utter weakness before the boundaries God has set for them. As the wind increases in fury the waves, with their mighty artillery, make a still grander and louder noise. They rise higher and higher until they hide the very moon from our sight. They spring at each other like fighting warriors, they howl like huge dragons, and like sea monsters ready to devour, rush upon you; those waves which but an hour ago played at your feet. Hear the grand breakers, listen to the trumpet sounds of the wind, sending its blasts boldly over land and sea. That is battle music; the wind is a great commander, and the sea is a mighty army.

But if God's earth is beautiful in its grandeur, it is also worthy of our admiration in the smaller forms of creation. There is sweet sound in the rippling waves, in the rustling leaves, in the whispering winds, in the chirp of the cricket, in the songs of the birds, for all these sounds are but so many stops in the great organ of nature.

Birds are nature's best and sweetest singers, and theirs was no doubt the first song of praise and thanks that arose to the heavens, for birds sang before man was made. Let me describe for you a bird concert. Spring-time is the season when the birds sing sweetest. It is in that pleasant time of the year when the hillsides are first green, when the cattle graze leisurely, causing the monotonous tinkle of the cowbells to be heard far and near, making the stillness of a May morn all the more apparent. The trees are covered with blossoms, and look like huge bouquets stuck in the ground. These are the halls in which the birds give their concerts. Not only have they elegant halls; they themselves are more beautifully arrayed than the most elegantly dressed prima donna or the most gaudily uniformed brass band. They charge no admission, they wait for no late comers, they care for no applause, neither do they mind your criticism. The birds give several concerts each day, the best of which takes place just before sunrise. Nature is yet still; even Mr. Rooster, whose voice was heard every hour during the night, is taking another nap with his hen family. He who is up that early and listens will now hear one voice and then another, as if calling out "are you awake? are you ready for the concert? let us begin"—and presently there are heard voices coming from out of the hedges and trees saying, yes, we are ready, and then begins the contest of song. There are the blackbirds, who come in small armies, who sing the choruses with their monotonous chirps. They are the monkeys of the bird family, with their incessant chatter. Then there is heard the merry voice of Master Robin, laughing aloud as he flies from fence-post to fence-post, and from tree to tree, as if saying, I am not afraid of you; you can't catch me. Then there is heard the whistle of the red bird, sharp as a piccolo flute, while Master Woodpecker, with his red military cap, beats the drum. The busy wren, ever moving, sings lustily, while the catbird, our sweetest and most modest singer, lets his voice be heard from the close pines. Then there is heard that voice of peace and sorrow, gentle and sweet, the coo of the dove—mournful but always tender. The richly colored jays, too, let their war-cry be heard, interchanging it once in a while with that modest and loving call for their mates. On the barn over yonder are sitting the martins; they form a straight line, first looking to one side then to the other, chatting and talking as if they were repeating the most important tales about their late trip from the Southland. Thus the singing continues for about half an hour, after which birds make their toilet and take their breakfast. The sun having risen, birds, like lazy fellows, now cease to sing, and, like idle loafers, they sit under cover of shady trees or go on foraging expeditions. Toward evening another concert takes place. Then the catbird does his best. He perches himself upon the topmost limb of a tree and sings as if his throat would split. Oh, how often have I stopped the piano for the pleasure of listening to our sweetest vocalist, the catbird. How appropriate were the little girl's words, who, when hearing a catbird for the first time, said: "What make he sing so; do he eat flowers"? Master Robin now goes for the late worm, and holding his head high, as becomes a free bird, he proudly hops along the closely mown lawn, until after finding his supper he rises with a merry laughter to the nearest tree. The redbird is not to be outdone, and his whistle is heard far and near, while poor disconsolate Mrs. White calls loud and long for her husband, Bob, to come home, a place he never seems to be. In the meantime the sun has gone down and birds begin to seek their shelter. One by one their voices are hushed, only the blackbirds are heard to chatter, like folks who must talk themselves to sleep. At last they too are quiet, only here and there one seems to call out: "Didn't we have fun though? Are you all in bed? Be sure and be up early! Look out for the owls," etc. At last darkness covers the earth, but silence does not reign, for now the owls cry for their nightly food. This unhappy bird always seems to be like the soul cast into outer darkness, where its piteous cry awakens sympathy. It is a remarkable fact that no bird of prey sings. So people who study only the things of this world, those who selfishly prey upon their fellows, generally have no music in their souls.

No birds have musically-arranged melodies. Many of their strains have been written down, and it has been found that most of them have a variety of songs. Hear the robin when he has a worm in his bill, and flies before you from fence-post to fence-post, in order that you may see his good luck. Hear his challenging sort of a chirp. Then hear the same robin when he is frightened from his nest, or hear him as he gives the little robin his first flying lesson. What a voice of warning, saying almost in so many words, "Don't fall; don't go to the ground; look out for the cat," etc. Then hear the catbird when singing his best, and again hear him when mewing like a cat, or listen to the jay when he blows his bugle, and again when he gently calls his mate. But enough of this. The finest singer there is to be found in all the winged kingdom is the nightingale. This bird sings at night, which fact, it is claimed, gives to its song a peculiar charm. There must, however, be something extraordinary connected with it, else poets of all ages would not have sung of the nightingale. He who hears it for the first time, if he has any music in his heart, will stand spellbound and listen. Its singing is the most characteristic of any bird's song, it is entirely unlike that of any others. Whether there is such a place as bird heaven or not, I agree with a writer who said, that if he were St. Peter he would exclude no bird from the blessed abode. The raven he would admit because of the poet, yes, even the owls would be welcomed, and each should have a hollow tree and as many mice as he could eat.

The songs of insects are numerous and varied. We hear their noises, but fail to appreciate the wondrous rapidity of motion required to produce them. The common house-fly, which, by the way, is said to sing always in the key of F, makes 320 vibrations per second in order to produce a sound, and if this motion continues only for one minute, not less than 20,000 vibrations are required. When listening to this thoughtless, careless insect after walking into the spider's parlor, one doubts not in the least that it produces 20,000 vibrations per minute. How proper that the treacherous, deceitful, bloodthirsty spider should be voiceless. Can any of my readers imagine what a spider's voice should be in order to give expression to its character?

Probably all of you will agree that the mosquito is the most noted singer; it never fails to arrest our attention, and it surely never fails to draw. There is, however, another and far noisier visitor of our bed-rooms who makes the night hideous. I mean Mr. Pinch-bug. Though he needs a bigger door to enter than the mosquito, he usually manages to find a place to enter. But no sooner is he in than he tries hard to get out again, and with an angry whirr and whizz he explores the ceiling, giving every now and then a dart against it, as if he meant to strike through and through. How delightful to lie in bed while one of these chaps gives us a serenade, expecting every minute that he will fall into our very face. How pleasant to the ear when at last he comes down, scraping the wall with his claws, as if trying in vain to hold on. The hornet and humblebee, those tigers of the air, whizz by you and actually make you dodge, as if they were pistol balls. When the humblebee settles upon a flower he appears to me like a grizzly-bearded western hunter, like an old, old bachelor trying to kiss a sweet-faced young lassie. His rough yet tender tones of courtship are something worthy of special notice. What a delight it must be to be nestled between rose leaves that diffuse delightful perfume, that supply sweet honey. 'Tis no wonder the humblebee sings merrily when he swings to and fro in his couch of roses.

The katydid has attracted everybody's attention, and many times I asked myself: What was it that Katy did? It must have been something terrible, else they would long ago have ceased telling us that Katy did. Like slanderers, these tattlers keep themselves hidden, but their slandering voices are heard half a mile off. Who was Katy anyway? Was she richly dressed in satins and silks, or did she go about in poor and torn garments? Was she meek, or did she act the part of a regular Tom-girl? Did she flirt and break some gentleman's heart, or was she disappointed in love, and did she die of a broken heart? What was it that Katy did?

We must not neglect the frogs, it will never do. I love to hear their monotonous song at night, for it is always a harbinger of good weather and pleasant spring-time. Don't call the frogs croakers, for they are merry fellows, cold-blooded fellows though they are. Don't say that a frog's home is dreary, for above him often blooms the pond-lily, while to the right and left are beautiful arbors of grass, where he sits and sings to his love, *good night, good night*, and as he looks up at the beautiful lilies, he cries, *how white, how white;* when the moon rises he tells his lady love that there is *the moon, the moon*, and so Master Frog goes on singing until he swells up with love and pride and becomes big, until at last he is sought by some prowling fellow on account of his tender legs. Then poor froggy must hang up the fiddle and the bow, and must go to the place where all fat frogs have to go.

The barnyard is alive with curious and interesting voices. The most talkative is the hen family. What a fuss and a noise a hen makes after the laying of an egg, like many people, who never do a good act without proclaiming it to the world. But listen to that same hen when quietly strolling along in search of a grain of wheat, and hear how her tones pine and whine, as if saying what a barren world this is, with nothing to eat. Again, listen to that hen when she calls her brood, and you hear a tender and yet a very commanding sort of a tone. Her husband, Mr. Rooster, is still more noisy. See him as he flies on a fence, spreading his wings and crowing lustily, as if he were the monarch of all he surveys. Next, observe him, when finding a good morsel, how gallantly he calls the hens to partake of it. He fairly seems to say, *quick, quick, here is something good to eat*, but if they fail to come quickly, Mr. Rooster eats the best morsel himself.

'Tis amusing to hear young piggie when waiting for his meal. What a discontented and injured sort of a cry he has, as if saying, 'tis too bad to treat an animal like myself in this sort of a way—I won't stand it any longer. But come unawares upon a porker and hear the *ugh* with which he starts off. Or hear him when a dog has him by the ear. What a cry of distress. The swine family have some connection with art. Louis XI, King of France, while listening to the grunting of some swine, expressed the desire that a pig concert be arranged for his enjoyment. His court musician at once went to work. He selected large and small pigs, had them put into boxes which stood in a row. Before these he fastened a keyboard, and arranged it in such a manner that by striking it pins would penetrate the skin of the poor animals. All arrangements being completed, a pig concert was actually given at Versailles. The music is said to have been very pleasing to the royal, and, I may say, piggish audience.

The horse has a merry laughter which runs through the entire scale. His voice always expresses impetuosity and courage. Place by the side of it the cow's lowing or the bawling of the calf, and we perceive in the difference of the cries also the difference in the characters of the animals. Even Master Donkey, the much-abused and wickedly despised brute, should not be forgotten in our visit to the barnyard. Mrs. Partington once asked the doctor whether Ike had a musical ear, and when he replied that he knew not, she requested him to take the candle and see. Surely we need no candles to see donkeys' ears, and from their size one ought to suppose them to be good for music. But even in this instance nature seems to have given the ears without musical purposes. Jack begins with a modest whistle, and then gradually rises to the top of his voice, and suddenly sinks to its lowest depth. He has been honored by poets and musicians. Mendelssohn imitated his beautiful cry in his "Midsummer Night's Dream." But I have said enough about assinine music, though the subject is by no means exhausted.

Let me tell you something about a cat organ that was built in the earlier part of this century. There lived a man in Cincinnati at that time by the name of Curtis, who conceived the idea of getting up a cat concert for the benefit of the river men. He resided near Western Row, where cats abounded and where he had no difficulty in procuring all the specimens he needed. They had kept him awake many a night, and often he threw stones, bottles and even his boot-jack at them, so he thought he would try and utilize their musical powers. First he made experiments with a few cats, sticking them with pins, pulling their ears, etc., in order to draw out the best sounds. At last he discovered that the safest way to make a cat scream was to hit its tail. Having made this discovery, he gave orders to a carpenter to build him an organ, on which he was to play the accompaniment for his cats. Next, he procured the cats and trained them. He placed each animal in a small box with four holes in the bottom, designed to let the animal's legs hang through, to prevent it from clawing. The head was fastened in a board above while the tails were enclosed in tubes upon which hammers worked. These were connected with the keys of the organ, so that by playing upon them the hammers were moved. At last Curtis was ready. He had procured a perfect scale of cats' voices, from the two months' old kitten down to the regular growling Tom bass. He hired the second story of a warehouse situated near the landing, and provided a sort of amphitheatre for his audience. At the appointed day he moved all his cats safely to the hall, except the two principal basses, who, being accidentally put into one box, had an awful fight on the way up, and were consequently forced to appear before the audience with bloody noses and rueful faces. Immense posters had been put up announcing a concert of forty-eight cats, and a large crowd with a good sprinkling of boys greeted Mr. Curtis. At last the curtain rose, exposing to the gaze of an eager audience two rows of cats' heads glaring with lustrous yellow and green eyes. They all had little ruffles around their necks. Miniature music-stands were placed before them. The two basses who had a fight had their heads ornamented with muslin bands, which added greatly to the gravity of their looks. At the organ sat Johnson, ready to start the music, while in front of the platform stood Curtis, gravely announcing that the first tune would be, as he pronounced it, *Auld Lang Zion*.

This announcement having been made, Johnson started off with his music, and there were heard sounds no mortal ear ever heard before. The audience shouted and stamped, which excited the fury of the cats all the more; they forgot all their lessons. They paid no attention to time or tune, to rhyme or reason; they squalled and yelled, they clawed and spit, and phizzed in the madness of pain, until the sound of the organ was completely drowned. Suddenly the leather strap of Johnson's organ broke. The music ceased, but the cats continued their song, until they too, one after another, became silent, winking and blinking at the audience in fear of a repetition. The audience, however, was completely overcome and enchanted. Shouts arose, yells were heard, such as only river men can give; they stamped the floor until the platform not only shook, but actually gave away. Then there was heard the wildest mixture of laughing and swearing. Not a few were hurt by the fall, who, in their anger, began dealing out blows. The boys, on the other hand, poked the cats with sticks, adding greatly to the confusion. Being unable to save his pets, Curtis removed the top board and gave the cats their liberty. The poor creatures at once darted off in every direction, some finding their way to the floor, moving wildly between the spectators' feet, while others ran over their heads or over their backs. Whoops and yells, hurrahs and shouts were heard from every throat, benches were broken, windows were smashed, and not a few were heard to cry FIRE! The terrible noise attracted the attention of the police, but with their best endeavors they failed to gain admission. At last the old engine, Liberty, No. 3, threw a good stream of water into the hall, which had the desired effect. Order was quickly established and the hall was empty in an extraordinary short space of time. Thus ended the first and only cat concert on record, an event which was talked of by the river men for years afterward. Curtis and Johnson, of course, were brought before the Mayor, but upon explaining the cause of the disturbance, his Honor heartily laughed and told them never to do so again, *and they didn't.*

But we will dismiss the animal world and turn to the home of man. How comfortable to be seated in a warm room on a cold winter's day while the wind howls and blows without. The wind, as has been said, is a great musician. He tries every crevice, every crack, every loose shutter, every swinging sign, to make his wild music heard, and if he cannot sing or improvise an instrument he beats the drum by slamming doors and gates. The wind tries chimneys, telegraph wires, in short, everything that is able to give sound he uses as his plaything. There is also music in the gentle rainfall, especially when snugly settled in a warm bed in some plain cabin, with the nose almost against the shingles.

When fall sets in, how cheery sounds the crackling of the fire. Listen how merrily the tea-kettle sings as you sit calmly in your rocking chair hearing the cold blasts without. Hear the solemn tick of the clock speaking ceaselessly of the flight of time. Ah, what good company a clock is, at times.

Having mentioned the rocking chair, I will say a few words about *it*. The rockers produce different sounds, according to who it is that moves them. If Grandma sits in the chair, knitting and swaying to and fro, the rockers keep up a sort of a contented purr, a drowsy sort of creak; but put your nervous gentleman into the same chair, either the one who lives on nothing but business or the one who forever wipes his hat and looks every few minutes at his watch; the gentleman who has for the tenth time tried to propose to Miss Sarah Jane, but who for the tenth time failed to muster up courage; when he sits in the rocking chair it produces a jerky kind of a Scotch tune. But oh, listen to that same old chair when it is freighted with aunt *Betsy*, the good aunty who weighs well nigh on to two hundred pounds. When she rocks you hear a long and melancholy whine from the rockers. But listen when two or three little ones sit in it: then the old chair goes *whicketty whack, whicketty whack,* as if enjoying the fun with the children.

Having taken a general survey of nature's sounds and musicians, I invite you now to the instrument which is the transition from nature to art, namely, the Æolian harp, the instrument made by the hand of man but played upon by the wind. Its tones impress me, according to the frame of mind I am in. Once they sound like an angelic choir, next they sing like the sad moans of a fairy that seems to be imprisoned in the little pine box. Again, they have sounded to me like the wailings of a maiden who has lost a true lover, or like the secret weeping of the mother who will not be comforted over the death of her little one. They often remind me of the wind as it plays through pine trees and weeping willows, growing on the graves of loved ones. Then the harp speaks to me of past greatness, of the valor of knighthood, of stately castles and turreted walls. While listening to those chords my mind often wanders to the far-off land of the South, where oranges bloom and magnolias perfume the air. If ever there was such a thing as a swan-song, it must have been as the zephyr-like tones of the Æolian harp. They can paint to my mind the world in the softest and gentlest tints; they clothe it with a romance that causes me to follow them whither they lead me. Oh, how they recall the ambition of the past and cause me to feel the emptiness of the present. The Æolian harp sings sweetest when the gentle south wind blows, but it wails and sobs when the rough north wind sweeps over its strings.

So the human heart loves best words of kindness and quickest responds to them, while when rudely touched by treachery, by unkindness, by deceit, or by the many adversities of life, its strings vibrate violently or break and cease to sound altogether. Is there a sadder spectacle in all this world than a broken heart. As the harp will only produce sweet harmony when the strings are tuned in unison, so will our hearts only produce sweet concord when our heart-strings are tuned in unison with God's will. Let then the gentle winds of prosperity or the bitter blasts of adversity blow upon us, we will at all times produce concord and our lives will be to others as sweet music.

But there is one more instrument I must speak of, *the bells*, the sweet bells, with their far-reaching voices. They, too, may be called voices of nature. Bells exercise a far greater influence in Europe than in this country. There, people usually remain all their lives in one place, and as bells are heard under many and diverse circumstances, they grow deep into the people's affections. The bell which calls them early in the morning to offer up their prayers always has a holy tone. Often have I stood on the high banks of the river Rhine watching the rising sun as it dispelled the veil of fog that rested on castles and river, and as I listened to the distant church-bells of a half-dozen villages, the sweet chimes turned my mind heavenward, and inwardly I said, "God bless the bells." When the cheery eleven o'clock bell rang, releasing children from the school-room, horses from the plough and the workman from the bench, I used to think that there was not a sweeter bell in all Christendom. But when, at 12 o'clock, the Angelus rang and the large bell tolled three times, and when I saw men and women stop in their work, offering a silent prayer, I felt as if I had heard a voice from above. Never shall I forget the sad bell which was rung every Friday at 3 o'clock, in commemoration of the death of our Lord and Saviour. Often I wandered in my childish mind to Calvary, while that bell rang, and viewed the uplifted cross. When the solemn death-bell rang announcing the departure of a soul, it was a warning voice to the living to be prepared also. But among all the bells there was no one so sweet as the evening bell. Poets have often sung about it and musicians were ever fond of reproducing it. Come, go with me across the deep blue sea; let us visit a German town, my native home, with its old-fashioned houses nestled as closely together as if they were unable to stand alone. The streets are narrow and crooked, the quaint old chimneys are inhabited by storks, while around the eaves there are rows of swallows' nests, for the German deems it a blessing to have birds make their dwelling under his roof. Hear the merry laughter of the children playing around the town-house; see, yonder comes a weary wanderer looking for an inn where he may find rest and shelter for the coming night. Farmers are now driving the cattle and horses to the creek, maidens come to the wells for water, and their merry laughter mingles strangely with the sound of the blacksmiths' anvils. Gently the curling smoke arises from chimneys, indicating that thrifty housewives are getting the evening meal ready. The laborers are coming home from the fields, the sun sinks slowly in the west, when suddenly there is heard the sweet evening bell calling weary laborers to rest and to prayer. All villagers now offer their devotions; the children cease playing, the merry sound of the anvil is hushed, people uncover their heads, old men and women reverently bow their heads, communicating silently with Him whom they must soon meet in judgment. When thinking of the sweet evening bells, I say *God bless the bells.* What can be sweeter than at eventide to hear the distant chimes as the sound comes over the quiet stream. Ah, they are like sweet dreams, telling the aged of youth that is past and fondly picturing to youth the future that awaits him. Much more might be said concerning the significance of the bell in European village life, but this must suffice. While I have forgotten the names and faces of many of those that were young with me, while early impressions have been weakened by a long absence from home, I can still recall the sound of the old church-bells. Whether I sit on the portico on a summer evening, or watch a cozy fire in winter, if I but will, I can hear those sweet bells as they ring and ring and ring, until their magic sounds sweep over thousands of miles and reach the ear of the far-off wanderer. Oh, ye bells; oh, ye sweet-sounding bells! Your never-dying voices speak to me of youth and home. You are indeed true and faithful friends. As Enoch Arden, when he came to the cold and chilly waters of death, beheld a vessel in his vision, and cried aloud, "*A sail, a sail, I am saved,*" and so fell back and spoke no more, so I often dream that when I shall come to the brink of the river I shall hear the bells, the bells of the heavenly Jerusalem, and crying out in rapture, "*The bells, the bells, the sweet bells of heaven are ringing for me,*" I shall fall back into the arms of Him who alone is mighty to save.

As there are sentiments which the poet never expressed, as there are scenes and sights as well as pictures of the imagination which no brush has as yet spread upon canvas, so there are sounds in nature that arouse and convey feelings which, in a certain sense, may be called music, but which have never been and never can be written in the language of art. Doubtless all of you have fond recollections of home and the scenes of childhood. Ah! how eagerly the mind turns homeward, especially when for the first time away. How strong is the desire to see once more a father's face and to feel again the touch of a mother's lips. What a powerful feeling is this longing for home. Oh, memory is a great artist! It draws the outlines of the loved faces and the scenes around the hallowed spot in the most enchanting manner. What once seemed scarcely worthy of our notice now becomes an object of our affections. Oh how great is the joy and how sweet is the hour, when returning home after a long absence! Alas, this joy was never to be mine. Many years ago I left my German home, fondly hoping that some day I might return to meet the loved ones again. Often I hungered for this pleasure, and a thousand times I pictured to myself a happy meeting. Alas, it was not to be so. I often wandered over the sea; yes, I even felt the pressure of my father's hand and heard my mother's voice. Alas! 'twas all a vision—*a mere dream.*

It is but natural that such feelings should arise when contemplating home and childhood. There are, however, other periods in life which make deep impressions, periods rich in pleasures never to be forgotten. I refer to the time when love's impulse first steals over our hearts, painting a world anew with colors too beautiful to describe. These are the times when we form new home-ties, and when we for a time forget even the places that first gave us shelter. The days of young love are sweet to the memory; they shed a lustre over everything connected with them;

they are days worthy of being placed by the side of our childhood's days on memory's page. Oh, blessed is the heart that *has* loved, and twice blessed is the heart that now loves. The joys of love are connected with a thousand objects and incidents, and time can never efface them from recollection. They are graven deeply upon the tablets of memory, and when we, perchance, walk alone or sit in the twilight hour looking upon the golden lines in the West, then, as if by magic, rises that tablet, and we read again the loved names and trace once more the outlines of those joyous scenes long since passed away. To visit after many years of absence the places in which we first loved, where we whiled away our time strolling on the banks of the river, where we had many cozy chats on the old rustic porch, is almost equal to a visit to the parental roof.

This pleasure I enjoyed a few years ago, when I visited Pennsylvania. The friend who promised to meet me being a physician, was unexpectedly called away, and it happened that I had the better part of a warm summer afternoon to myself. I decided at once to visit the old church on the hill, where I used to play the organ, and where I took upon myself the marriage vow. Silence reigned over all that broad sweep of country, and a solemn feeling took possession of me as I stepped into the old graveyard. Turning toward the village nestling at the foot of the hill, I eagerly looked for the house of this or that friend, but in looking around upon the graves I was also reminded of the fact that many of these dear friends had departed from this life and were now resting in God's acre. To my right and left were the graves of those who, once young and joyful, graced a merry circle of friends. In my imagination I again heard the sound of the old church-bell that used to call me to that hill to worship God. Again I heard the choir chant, and the tones of the little organ I used to play rang loudly in my ears. My heart throbbed wildly as I recounted the many changes that had since then taken place. Sadly I seated myself under a pine tree, and while there musing I heard the hum of many insects, and a sad, low breeze played through the pines above me. Was there music in it? yes it was music; music which I shall never forget, music that can never be written down, music inexpressibly sweet, music that touches the heart to its deepest depths. I know not how long I sat there, but I know that the reveries of the hour were sweet. Raising my head, my eyes naturally fell upon that building where I formerly lived, and where I spent so many happy years; where I first met her who since has traveled with me on the journey of life. With a sigh I said farewell to the loved friends sleeping their last sleep, and started to visit the old house so hallowed in my memory. As I opened the gate the sound of the old latch almost paralyzed me. Involuntarily I stood and listened—as if I had heard the voice of one of the friends long since departed. Strange recollections crowded upon my heart as it responded to that familiar click. How I used to love to hear it when friends called, but especially when returning home after a long absence. Sweet gate, sweet sound, sweet memory, sweet days of love! Years had passed, and lo! I stood with a quivering heart and a trembling hand by the side of that old gate. Was there music in that click? Yes, there was a power in that sound, that, like music, suddenly opened the sluices of memory—those sluices that had long been closed—and feelings and thoughts like a wild stream rushed upon me.

But on I went, and as I walked over the old and well-worn flagstones my steps resounded as if I were walking in a vault, with the dear ones resting to the right and left, and when I reached the door with its time-worn brass knocker, I scarcely knew how I had come there. The sound of that old knocker seemed to come out of the grave, it seemed to say, "be ready, for soon you, too, will have to depart to meet your many friends." The tolling of a bell when they carry a friend to the grave was not half so solemn as was the sound of that knocker. It was well that no one came, for I could not have said a word, because my heart-strings vibrated wildly. Was there music in the old knocker? Oh, yes, it sounded like a funeral dirge. And thus I was again left to my dreams. Sadly I reviewed the past, sorrowing o'er the follies of youth, and tenderly whispering the names of those who used to sit with me upon the old bench on that rustic porch: The dark clouds which then at times overcast my path with threatening aspects, now had more than a silver lining, and sadly I said: "Short-sighted mortals we are." Deep, deep into the heart goes the music of nature, for it takes us out of our every-day life and leads us, as it were, up the mountain from whence we may behold the distant landscape through which the journey has led us. Oh, how strong the yearning once more to tread those paths so wrought with youthful pleasures, and how stern and irrevocable the command to pass on to the end of life's journey. Our imagination may take us there; the gale sweeping over the pleasure-grounds of youth may fan our weary brow; alas, it fails to bring us the fragrance of the flowers as once it did. As the sun of the Indian summer shines in vain upon the tree that is fast losing its foliage, making it glisten in untold beauty but failing to awaken new life, so is the recollection of youthful pleasures to the heart that has made the larger portion of its life's journey. Oh, that I were a poet, so that I might tell in fitting words what I then felt. And so I left the little town and said farewell to the hallowed spot, praying that peace may ever reign there, that the freshest flowers may bloom and the sweetest birds forever sing where I spent so many happy days. A writer compares our lives to ash-heaps, where our days lie consumed and where we have buried many unrequited affections, many disappointments and sorrows. Still, we fondly stoop from time to time over this ash-heap, for there we also find many diamonds, jewels of friendship and happy hours which we once enjoyed in our every-day life, and the recollection of which is dear to our weary hearts. Though we can no longer wear these jewels, we may at least feast our eyes upon their lustre. So, though we can no longer enjoy the pleasures of youth, we may at least recall them, for were it not for the pleasures of memory and hope many poor hearts would break and die.

A legend says that when Adam and Eve were about to be expelled from Paradise, God pitied them, and to alleviate their sufferings while battling with life's bitter blasts, He gave them a harp made of wood taken from the tree of life, ordaining that its sweet sounds should ever be a relief for their sufferings. Hence, it is that all human hearts are so tenderly touched by sweet music's power. And the poet who listened spell-bound to the charms of song correctly said: "Oh, music, thou art either a recollection of Paradise or a foretaste of heaven."

Though music like a harp is not heard in the realms of nature, yet there is the bird that sings, there is the wind that sighs through the pines and whistles upon reeds, there is the wave that moans, the rivulet that laughs, the thunder that peals and the ocean that roars, all of them voices speaking to our hearts if we will but listen. The painter loves to reproduce the beauties of nature, with its mountains and rivers, the flowers and trees gorgeously clothed in rich colors. He delights to paint for us the beautiful sunset, when the sunbeams melt along the silent horizon and when the various colored strata of clouds seem to be like so many steps upon which we may enter heaven itself. The sculptor delights to portray the beauties of the human form, and, like his brother artist, goes to nature to school. The poet sings sweetly of the things God made, putting a halo around every object in nature. Yes, he even weaves the voices of nature into fairy tales. If, then, the painter, the sculptor and the poet delight in nature and its sounds, why should the musician not do the same? I have simply tried to show you what a musician hears in nature, and if I played only short tunes upon the several stops of this vast and mighty organ of nature, it was because there are too many of them to play more. If I shall have induced any of my readers to give a more willing ear to the sounds of nature, if I shall have enabled any one to derive more pleasure from the beauties of nature and its music, I shall feel amply repaid for my labors.

HEAD AND HEART.

When speaking of head and heart I mean yours and mine, not those of a select few. In our intercourse with men we deal either with their heads or their hearts, generally with both at the same time. The fact that we *know* too little of either, or, perhaps our unwillingness to regard the thoughts and feelings of others, causes much unnecessary trouble in life. My subject, therefore, is a profitable one for discussion, and I trust I may be able to make it equally interesting. Pope has said, "The proper study for mankind is man." If it is useful and necessary to study the sciences, it is still more so to study man, for this is the deepest of sciences. We look at men's faces much as we look at the face of a clock. From the one we endeavor to read character, from the other we learn the time. In neither case, however, do we think of the wonderful works that are concealed behind these faces.

Everything that is noble and good springs from the heads and hearts of men, and *these* are also the sources from whence comes all the wickedness that curses the human family. Therefore, I invite your attention to some reflections upon the relative influences of the head and heart upon our actions.

The head is the seat of the thinking powers. The Chinese claim this distinction for the stomach. When speaking of a well read man they say, "he has eaten many books." Buffon has said—"The stomach is the seat of thought." Doubtless the condition of our stomachs gives coloring to our thoughts, but from this it does not follow that we think with our digestive organs. Man thinks with his brain ; *it* takes cognizance of objects, *it* realizes conditions and situations, *it* reasons and concludes. When a man has but little thinking power we do not say of him that he has a weak stomach, but rather that he has a thick head. When a man displays great presence of mind in the hour of danger we do not say that he has a cool stomach, but rather a cool head. When men are angry we do not say to them keep a cool stomach, but rather keep a cool head. If a man is shrewd enough to gain an advantage over his fellows we do not say that he has a long stomach, but rather that he has a long head. In our common parlance, therefore, we accord to the head the thinking powers.

The heart is called the seat of the emotions, but it cannot be regarded as such in the same sense as we call the head the seat of the thinking powers. The heart is the seat of our emotions only in a symbolic sense. The heart of flesh is merely a muscular cavity through which our blood flows. As all violent emotions affect the flow of blood, these, naturally enough, make themselves felt in the heart of flesh, hence we call it the seat of our emotions. The emotions which quicken the flow of the blood must, however, have an origin somewhere. Where do they originate ? There is within us a power which prompts us to action, which produces emotions, and this power is the *will* of man. This is the greatest power; indeed the will is man himself. It is the will of man that is prone to evil; it is the will which shapes our final destinies. Despite the fact that the will is a most dangerous power, a power which has wrought untold misery from the time of Adam down to the present day, God left it free; to destroy or to fetter it would be equal to the destruction of man as a free agent. The will affects the mind, it governs largely our thoughts, it is the source of all that is good and evil within us. The will is responsible for our acts and not the brain, for the will gives coloring to our thoughts and actions. It is the will that is corrupt and not the brain; the latter is only in so far prone to evil, as it yields to the dictates of the will. This will power produces desires, it prompts us to action, it is the source of our emotions, and it is in reality what we commonly call the *heart*. It is said man hates, but not without a cause, for he simply *wills* to hate, and so we love because we *will* to love. A bad or a good sentiment must have a bad or a good cause, and the *will* or the heart is this cause. Commonly we speak of a bad or a good heart, but in reality we mean a bad or a good will. We speak of kind-hearted people, says Schopenhauer, and we mean those whose wills are favorably disposed toward mankind. We speak of hard-hearted people, and we mean those whose wills are unfavorably disposed toward their fellows. A broken heart is a broken will, a human being without those powerful desires that are common to mankind.

We must control this will, and this duty places upon us a heavy and almost frightful responsibility. Were it not so we would be blameless in the midst of our evil doings. Says a famous writer, "The head is as the rudder of the ship, while the heart or the will is the power that propels it. Both rudder and sail are needed in order that a vessel may safely travel on the waves, so a good heart and a clear head are needed in order that we may successfully pass through life.

In the animal the instinct rules supreme; in the educated man the will rules supreme. The *will* is the source of all evil, and, as has been said, must be governed and directed. It is the object of education to so train the mind that it may govern and guide the will, much as a rider governs the horse. With an uneducated man it is difficult to reason, for his will assumes the form of passion; he simply *wills* to have his own way. With an educated man we can discuss a question, for the brain acts as moderator of the will or the heart. To get a good education, therefore, means not merely to stock your mind with facts as men fill scrap-books or pigeon-holes with items of useful information; nay, it means the strengthening of the mind, so that under all circumstances it may be a safe guide to the will, so that it may under all circumstances see the ways that are wise and prudent.

Men differ in their valuation of head and heart. The one is preëminently an admirer of the thinking powers, and he is a man that must be convinced in order that he may follow you. The other is more an admirer of the emotional man, and he needs only to be persuaded to follow us without much reasoning. The one yields quickest to the head, the other to the heart power. And so men choose their friends, the one seeking his companion among thinking men, the other among those whose hearts are the stronger parts of their natures, and all this we do without any forethought or previous consideration. There are those who speak lightly of the operations of a profound mind, proclaiming thought to be cold and unfeeling, while others denounce emotional natures as weak or feminine. Doubtless, thought is cold, but if it is as cold as ice it is also as *clear* as ice. The emotions are warm but they are often unreliable, they need to be guided and checked; therefore it must be acknowledged that the heart or the will alone can impart life-producing power to thought. All men admire great minds, but there are those who cherish a sort of an enmity against men of superior brain power. They prefer the stupid fellow who stands beneath them, to the scholar who outranks them. In such a case the envious heart and not the brain is to blame. The noble heart would rather associate with its superiors; the low and vulgar would rather be leaders among ignoramuses than followers among the wise. The heart is greater than the head. The latter becomes feeble with old age, and judgment is no longer reliable when men are in their *dotage*. According to a certain writer, the mind of man is not immortal, the will, however, is. The heart or the will is causeless, it operates at pleasure and remains active till the end of life, hence, we speak of the "ruling passion strong in death." God does not ask for our minds, but he constantly demands our hearts. He says, give me thine heart, which means, give me thy will-power, let thy will be in accord with mine. That we attach more importance to the heart than to the head is plain from the fact that we pardon an error of the head quicker than an error of the heart. We would rather be suspected of stupidity than of dishonesty. We would rather be accused of an error of the head than of an error of the heart, for one ounce of the heart's intentions outweighs a whole pound of the head's action. Seneca said that no action could be blameless unless the will is blameless, for the will or the heart prompts us to action. We forgive a man more readily for suspecting us of stupidity than of wrong intentions, though in either case we are lowered in the human standard. The reason we resent the one more quickly than the other is, that a charge of ignorance does not affect our character and standing as much as a charge of badness of heart. If a man lacks education or talents, he simply lacks that which, under more favorable circumstances, he might have attained, but if he is bad he falls below that standard of morality which all men should reach. An uneducated but a kind-hearted man we may take to our hearts, but no one loves an educated scamp or deceiver.

The heart or will prompts us to action, and in this it is often so powerful, quick and sly that the mind is led captive before it has time to consider, before it can fulfill its mission of judgment. The mind loves to be idle at times, but the heart is always active. The idle mind is easiest led into evil deeds, hence the saying, Satan finds some mischief still for idle hands to do. The busy, active brain that battles with the world, that is engaged in study or scientific research, is not so easily overcome by the ever-active heart in its evil promptings and sly temptations. The head has not the time to listen to the heart.

Little children never think deeply, their attention can, therefore, easily be diverted from one object to another, yet their wills are always active. If the heart or the will becomes a great factor, if the child wills a thing decidedly, we fail to divert its mind. The heart controls the head. Of such a child we say it is *self-willed*. The dullest intellect is set to work by the will, our wants and necessities drive us on, they cause us to set our wits to work, hence, the familiar saying, that necessity is the mother of invention. The superiority of the heart power over that of the head may also be seen from the fact that some men's appeals fall coldly upon people's ears. This is owing to the fact that the speech of the one lacks emotional power while that of the other does not. The fiery heart of some speakers makes itself felt in word, look and action, and the hearts of the audience respond to his own. It is this heart-power that men use to sway the masses to action. If it is used for the right it becomes a blessing, if for the purpose of dethroning reason, or for the purpose of beclouding judgment, it is a curse. It is the heart power that makes men leaders of others, hence, when sending men on missions of persuasion we choose men of emotional powers.

We imagine that the head conceives projects, but it is generally the heart that does so. When the heart decides to do a thing it sets the mind to work, compelling it to devise plans for the execution of the new scheme. The good old proverb says, "Where there is a will there is a way." When the mind is searching out the way, we are in a brown study, we are cogitating over a thing. When another man's heart proposes something aiming to set our heart to action, we say, "Let me sleep over it," that is, give my mind time to consider. He who fails to consult his mind before acting, is hasty and inconsiderate. To enable the mind to give the heart good advice is the object of education. The heart often leads men into trouble by its strong promptings, and, when man finds himself in a difficulty, having failed to think before he acted, we say, "He has put his foot into it." If a man thus finds himself in a snare, the cowardly heart is apt to retreat, it surrenders control, and appeals to the mind to find a way out of the difficulty. If the mind raises its warning voice against the heart's foolish projects and desires, there often follows a bitter combat between head and heart. The head counsels one thing and the heart desires another. When in this condition we say we are undecided, and in order that we may arrive at some conclusion we seek the counsel of a friend to sit in judgment over our heart's project. We rarely ever appeal to another's heart in such cases, for the heart usually is full of motives, it is apt to give advice selfishly. The mind alone is unbiased. The heart generally prefers that advice which is favorable to its own projects, and it is apt to call him a fool who counsels the contrary. 'Tis not always easy to give advice, but, as a rule, it is easier given than followed. Swift says, "No man will take counsel, but every man will take money; therefore, money is better than counsel. There is a class of persons whose minds are always made up. We had better say that their wills are always made up. This may show superiority of mind and it may not. It more generally displays a hasty and a dogged will. "The heart of a hasty and self-willed man," says Schopenhauer, "is like a runaway horse that takes the bit between its teeth and starts off without knowing whither it goes. Usually it runs on until injury is done to self or others." When the heart is stubborn, and, like a runaway horse, takes the bit between its teeth, the head or reason can do no more than hold to the saddle, no matter how good a rider it has hitherto been. Men who are unyielding to reason are called *headstrong*, but it is more proper to call them *self-willed*, for it is the heart that is stubborn, not so much the mind. Try to convince a stubborn man and all your arguments will fail, *not* because they are not good, but because his *will*, his *heart* is not ready to surrender. Says the good old proverb, "Convince a man against his will and he is of the same opinion still." It is simply against human nature to curb the will and to give up, hence, men will stand on the most untenable ground and stubbornly hold fast to their expressed opinions. Stubbornness is not firmness, though many mistake the one for the other. The firm man stands upon a principle because it is true and correct; the stubborn man stands upon his own opinion and holds to it simply because it is his own opinion, no matter whether it is true or not. The firm man is worthy of our admiration, but the stubborn man deserves our contempt and pity. 'Tis no shame to give up, 'tis no disgrace to acknowledge that we were in the wrong, but it is weakness to adhere to a wrong opinion knowing it to be such. Some people are so conceited that they deem themselves always in the right. They are your dogmatic, arrogant men, who are ever ready to set up their *own* wills as laws for others. These are the bigots, a few of whom are still running at large in this world.

I have said that the heart is sly. Let me add that it is often so deceitful that it is difficult for the mind to find out the first cause for action. The old saying is—" The truth lies at the bottom of a well," so our motives for action lie at the bottom of the heart, and *it* is terribly deep. Out of this depth arise promptings that cause us to blush, and so indistinct at times are these motives, so difficult are they to discover, that people often say they cannot understand their own feelings. Is not the mind prompted at times to actions, while the heart tries its best to hide the true motives? The heart is not only a sly, but also a hasty actor. Like children, we come quickly to conclusions, because it is easier for us to do what we wish to do than what we are told to do. Children often do directly the opposite of what they are commanded to do, simply because they would rather follow their hearts' desires than your head's counsel and law. When taken to account for disobedience they give it as their excuse, that they forgot; thus you will notice that they accuse the head and exonerate the heart. In the one case they would have been guilty of willful disobedience, while in the other it was mere thoughtlessness. It is a question worth asking, how it comes that children, who know little or nothing of the operations of either head or heart, make such a fine distinction when excusing themselves for not having done what they were told to do. Tell a boy to saw some wood or to pull weeds on a hot summer day, or order him to do some other unpleasant labor, and your command is soon forgotten, or the work, if done at all, is but poorly executed, and that simply because your command was in opposition to the boy's will—because his heart was not in his work. But promise this boy a dime or a circus ticket, and he will remember your word, simply because he desires—his heart wishes to possess—what you have promised him. What he *wills*—what his heart *desires*—he has indelibly written on memory's page; what he does *not wish* to do he either wrote so faintly that it was easily erased, or perchance he never wrote it there at all.

Youth, as a rule, yields preëminently to the heart power, hence it often hates and loves without cause, and its emotions are easily swayed; youthful love is quickly turned into youthful hatred. Hence it is that youth is also often *stubborn, conceited*, and easily roused to passion. As youth lacks the cooler reasoning of older people, it is quick to judge and quick to act. Hence it is that boys come so easily to blows. Youth readily attempts *that* from which older men shrink with fear, for the riper judgment of advanced years tells them that failure is a possibility. We learn that the heart of youth generally has accomplished the great deeds recorded on history's page. Youth reasons but little, but it feels intensely, and acts both quickly and inconsiderately. With older men the opposite is the case. So common is it for youth to act without forethought that a calculating and prudent boy attracts our attention, and we say of him, that he has an "*old* head on him."

Impulsive youth, with its energetic will, is ever ready for combat, for criticisms, for daring speculations, but when riper years come men do not trust themselves so freely. Said a farmer—"When I was twenty-five years of age I felt that I needed *no* man's advice. It never occurred to me to ask my father what he thought of my enterprises. When I was thirty years old I would sometimes ask Father, just to see whether he would approve of my ideas. At the age of thirty-five I was in the habit of asking my father's advice, while at the age of forty I never undertook anything without first seeking counsel." What mistakes the farmer might have avoided had he done at twenty-five what he finally did at forty.

That the heart rules the intellect is plain from the fact, that when a friend is in trouble we tell him to drive unpleasant thoughts out of his mind. The question now is, who is to drive the unpleasant thoughts out? When we change the current of our thoughts we do so in obedience to the will-power, and not so much through the action of the mind itself. Luther said—"I can no more prevent thoughts from arising in my mind than I can prevent birds from flying over my head; but I need not allow them to make their nests in my hair."

Great minds we admire, but great and noble hearts we love. Great intellects and powerful hearts do not always go together; they are not often found united in one person. It is always unsafe to judge of the head from the heart, and *vice versâ*. Stupidity does not presuppose vice, nor is great learning a sure indication of virtue. We all love to be associated with kind-hearted people, but, says a writer, while we admire men and women of strong minds and powerful wills, we prefer to look at them as we look at lions and tigers in a menagerie; none of us would like to be locked up with them. Great hearts make great leaders of men; great minds are the thinkers, the revolutionizers of the social and political affairs of the human family. They are the men who see what the world really is, while heart-people usually see it through the lens of their emotions.

The masses are easiest moved by the heart, for men usually like persuasion better than conviction, but conviction in the end is always more enduring in its effects.

There are found everywhere good-hearted people who lack culture. They are as rough diamonds, which, if they were cut (that is—educated) and set in the surroundings of refinement would be more useful citizens; they would enjoy life more.

Man's emotions often are the source of his troubles. Imagine two men conversing on politics or religion, or perhaps they are arguing a question of property right. As long as the head rules, the parties are calm and dignified in their discussion, for the mind acts as a moderator—the mind is chairman. How appropriate the use of this word moderator, when applied to presiding officers. But watch these men when the heart begins to take part in the discussion. Notice how the voice changes, see the flushed cheeks, observe the increasing state of irritation! Unless the two will soon part there is danger of hearing bitter words. When two men discuss politics at ordinary times they can do so with calmness, but during a hot campaign the best of friends sometimes fall out, and that because the heart takes part in the discussion, while at ordinary times it does not. When arguing in the court-room, the lawyer whose mind rules supreme usually keeps calm, but the advocate whose heart is a powerful factor in the case becomes easily excited and even angry. Then it is that his adversaries taunt him by saying, keep your head cool; don't lose your balance. In a well educated man head and heart are equally trained; they are balancing each other like the two sides of the scales. If the heart swells up with pride or becomes turbulent with anger it outweighs the head, and thus it is correct to say of such a man, that he has lost his balance. There are men who purposely make others angry, for then men's tongues go off like guns that are half-cocked. When in anger reason loses its control, and men then reveal secrets which in calmer moments they never would divulge.

So skillful lawyers sometimes endeavor to arouse the anger of their adversaries or of troublesome witnesses, and that for no less reason than to weaken their judgment and to cause them to say that which might injure their cases. On the other hand, many lawyers pretend to become excited, in order to make their clients believe that their hearts are deeply engaged in their cases. Ministers, too, often become unduly excited while preaching the gospel of peace and love; their hearts run away with their heads. Indeed, I have heard a certain great divine say that when he was least prepared for his sermon he generally became most excited and spoke loudest. When man thus yields to his emotions and allows them to run away, the mind becomes clouded like muddy water, or, to use another illustration, head and heart are like a ship in a dense fog, there is no telling when or where they may collide one with the other.

Thus we see that the reasoning powers, through education become, as it were, a lever that keeps the heart's passions in their proper channel. But if this lever breaks, if the passions leave their bounds, what destruction follows! Then men commit foul deeds. As the muddy waters of a flood leave their marks upon the inundated land, so the frequent outbursts of the passions leave their stains upon the human mind and character. If the passions of a whole community break through the levee of reason and law we have the mob, the deeds of which are unaccountable. Then men resort to lynch law, and commit violence against those who are suspected of wrong doing. Thus we see that lynch law yields to the heart and its passions, while in the court-room reason alone prevails, or ought to prevail. In a university it sometimes happens that some of the students deem themselves wronged by a rule which, in their estimation, has a tinge of injustice. Straightway a wave of excitement and passion rolls over the school, reason is clouded, while only a few keep their heads clear. But strange to say, those few, who take in the real condition of things, are always denounced as the weak-kneed ones.

A prejudiced heart beclouds the mind, so that it fails to see things in their true light. The heart has bribed the head, and the head argues falsely in order to please the heart. Thus the prejudiced heart regards that as ugly which in reality is pretty; it pronounces that to be mean which is good. The selfish heart, too, beclouds the mind. Selfishness is like a thick veil which prevents the mind from looking beyond its own interests. There are men who can see nothing beyond their noses, except it be a a shining dollar or a promissory note. The selfish heart is a mean heart, but the meanest of all hearts is the malicious heart, the one that rejoices over the misery of others. It is sad to think that a human heart can shrivel up to such a degree that all sympathy is obliterated. Public judgment is unreliable in matters of art and learning, but in matters of morality it hardly ever goes far astray. Thus the selfish man is quickly known and sincerely despised. The suspicious and jealous heart is a petty little heart. Such a heart is never at rest, it is its own torment.

How many hearts are guilty of pride! It is the heart first that is guilty of this weakness, and when the heart of a man is thoroughly filled with it then it affects the head, and we say that pride has turned his head; that is, it has dethroned reason. Oh, what is there in this life to make man proud? Is it good looks? If so, how long will these endure? Are we proud of learning? Remember that no matter how far we advance upon the road of knowledge, there has, after all, been but little accomplished, and much remains to be done. No matter *how great* we may be, there are others who are our equals and superiors. Are we proud of wealth? How foolish! Have not gamblers, thieves, and dishonest speculators great possessions also? Are you proud of social standing? Remember, the grave levels all, and even here on earth many an humble man who is socially not much regarded, weighs more in the scale of public opinion than you with all your proud, high social standing and family connections. Pride may be a virtue—usually it is a vice. Keep it out of the heart. When sending a man on an important errand we say, try to get on the right side of him whom you are to see—that is, try and reach his heart; seek to obtain control over his will. This leads men to use flattery, a dish of which the average heart is exceedingly fond. The flatterer is a deceiver; his potion is designed to destroy the action of the mind; it intoxicates the will. No honest man stoops to flattery.

People with strong emotional natures usually are very impulsive; people with great brain power often are freezingly cold. Despite their excitability we would rather trust heart people, for they exhibit their natures, we can read their dispositions, while it is very difficult to read the character of purely brain people. The heart usually makes the deepest impression upon our faces, and the Germans are correct when they say that in the eye lies the heart. I would at any time trust facial expression as a key to character more than language. Words are often used as a means of deception, and if but sparingly used we have no means of knowing whether such people may be trusted.

This corruption of the human heart is no invention of mine. Ever since philosophers have studied man has the proneness of the human heart to evil attracted attention; nay, more, many of them have diligently sought for a remedy. Men have earnestly endeavored to subdue and to deny the will, hence, they entered monasteries, they chastised their bodies, they educated the mind, they lived in poverty and solitude, but while they have attained great self-control they have not succeeded in *changing the heart.* Thus, you perceive that philosophy and religion teach the same doctrines concerning men's hearts, but they differ in their remedies. Religion teaches that the divine power alone which made the will can change it, and this is the doctrine of regeneration.

The heart of man is the same in all climes and ages—the Bible being the story of the human heart, is, therefore, suited to all climes and ages. So music, being the language of the heart, is practiced by all nations and tribes. When preaching religious truths always appeal to the whole man, both to head and heart. Religion is not exclusively emotional, neither is it purely thought. While the church frequently appeals too exclusively to the emotional man, our public schools, in many places, go to the other extreme by cultivating the mind only. The true educational plan is to see to the wants of the whole child, those of head, heart and body.

Doubtless, the home and Sabbath school are the places where heart culture should begin, but for all that our public schools have a great work to do in this direction. There are many means at the teacher's command designed to develop the child's heart power. The love element is a great aid in governing a school, and the teacher who cultivates this element has fewer cases of discipline and does better work. Men who have made horses a study have long taught the lesson that the best mode of breaking a colt is to use kindness. Alas, in many homes and schools children are not treated as well as colts or horses. Many parents and teachers commit the unpardonable blunder of trying to *break* the child's will—rather than strengthen it and guide it, so that it may choose that which is good. Many parents punish only when angry. What good can come from such discipline? What can a teacher do with children who have grown up at home almost like wild animals, whose hearts are mere waste places? For all that, it is my opinion, based upon experience, that every heart *may* be reached and led if the proper means are used, and I give it as my decided opinion that the teacher who fails at least to aim at establishing a love atmosphere in his school-room falls short of his mission, no matter how well qualified he may be to impart instruction. The same is true of parents and homes. Education alone cannot make a perfectly good heart out of a bad one, but education and proper training doubtless improves it. Education is always advantageous to morality, but book-learning alone cannot bring it about. Men may be thought to understand the Bible and the best theology and at the same time be rascals at heart.

It would be terrible if all heart-training were neglected. If it were, who could abide here on earth? Of the few virtues we can notice the first is *friendship*. This is a plant which grows only in a good heart. Friendship is more than a mere attachment, its roots strike deeper than mere liking, and it is as different from mere acquaintanceship, as night is different from the day. It is a jewel well spoken of by the Bible and is highly praised by the philosophers: Would you call your friend a *bosom*-friend, let the heart choose him, but let the head decide whether you have wisely chosen.

Would you retain the friendship of one whom you have taken to your heart, let the head teach you how to keep him. To disturb the friendship of two persons is one of the lowest things man can do. Most men can be lovers, but it is not given to all to be good friends. Most men like to win the friendship of others, but they are not quite so ready to bestow their own. Ask not for that which you cannot return. Those who attempt to buy the friendship of others show what a low estimate they place upon their own. Tell me who your friends are and I will tell you what manner of a man you are. Blessed is the heart than can boast of a true friend, but the heart that knows not true friendship misses much of the joy this world has in store for us.

Charity—sweet *charity*—who can sing thy praises better than the Bible? Floods, fires, earthquakes, pestilence, poverty, are indeed great afflictions, but these evils are more than counterbalanced by the deeds of charity they call forth. The heart must propose acts of charity, else giving or doing is not charity. But while the heart proposes acts of charity the head should sit in judgment over these acts. You may waste a fortune by giving and not bestow good charity. Ill-bestowed gifts and unwise assistance are not charity.

The spirit of *forgiveness* is indeed a noble one, and I often think that he who *can* and *does* forgive an injury has done more than he who has given away much money. He, however, who is unwilling to forgive, as a great man said, burns down behind him the bridge over which he himself will eventually wish to cross. The Lord's prayer says: "*Forgive, as we forgive.*" It is the heart that must forgive, and it is the heart that cherishes enmity, not the head.

Patriotism is one of the noblest virtues of the human heart. He who is devoid of it is worthy of that detestation with which all right-minded men regard him. But I must not lengthen my paper by enumerating the heart's virtues.

I [must touch on a subject which ever has been and ever will be of extraordinary interest to the human family. I mean love and marriage. They should be affairs both of head and heart, and not of one alone. Love, so say the philosophers, makes men blind, and blind people are always exposed to dangers. Purely *heart* matches, that is, *genuine* love affairs, are liable to be stormy, for it is difficult to get along with people whose hearts rule supreme. Head marriages, on the other hand, are mere convenience matches, they are often selfish, they lack the true elements of love, hence, everything that transpires in such families rests upon the basis of cold politeness. The heads of the two contracting parties rule all their actions; the heart-fire does not burn, hence, there prevails an even but also a cool temperature of mere civility. Such marriages usually are calm, but they lack the noblest sentiment, the noblest fire, one spark of which compensates for a good-size family broil. I have said that love makes men blind, which means that the heart refuses to hear reason. Says a great poet:—

"To be wise and love
Exceeds men's might."

Shakespeare says:—

"Love is blind, and lovers cannot see
The pretty follies they themselves commit."

In another place the immortal William says:—

"Men's vows are women's traitors."

But, then, dear woman loves to listen to these vows; woman's ear is generally open to the lover's smooth tongue, and knowing how attentively it is listened to, it rattles off words which in a calmer moment would be regarded as evidences of insanity or foolhardiness. Still, love's language is delightful to utter and to listen to. While I do not condemn it indiscriminately, I make free to say that much of it deserves to be branded as mere lies, or, at best, as a pack of exaggerations.

People that are in love are not at all disposed to listen to the language of reason, not even to that of their parents. This often leads to runaway matches and to unwise unions. At last calmer days come, when reason assumes control, and then the head brings a bill of indictment against the heart. Then follow tears and lamentations, and the fact is realized that two blind lovers ought to have considered the results before acting. By all means love when you are about to marry, but let me advise you not to trust the heart alone—it is not worthy of such confidence. Give the head a little show, also.

The heart-power is indeed great. It is *that* which makes the world either better or worse. Oh, what have great men not said about love? How many dramas, poems and novels have been written, how many pictures have been painted and songs composed, all of them setting forth the ever fresh theme of human love? Though we have heard the story time and again, it is always interesting whenever it is presented to us in new forms. He who has loved hears in these tales an echo of his own passion, he who has not yet loved hopes some day to be swayed by its magic power. Even idle gossipers seem to take a special delight in discussing other people's love affairs, and perhaps some of you know from experience how exasperating it is to be watched in one's courtship while we imagine our tracks to be well covered. Men usually take it more seriously with love before they are married, ladies take it seriously throughout life. Men's love seems sometimes to have cooled off after marriage, yet such, upon close examination, would be found to be untrue.

Man yields more to the brain than to the heart; he is more a creature of interest and ambition, says Washington Irving. His nature leads him forth into the struggle and bustle of life. Love is but the establishment of his early life, or a song piped in the intervals of the act. He seeks for fame, for fortune, for space in the world's thoughts, and dominion over his fellow-man. But a true woman's whole life is the story of her affections. The heart is her whole world. It is there her ambition strives for empire; it is there her avarice seeks for hidden treasures. She sends forth her sympathies on adventure; she embarks her whole soul in the traffic of affection, and if shipwrecked her case is hopeless, for it is a bankruptcy of the heart. Says Byron :—

"Man's love is of man's life a thing, a part,
'Tis woman's whole existence."

Man reasons, woman judges by intuition. The love-power is the lever that lifts mankind to a higher plane, and sweet woman is its representative. I mean now that pure and noble love for all mankind; that love which is one-half of religion. Woman is this love-power; she is the heart element of the human family. If woman loves the pure and the good she is a part of that great moral power that moves the world upward, *but*, if she loves the evil she is apt to sink lower than man, and she is almost sure to drag everything down that comes in contact with her. Man, as a rule, stands lower in the scale of morality than woman, but he will have to take many steps in order to reach that point of degradation which a woman *may* reach with one step. Says a writer—"Woman comes into the world with higher ideas than man, but she often goes out with lower." Woman's love-power is the loadstone of the world : it attracts that which is good and repels that which is evil. The words mother and wife are two of the dearest words in our language, and as woman's domain is home, the words *Home, sweet home*, have a sweet ring in our ears. It is woman's heart-power that subdues the rudeness of men where other remedies seem to fail, hence we notice often that rowdies try to act the part of gentlemen when coming into the presence of a refined woman. When gold was discovered in California, men rushed wildly to the places where the precious dust was found; there was no place for woman in those earlier settlements, and as the miners were deprived of her influence they often sank to a state of degradation that was shocking. When, at a later period, a settler brought his wife along, we are told that men came for miles just to see her face. What was it that attracted them? It was woman's love-power, that looks out of her gentle eyes. Man's heart turns to it as the needle turns toward the north. It is always good for man to come in contact with the character of pure women. Did not our Saviour love Mary and Martha? The best friends young people *can* have are their mothers; those who neglect this friendship surely are not worthy of other friends. Woman's love-power is the strength of the church and the mission; it is a blessing in the school-room and the sick chamber. Deprive the church or the cause of missions of woman's influence and see what the result will be. Pure woman's heart is as the sun of life, under whose benign influences all good causes develop; it is as a burning torch that kindles love's fire wherever its sparks fall. To kindle love, to keep its fires burning, to make this world better through love, this is woman's mission. Every true man loves her when she is true to this mission. All right-minded men love woman's heart-power, but most men cease to love woman when she substitutes superiority of the head for that of the heart. A woman who suppresses the heart-power, a woman who aims to rule by force of thought—a strong-minded woman—a "blue stocking," if you please—puts herself out of the ranks of women and places herself on the side of the sterner sex. Sensible men advocate woman's highest possible culture. Yes, let her write books, paint pictures, carve statues; open to her all those avenues in life for self-support that are suited to her capacity and strength, but never let her unsex herself by substituting superiority of the head for that of the heart.

It has been said that man is more a creature of head than heart. Says a writer, "He must battle with life, he must develop his wits, he must often be stern and cold; he meets with many rebuffs in life, much unjust and severe criticism is meted out to him, all of which tends to make him hard-hearted and selfish." Is it a wonder that men love to return home in the evening, there to rekindle their own love-power? Alas, what strange altars some women erect in their homes, on whose fires they expect their husbands to rekindle their love-powers which have been checked during a weary day's toil! The *tattling* woman, who regales her husband's ears with idle society gossip, the contentious woman, whose words are as a consuming fire, are still to be found. Such women have driven many men out of house and home, and have forced them to seek relief in the intoxicating cup. On the other hand, how much love-power is wasted in homes where husbands fail to appreciate woman's mission and character. Happy is the home that is presided over by a loving woman, but thrice cursed is the family which is tormented by a contentious, fault-finding, unwomanly woman.

When looking for wives men are too often influenced by wealth and beauty, and not sufficiently by character. Remember good looks vanish, and woe to him who has staked his all on a beautiful face! There is a nobler beauty than that of the face; I mean the beauty of the heart, which never fades, and which makes an aged countenance, wrinkled all over, appear at times more beautiful than that of a maiden of sweet sixteen. The heart that has cultivated love and peace looks out of a loving and peaceful face, and so the passionate heart, ready to burst out in anger, the heart full of cunning and deceit, reveals its own character on the face. He, therefore, who marries a good heart will ever deem his wife pretty, for the heart beauty cannot fade.

It would seem impossible to mention anything in connection with human existence that is heartless and headless, yet flirting comes under this head. Do not indulge in it; it is foolish and bad; no good comes out of it. Would that woman could realize the fact that she is the greater sufferer from this senseless amusement. Man is a rougher creature, hence he can stand such sports much better than delicate woman. The flirt's heart is like a garden-spot that has been burned all over, until not a pretty flower will grow upon it again. Young men who indulge in flirtations are as stupid and giddy flies that find a dish of honey standing about. They come and taste, fly off, and come again, until at last, being too full of sweetness, they fall in and are caught. See the thoughtless fly as it slowly crawls out of a dish of honey. Is it not an object of pity and ridicule? See how it moves slowly on, covered with sweetness. That which it once enjoyed has now robbed it of its freedom. So appears to me the young man who has been caught by a flirt; who has been made a husband against his will. A philosopher once said that men in matrimonial matters are like flies on the window—those that are in try to get out, those that are out try to get in. But the woman who thus led him to speak harshly of the marriage relation must either have been a shrew or a flirt, for man can love neither.

Young ladies and gentlemen beware of flirts, for they indulge in heartless and brainless sport. Seek the *good* heart, it alone keeps the affections warm, *it alone* brings happiness and is able to endure the trials of life.

The heart brings men together, thought, or the brain, drives them asunder, All differences in religion spring from the head. The heart, or the love of Christ, brings all Christians together. It is the head that drives political parties asunder, but the heart—the love for country and the flag—unites all citizens in its defence. We speak of a *republic of letters*, and thus we learn that the head, or learning, unites us like citizens of one *country*, but we also speak of the brotherhood of man, showing us that the heart—the love for mankind—unites us as members of one family. He who realizes this principle of the brotherhood of man, and lives up to it, has gone a great way toward the love of God. He, however, who does not love his fellow-man, has no right to say that he loves his God.

I have laid before you some reflections upon head and heart, and now that I have finished my task I feel that the theme is too great to be treated effectively in a lecture. I have pictured the human heart in colors that are not flattering to it. In doing so I have spoken not only from experience and observation, nay, I have higher authority than this, for the Word of God pronounces the heart deceitful above all things, and desperately wicked. I have shown you how low the heart may sink, I have disclosed to you its own dirty bottom, so as to put you on your guard against its wiles. On the other hand, I have shown you also some of its good sides—its capabilities—so that you may not be discouraged, but seek to rise and to move onward on the path of duty.

Hear, then, the conclusion of all. Lessing said: "Build up within you a dominion in which you may be kings and subjects at the same time, for the only possessions which you *may* govern are your hearts." Finally, hear a familiar old word—one that is ever true—*a text*, which, had I preached a sermon, would have been placed at the head of my discourse, but which I now place at its close, so that it may make all the deeper impression, namely; "*Keep thy heart with all diligence, for out of it are the issues of Life.*"

THE SANCTITY OF MUSIC.

I have chosen the subject of the sanctity of music for the purpose of impressing your minds with the importance and the seriousness of your work. No one of the arts is so popular, no one is so generally practiced, as the art of music, yet not one is as much abused as it, and that for the reason that its high meaning is but little understood, not only by the masses, but even by musical students and teachers. The art is used too much as an amusement, as an exhibition of skill, as a means of attracting attention, and too little as a means of education. Musicians often revel in their art, they even worship it, but they fail to go beyond the pleasurable sensations produced by it. Music is a means of culture; it is one of the greatest, and perhaps the greatest factor in human civilization. Not until men shall use the art with the spirit of reverence will it exercise those powers for which it is designed. The present generation of philosophers and teachers are only beginning to search for the real meaning and explanation of the art, and they have not advanced sufficiently to answer even these simple questions: What is music? Wherein consists its great power? Many definitions of music have been given, but they, without an exception, are imperfect. I desire to show you that there is a higher meaning and a loftier purpose attached to this mysterious art, and for this reason I shall review it from various standpoints.

Nearly every one will agree with me that a revelation was necessary for the progress of true civilization. Learning alone does not, and cannot, bring about this result, nor could the arts alone accomplish it. He who studies the influence of Christianity must confess that something higher than human learning was required to advance the world. The ancients certainly were profound thinkers. The philosophers of Greece, at least, had reached a high degree of learning, and no one would deny that Hellas enjoyed an unusual degree of art culture. In many particulars we must still go to them for instruction. Yet, despite the fact that these great men had made great advancement toward the horizon of human learning, in philosophy at least, the best of them felt that something else, something higher, was needed to explain life. Moreover, their wisdom failed to reach the masses; it was designed for scholars only, and it could not benefit the people. It must be acknowledged that human wisdom and speculation came to a limit, as it always must when it attempts to fathom the infinite. Human learning is profound, but, despite its depth, it leaves the mind unsatisfied. There is a universal longing to look into the beyond, a desire for progress, a cry for relief from oppression, from sin, a wish for a higher existence. This yearning and longing could only be satisfied through revelation; hence, the tremendous power of Christianity; hence, its ability to satisfy and to reach the masses; hence, the devotion of its followers, the swiftness of its progress, and that, too, despite the most violent opposition. Compare the poor fishermen with the Grecian philosophers as regards their learning, and it must at once appear as a surprising fact that these unlearned preachers revolutionized the world, while the deep learning of the philosophers failed to do so. Their divine doctrines fell upon human hearts, as gentle rain falls upon parched ground.

Compare the Apostles with a Socrates, an Aristotle, a Plato, or a Pythagoras, and then ask the question, Whence comes their great power? How is it that these simple men, who lived in want and poverty, who were untutored, aroused Greece and Rome, while these great philosophers failed to do so. A great philosopher teaches that the human mind has a methaphysical want, yet metaphysics has never become a panacea for the world. He should have said that the human mind has an inborn desire for revelation.

Something else was needed, and this something was revelation. Through it alone the human family could reach its present state of civilization. The world was ready for its reception, hence it spread most rapidly, despite the slowness of communication between states and countries. In its onward course it had not the aid of the sword to hew a way for it, it was not protected by the strong arm of government; on the contrary, it was opposed by those in power. Yet Christianity seized upon the human mind and heart, it revolutionized the masses, it improved their conditions, and why? Simply because of its supernatural powers. How many lives were lost in the establishing and maintaining of the Roman Empire? How many cruel deeds were committed in aid of Islamism? yet the new doctrines spread, despite the fact that their adherents were often compelled to surrender life. Hellenic, Roman, Egyptian, Persian, Hindoo and Arabic culture was protected by the strong arm of the government, and by the mystic power of the priesthood, yet it failed to reach the people; it never elevated them; Christian preachers, however, proclaimed the gospel and the poor accepted it, because it filled the aching void of their hearts; because they had faith in the new doctrines and their indestructibility. Man's attempts at civilization were a failure, and now God took up the work. Men had sunk into a state of degradation; the race was oppressed and tyrannized. Had not the Grecians claimed that all non-Hellens were barbarians, and that they were born to serve? Did not Rome foster slavery? Did she not indulge in all manner of cruelties and subtle immoralities? Men were regarded as cattle, and woman occupied an extremely low position. The bonds that kept the masses in a state of low degradation and subjection were strong, and mankind cried for relief. How appropriately Händel begins the Oratorio of the Messiah with these words: "Comfort ye my people, saith your God; speak comfortingly to Jerusalem, and cry unto her that her warfare is accomplished, that her iniquity is pardoned. Prepare ye the way of the Lord; make straight in the desert a highway for our God. Every valley shall be exalted and every mountain and hill made low, the crooked straight and the rough places plain. And the glory of the Lord shall be revealed and all flesh shall see it together, for the mouth of the Lord hath spoken it." The promised relief came, and it was ushered in through revelation and *not* through philosophy. No one who believes in Christianity will deny that it is the foundation-stone of modern civilization, and that it must finally be its capstone. Let rationalists say what they will, this fact *is true*, that *without* Christianity our civilization would not be what it is. The world had its Buddha, its Confucius, its Zoroaster; it had the great thinkers of Egypt, Greece and Rome; yet, what was the condition of the world at the time when Christ came? Christianity is the kernel out of which our civilization grew. If this is *not* true, why did the human family fail to reach it after centuries of struggle? Only through revelation, with Christ as its centre, could the human family rise to the present high state of culture.

But what has all this to do with music? Let us see! It is a significant fact, that the good book is full of allusions to music. If there is nothing contained in holy writ that is not of importance to man, if it contains the much needed revelation, why these repeated references and allusions to music? Why is music used in connection with many important events? From the book of Genesis to Revelation music is mentioned. This fact is not without meaning, nay, it attaches a great importance to our beloved art which no other enjoys. That there is a close connection between religion and music is a fact too often overlooked or even denied by many musicians; yet it is nevertheless true. I am happy to state, however, that the number of those who view our art in its proper relations, is constantly on the increase. In its relations to religion music attains its highest meaning. This does not imply that all music must be wedded to sacred texts, or that it is to be used in connection with worship, but that all pure art, and hence all pure art music, is *sacred* or *religious* in its character and mission. If the Bible is the foundation of our present civilization, music has, undoubtedly, a most important mission to perform in this work. This is not a popular idea among those who make music its own finality; yet we firmly believe, that eventually this will be the common view taken of art in general, and especially of music. Who can doubt that music, when it is practiced in this spirit, reaches its true meaning.

Next to religion, music is one of the greatest civilizing powers. You cannot point to a nation that is totally devoid of religious ideas, neither can you discover even a small tribe, be it *ever* so crude in its customs, but has its music. Wherever religion has a foothold, there music is found. There is an inborn love for song in all men. The power of music is so great, that in the legends of all nations, the invention of the art is ascribed to the gods. Among the children of Israel music was used *only* in connection with worship, and is it unreasonable to believe that there will come a time when all art practices will be worship?

In the fourth chapter of the book of Genesis, the invention of music is recorded. If music is merely a plaything, if it is merely an amusement, merely a means to arouse pleasant emotions, if it has not a higher mission, why does the book of God mention its origin? Is the creation or origin of any other art recorded? That the power of music was early felt and appreciated, is evident from the fact that David played before Saul to drive away the evil spirit. Is the Bible true, or is it merely a myth? If it is the truth, does this instance not show that what Luther said is true also, namely, that the devil hates music. Now it is a natural question for a musician to ask, why was music used to drive away the evil spirit? Why were not prayers, exhortations and incantations used in order to accomplish this work of mercy? The Germans say that where they sing, there you may safely rest, for bad people have no songs. Of course, bad people sing, but they sing not with the spirit of love, which, as I shall show you, is the one power that must underlie all musical practices.

In Second Chronicles, chapter five, we read, that when the Levites were "arrayed in white linen, having cymbals and psalteries and harps," and when they "stood at the east end of the altar, and with them the 120 priests, sounding with trumpets, it came to pass, as the trumpeters and singers were as one to make one sound, to be heard in praising and thanking the Lord, and when they lifted up their voices with the trumpets and cymbals and instruments of music, and praised the Lord, saying (or singing), 'For he is good, for his mercy endureth forever,' that then the house was filled with a cloud, even the house of the Lord, so that the priests could not stand to minister by reason of the cloud, for the glory of the Lord filled the house of God." This is a divine manifestation, but why did it occur during a *musical* performance; why not during the offering of sacrifices, or during the act of prayer; why did it not occur during the act of placing the ark in the temple? Does not this divine manifestation attach a great and a serious importance to our art?

But still another illustration. In Second Kings, 3d chapter, we read of Elijah having been asked to prophesy. When he consented to do so, he did not pray for the Spirit to descend, he did not confess his sins, nor did he ask Saul to do so, but he said, "'Bring me a minstrel.' And it came to pass that, when the minstrel played, the hand of the Lord came upon him." Why was music required to bring down the Spirit of God? Why was not another art, why were not burnt offerings used? It is indeed a most remarkable demonstration of the great power of music. Recall the fall of the walls of Jericho. Music was chosen as the power to accomplish this act, and through music this miracle was wrought. The Lord could have chosen any other means, yet he chose music to bring it about. Has this not a deep meaning?

When God gave the Decalogue, lightning was seen and loud thunder was heard; yet we are informed that above all this were heard trumpet sounds. Why was the sound of music added to these manifestations of nature? Why was it introduced at so important and never to be forgotten an event?

When the angels proclaimed the birth of Christ, they, no doubt, sang that beautiful sentence, "Glory to God in the Highest, on earth peace and good will toward men." This is the proclamation of the divine work of civilization. While in Old Testament history music is connected with many important events, and also with religious worship, we learn from the New, that music is to be used in the blessed abode above. Whether this is to be music such as we practice, I will not say, but then it is to be music. Perhaps in the last days, when everything shall be changed in the twinkling of an eye, our beloved art also will be changed, but this does not lessen the force of the Bible truth. Does this not prove that music is the one favored art of God? Ever since the time when the morning stars sang together, until now, music has been a means of praise, and this honorable position our art shall enjoy throughout all eternity.

Music was admitted into all churches, a few being excepted; and even these are yielding in this direction. It has ever been a language of praise, a language for the expression of our inner soul-life. Now is all this accidental, or has it a meaning? Undoubtedly we have a right to claim for our beloved art a high position and a most noble mission.

But turn from the Bible and read the ancient heathen writers. Though the idea of the true God had been lost, the art of music was still practiced, and was regarded as a means of civilization. Pythagoras calls music the emblem of the Cosmos. His disciples claimed that music was designed to restore the original harmony of the soul. How near he came to the truth, and yet how far he was from it. At night, before retiring, his followers cleansed their souls through calm music, and in the morning they strengthened themselves through the same means. Plato speaks of a music of the spheres, and goes parallel with the Psalmist, who says that the heavens declare the glory of God, and with Job, who speaks of the morning stars singing together. The ancient Grecians took great pains to instruct their children in music. Plato said that youths should be trained through music to do *that* which is seemly, for music, according to his ideas, is useful in all serious undertakings, but especially so in war. Soterichus speaks of the fact that music leads to that which is great, beautiful, noble and sublime; and through it, he says, we are benefited. All states, he adds, which are distinguished for the best laws also show the greatest love for music. Socrates claimed that true education means gymnastics for the body and music for the soul, and, says the same sage, music must begin earlier than gymnastics. The Grecians attributed peculiar powers to certain keys; some were suited for peace, some for war. They had a profound knowledge of rhythm and its powers, through which they cultivated their sentiments, making themselves receptive for the pure and good, and teaching themselves to abhor the ugly. But enough has been said to show that the ancient Grecians had a high regard for music, although they knew not the one true God.

Let us now turn from the good book as a revelation, and realize the fact that genius, which is the gift of God, is in a certain and, of course, in a limited sense a revelation also. Men of genius have been sent into this world as beacon lights, that men may also by *these means* be helped on their upward course. Undoubtedly Shakespeare was such a genius. Who can deny that when he was yet in his cradle he was already the Shakespeare who, by his divine gifts, has given utterance to so many profound sayings? Neither schools nor example made him what he was; he was divinely gifted, and his utterances in many instances have the character of divinations. His works are full of allusions to music, only a few of which I shall quote. Bear in mind *this* fact, that in Shakespeare's time but little of art music was known, yet in his precious writings we discover sentiments, and read wise utterances about music which attribute to it great powers. Listen to a quotation from "Richard II." In his monologue in prison the monarch says, while listening to music—

> "For music mads me, let it sound no more;
> For though it have holped madmen to their wits,
> In me, it seems, it will make wise men mad;
> Yet blessings on his heart that gives it me,
> For 'tis a sign of love, and love for Richard
> Is a strange brooch in this all-hating world!"

Observe the great writer recognizing the fact that music has cured insanity! What art is this which follows man, as a sweet blessing, into the greatest depths of misery, those depths where even religious instruction, the kind words of friends, can afford no consolation or aid? When man's mind is disordered, when reason fails, then the divine art is still a blessing; it affects both mind and heart, and often has restored what was lost. What a blessing music is to-day to the thousands locked up in asylums? Yet, notice also the first saying of the king, namely, that music *mads* him. With its gentle and persuasive tones, no doubt, it opens the sluices of memory; it brings back the recollections of youth, with its blessings and innocence, and thus it causes sad reflections upon an ill-spent life. Music leads the hearer to draw a contrast between the past and the present; it awakens conscience, and *this* no doubt is what the author means when he causes King Richard to say that this music makes a wise man mad. But notice also the fact that the king, who is weary of life, who is bowed down by misfortunes, goaded by his own errors; who is kept in prison for his wrongs, in the midst of these trying circumstances, is suddenly led by music to pronounce a blessing. When hearing music, he, who is on the verge of despair, says: "Blessings on his heart that gives it me!" See the noble influences of our art; see the good a simple musician is permitted to do. Though heavy walls separate him from the one for whom he played, his music calls forth a blessing from the lips of a despairing sufferer. Who can doubt that thousands of bleeding and suffering hearts, that were on the verge of uttering a curse, were through music made to utter a blessing? Who can deny that thousands of hearts have found consolation in music, when no other earthly language would have reached them.

And now follow the poet a step farther, and notice that he regards music as a sign of love! Ah blessed Shakespeare! Here one sees a spark of thy powers of divination. Knowing nothing about art music and its powers, he ascribes to it the spirit of love! In these words he utters the greatest truth with regard to music, for music is love, religion is love, and blessed love is the link that binds the two inseparably. Yet, let us not overlook the sad fact, that while music and love are divine gifts, they both are, also, shockingly abused. Both religion and music aim to spread the spirit of love, which is the atmosphere of heaven, and when love shall once reign supreme, then also will music exercise its greatest power, for then shall we have reached the highest point of civilization.

Permit me to give you a few other quotations. King Henry IV, the dying monarch, says:—

> "Let there be no noise made, my gentle friends,
> Unless some dull and favorable hand
> Will whisper music to my weary spirit."

What a picture! A departing monarch, after enduring many struggles in behalf of his crown, at last comes to the brink of that cold, chill river which divides the known from the unknown. Though the possessor of a kingdom with all its wealth, he asks only that some one will whisper music to his weary spirit! This, and nothing more! Why did he merely ask for music? Ah, it was to be an invisible bridge for his pain-racked mind, on which he might cross this chill river; it was to be a soothing voice, that should enable him in peace to enter the long sleep! Oh, what is music, when dying kings are made to ask for it as their last request? The monarch did not ask for the consolation of friends, he did not long to hear his deeds of valor recounted, he did not ask for homage as a sovereign, nay, all he wanted was a whispering of music—that and nothing more. What a tribute to the secret powers of our art! Should we not revere and love it, should we not use it with genuine devotion? But then King Henry's last request is the same as that of millions of Christians, who, when about to exchange mortality for immortality, ask for no more than a simple song of praise. They wish to die with the fragrance of religious song on their lips, or, if perchance the voice is *too feeble* to sing, they wish to hear sweet song from the lips of the loved ones, and with *it* in their hearts, they desire to reach the other shore. On the pinions of song, they wish their souls to rise to the throne of Grace. Ask ministers how many hymns there are that are wedded to death-bed scenes.

Still another quotation. In the "Twelfth Night," the Duke says to his musician—

"If music be the food of love, play on,
Give me excess of it; that, surfeiting,
The appetite may sicken, and so die.
That strain again; it had a dying fall:
Oh, it came o'er my ear like the sweet south,
That breathes upon a bank of violets,
Stealing and giving odor."

In another place he says—

"Give me some music; that piece of song,
That old and antique song we heard last night;
Methought it did relieve my passion much;
More than light airs and recollected terms
Of these most brisk and giddy-paced times."

One might write a whole lecture about Shakespeare's wonderful utterances in connection with music. Notice that the Duke asks for the antique song, and that he preferred it to the light airs of the giddy-paced times. Learn from Shakespeare, and use but that which is good; avoid the giddy, the flashy and silly in music.

Only one more quotation and I shall dismiss the immortal William, as our good and learned Dr. Black so fondly calls him. In the "Merchant of Venice" Lorenzo says—

"How sweet the moonlight sleeps upon this bank!
Here will we sit, and let the sounds of music
Creep in our ears; soft stillness, and the night,
Become the touches of sweet harmony.
Sit, Jessica: Look how the floor of heaven
Is thick inlaid with patines of bright gold;
There's not the smallest orb, which thou behold'st,
But in his motion like an angel sings,
Still quiring to the young-ey'd cherubins:
Such harmony is in immortal souls;
But, whilst this muddy vesture of decay
Doth grossly close it in, we cannot hear it.

> The reason is your spirits are attentive:
> For do but note a wild and wanton herd,
> Or race of youthful and unhandled colts,
> Fetching mad bounds, bellowing, and neighing loud,
> Which is the hot condition of their blood;
> If they but hear perchance a trumpet sound,
> Or any air of music touch their ears,
> You shall perceive them make a mutual stand,
> Their savage eyes turn'd to a modest gaze,
> By the sweet power of music: Therefore, the poet
> Did feign that Orpheus drew trees, stones, and floods;
> Since nought so stockish, hard, and full of rage,
> But music for the time doth change his nature:
> The man that hath no music in himself,
> Nor is not mov'd with concord of sweet sounds,
> Is fit for treasons, stratagems, and spoils;
> The motions of his spirit are dull as night,
> And his affections dark as Erebus:
> Let no such man be trusted."

Here we see the poet describe the magic effect of music upon the animal creation, and, indeed, there is scarcely any animal but does yield to its charms. Even the crawling serpent with its poisonous fangs is tamed by sweet melody. Well may one ask: Is all this meaningless?

Does God do a purposeless thing? Why do the human and animal creation yield so willingly to the charms of music? Undoubtedly it is the divine will that it should so be. And now comes the question, why did he create this love for music, and why did he give us music itself, unless it is to be an educational factor? Ah, music is more than a mere amusement. If it were only this, we would be deceived, all our musical practices would be the emptiest and most meaningless performances imaginable. But can this be so, in view of all that has been said? Surely not! God has given us this art for a high and noble purpose, he has inclined our hearts toward it, and if we fail to realize all the noble influences that may be drawn from it, it is because we have not studied the art as we should, because we ourselves are not prepared for its blessed influences.

But listen to these words once more: "Such harmony is in immortal souls; but, whilst this muddy vesture of decay doth close it in, we cannot hear it." Ah! this music of the soul or the heart is a wondrous power, and if it has once been heard, it will never be forgotten. He who has been under its influence, has tasted greater joy and deeper sorrow than can be expressed in words. Would you hear this music, seek solitude and silence, retire from the world of laughter and merriment, and enter the world of love, sympathy and meditation. *There*, listen to your heart and you may hear music that is calculated to arouse your emotional nature to its deepest depth. When the sun has gone down beyond those red and gorgeously colored clouds that appear like so many huge steps leading into Heaven itself, when the birds have ceased to sing, when silence reigns, and when the stars look down upon you like so many loving, watchful, but also *soul-searching* eyes, then the heart vibrates most readily. Listen! and perchance you will hear your mother's voice singing again those songs you loved to hear from her lips. Then you may also hear the old familiar Sabbath-school hymns, the songs of the sanctuary as well as those of the school-room. Presently the vibrating strings will also reproduce those strains you sang when a child among many children, gathered around shady trees or sitting on the porch in the twilight of the evening. Then you may also hear the song you sang so sweetly when love's impulses were first touching your youthful heart. The longer one listens to this silent music, the more powerful it becomes, until at last all communication with the outer world ceases. Then the mind reaches beyond the present, and, in its flight, it searches for those things that are hidden.

When we yield to such influences, it seems to me I hear the old church-bells of my far-off home, I hear the sweet and majestic tones of the organ my youthful fingers played with so much reverence. Many a lost chord, many a long-forgotten melody then makes itself heard, chords and melodies which for years had been crowded out of the heart and mind. Sadly I hear the choir chanting the requiem for the dead, and quicker beats the pulse as I hear again the Te Deum as it was sung on Easter and Christmas festivals. While thus in a reflective mood, scene quickly follows scene, ever changing like the figures of a kaleidoscope. The heart music changes from the soft minor into the bright major, and back again into the sombre minor. The grand and passionate Allegro is succeeded by the gentle Adagio, and the painful scenes of the past are softened and blended with those that are pleasant, as the dominant chord resolves itself into that of the tonic. One after another the sluices of memory are opened, bringing back old friends, events and situations, which the busy world had long ago crowded into the rear chamber of memory. But then the silent music of the heart is not always sweet and gentle. Discords, too, are heard, and painful melodies are sung. The heart-strings often quiver, and the tones produced by them are often loud and shrill, like those of the æolian harp when blown upon by the fierce north wind. This is music of sorrow over wrong deeds, over life's errors. Then are heard the dirges over ill-spent hours and over wasted opportunities. Who can long endure such music? Its effects, however, are softened by the sounds of a sweet anthem that is wafted into the heart with the consoling words, "Come unto me, all ye that labor and are heavy laden, and I will give you rest." When this sweet and promising music is heard, the heart takes courage again, it becomes calm once more, and while listening to it, its inner chambers become bright and shining. Verily, at such an hour the heart realizes more of the true meaning of life than philosophers ever revealed. This is music *not* to be found in books, this is music which the deaf ear can hear, music which the heart is always ready to produce, if we but give it an opportunity. This music is heard in its greatest beauty by those whose emotional natures are best developed and most refined. This is the music which Beethoven heard all the more strongly, because the sense of hearing had been destroyed. Having lived a life of isolation for many years, having communed much with his own soul, his heart music became more powerful. He diligently listened to it, he faithfully caught it, and by the aid of his genius he gave it to the instruments. Hence it is that his tones speak with such irresistible force. They come from the depth of a noble heart, and for this reason they never fail to touch and to arouse the emotions of all fine feeling people. What soul music must he have heard as he wandered lonely through fields and valleys, with no sound from the outer world to disturb the music within? The great tone masters were men of noble souls, they were endowed with deep emotional natures; hence it is that their music lifts us up to a higher sphere as we listen to the beatings of their own hearts. We commune with them in the spirit, and are made better by them.

But if the masters wrote from the heart, if they heard much silent music within, which they wrote down for us, those who aim to perform it must in a like manner sing and play with the best powers of their hearts and minds. No matter how simple may be the strain that is awakened by the musician's touch of the instrument, if the player expresses the composer's feelings and full meaning, the performance is artistic. Every student should aim at this power of reproducing the true heart music as it lies hidden in the notes.

When those who have communed much with their own souls, those who have cultivated heart music, come to the end of their life's journey, they often see sweet visions and hear sweet sounds that afford them consolation and joy. Though speech, sight and hearing have failed them, making it impossible for those who stand sorrowing around the dying to communicate with them, though they can neither see loved faces nor hear the gentle accents of beloved voices, though their lips are parched and their voices are broken, yet in the midst of their suffering and mortal loneliness we see their faces light up, and in rapture almost they whisper: How beautiful! How beautiful! It is at such a time that they hear the music of the soul, that silent music I spoke of, that music which the Scotch believe comes from the spheres. Of course, only those who in life have cultivated this heart music may also hear it in their dying hour. Well did Shakespeare say to Jessica:—

> "Such harmony is in immortal souls;
> But while this muddy vesture of decay
> Does close it in, we cannot hear it."

But listen and you will hear beautiful music—that is, if it is in your hearts.

Having quoted the Bible, having heard what Shakespeare had to say about music, let me now turn for a moment to the great Reformer, Luther. He surely was chosen by God to do a great work, he gave a new impulse to that civilization which Christianity had begun, but which had been retarded in its onward course through man's love for oppression and gain. It surely is of interest to hear what so great a man, a God-chosen instrument for a great and important work, has to say about music. One of the first acts of the great Reformer was to introduce music in the public schools of Saxony. Thus we see the great leader, who was no doubt guided by God, bring music right down to the people. Not only did he introduce music into the public schools; nay, he allowed the people to sing in the church, a privilege hitherto denied them. Thus he at once brought music to the old and young, and he made it a blessing to the people. Of him it is justly said, that he laid the foundation for German musical art. The first impulse for *German musical art* came in connection with a great religious movement, hence it rests on a religious basis, for out of the Protestant choral grew Bach and Händel, the roots and trunks of the German art tree. But then see how the

Reformer uses music as a means to spread the Gospel. The Reformation was not only a revival of religion, but it was also an awakening of song. I will quote only a few sentences from the two essays he wrote on music. Aside from these, he often alludes to the art in his voluminous writings, and always professes for it the deepest reverence and love. Says he, "I scarcely know where to begin and where to end in singing its praises." He claimed that God takes care of man and of art, and he strongly enjoins it upon the church to foster the latter. "Song," says he, "makes the sad joyful, it gives courage to the faint-hearted, and the haughty it makes more gentle." In his opinion there is nothing 'so well calculated to control the emotions as music, hence he calls the art a disciplinarian, calculated to make children gentle and meek minded. He teaches that God has honored music throughout all ages. Those who love not song, Luther calls, in his blunt language, "blockheads, who ought to be treated to the bawling of donkeys, the barking of dogs, and squealing of pigs." Those who use the art for selfish purposes he calls "degenerated children and changelings." He places music next to theology, which is its proper place, and adds that, "the devil hates it." "Where music is sharpened by art," says he, "one sees the great and perfect wisdom of God in his wonderful work." Yes, he goes so far as to call music "the transfigured daughter of heaven," a solace to him in his arduous task. Now, is it not a singular fact that the great Reformer, whom God had chosen to renew the work of civilization, was a musician also, a lover of the art, a man on whom rests the entire German musical art work? Is this fact not significant? and, in view of what has been said, can it be meaningless? And if it has a meaning, what is it?

But are not the poets in a sense inspired? They are the sweet singers who are also designed to help along the great work of civilization through their inspirations. If I were to gather what has been said by them in praise of music, I might fill a volume. Only a few quotations shall be offered, to show what fine feeling poets have said about our beloved art.

Collins wrote :—
"Music, sphere descended maid,
Friend of pleasure, wisdom's aid."

Montgomery said :—
"Through every pulse the music stole,
And held sublime communion with the soul,
Wrung from the coyest breast th' imprisoned sigh,
And kindled rapture in the coldest eye."

Pope sang thus :—
"By music minds an equal temper know,
Nor swell too high nor sink too low;
If in the breast tumultuous joys arise,
Music her soft assuasive voice applies,
Or when the soul is pressed with cares,
Exalts her in enlivening airs.
Warriors she fires with animated sounds,
Pours balm into the bleeding lovers' wounds,
Melancholy lifts her head,

> Morpheus rouses from his bed,
> Sloth unfolds her arms and wakes,
> Listening envy drops her snakes.
> Intestine war no more our passions wage,
> And giddy factions bear away their rage."

Thomas Moore, Ireland's sweet singer, writes:—

> "Mine is the day that lightly floats,
> And mine are the murmuring dying notes,
> That fall as soft as snow on the sea,
> And melt in the heart as instantly.
> And the passionate strain that's deeply going,
>   Refines the bosom it trembles through,
> As the musk wind, over the water blowing,
>   Ruffles the wave, but sweetens it too."

In another poem he says:—

> "Music! oh, how faint, how weak,
>   Language fades before thy spell,
> Why should feeling ever speak,
>   When thou canst breathe her soul so well.
> Friendship's balmy words may feign,
>   Love's are e'en more false than they;
> Oh, 'tis only music's strain,
>   Can sweetly soothe and not betray."

Holmes writes, after listening to an organ concert:—

> "I asked three little maidens, who heard the organ play,
> Where all the music came from that stole our hearts away.
>
> I know, said fair-haired Edith:
>   It was the autumn breeze
> That whistled through the hollows
>   Of all those silver trees.
>
> No, child, said keen-eyed Clara,
>   It is a lion's cage;
> They woke him out of slumber,
>   I heard him roar and rage.
>
> Nay, answered soft-voiced Anna,
>   'Twas thunder that you heard,
> And after that came sunshine,
>   And singing of a bird.
>
> Hush! hush you little children,
>   For all of you are wrong,
> I said, my pretty darlings,
>   It was no earthly song,

THE SANCTITY OF MUSIC.   85

> A band of blessed angels
> Has left the heavenly choirs,
> And what you heard last evening
> Were seraph lips and lyres."

Only one more of the many I might offer you.
Says Miss Carter :—

> "The world is full of wondrous song;
>   We pause to hearken, and we hear,
>   Forever sounding far or near,
> Those sweet vibrations soft or strong ;
>   Yet sweeter sound and far more dear
>   Than to the outward sense can hear,
>   That rings upon the inward ear,
> The loved old songs of home.
>
> We catch the music of the May;
>   The tender voice of bird or breeze,
>   That trembles tuneful through the trees,
> And faint and sweet from far away,
>   The mingled murmur of the seas;
>   Yet *sweeter*, *dearer* far than these,
> Though Sirens sang across the foam,
>   Are echoed, through life's silences,
> The loved old songs of home.
>
> The *old*, *old* tunes, the sweet old words
>   That lips grown silent loved to sing ;
>   How close around the heart they cling,
> Smiting its truest, tenderest chords ;
>   Let all the world with music ring,
>   Where'er we rest, where'er we roam,
>   Not one can touch so sweet a string,
>   Or to the heart such rapture bring,
> As these loved songs of home."

But I must cease quoting. Read for yourselves, and notice that, whenever poets try to catch in words the spirit of music, they write their tenderest lines.

Now behold music as the companion of man. It follows him through joy and sorrow, it is with him in sickness and health, it is a delight in the prison as well as on the pleasure ground, it is heard in Sabbath-school and in church ; we love it in youth as well as in old age, it is welcome in peace and in war, it delights us in the school-room as well as in the home-circle ; we hear it while resting on our mother's breast, it greets the bride at her wedding and follows us even to the tomb! Is there any other power or created being that is such a steady companion to man's life, the word of God excepted? Is there another companion as tender, as faithful, and as soothing as sweet music, except the word of God? Is there another power that awakens and holds the human heart as does music?

And now, if God in his word speaks so frequently and so highly of music, if in sacred history it is coupled with so many and with such important events, if it is the art that goes with us to heaven and that is practiced before the throne of Grace, if it is the art which all ancient writers delighted to praise, and the invention of which they ascribe to the gods; if music, like religion, is found among all tribes and nations, no matter how uncultivated they may be; if Shakespeare, as if through divination, spoke in rapture of music's power, if Luther, the great reformer, assigns to it a place by the side of theology, if the poets sing sweetly of the art, if painters and sculptors have delighted in representing it, if all right feeling men love it and yield to it, if even the animal creation is charmed by it, if nature is full of it, if man's heart seems to have been made for it, then one may well believe that God had a great and a wise purpose when he created music, and hence it is that every serious musician seeks for something beyond the vibrations that produce the sweet sounds.

What is music? If we could tell as much of it as we feel when hearing it, we might easily answer this question. Is it an eternal sentiment laid within our breast, that is aroused when sounds are produced? or are the sentiments hidden in the sounds? or are our hearts and the sounds, like opposite poles, attracting one another? Says Jean Paul Richter : "Oh music, thou who bringest the receding waves of eternity nearer to the weary heart of man as he stands upon the shores and longs to cross over; art thou the evening breeze of this life or the morning air of the future one?" Or, as another put the question : "Art thou a recollection of Paradise or a foretaste of heaven?"

Who dares to abuse such an art? who dares to belittle its powers? He who uses it only for his own glorification, shows how little he values it as a gift of God. Let us study it as a most powerful and mysterious gift, as an art which is designed to enhance the civilization of man. I often think of music as a soul-language; it utters what words cannot express. Is it possible that music shall be the language of heaven, and that, thereby, our daily or hourly utterances become praise? No matter what definition of music we *may* give, so much is sure, that the essence of the art is love. It comes from God, hence it leads back to God, and its mission here can only be that of peace. Love never rests, it forever moves, it constantly seeks new territory to spread happiness; hence, music, like the Gospel, is heard everywhere. Mankind leans toward love, and whatever brings it to us we take to our hearts.

As the love of God is immeasurably great, so no one has as yet fathomed the depth of music. It is the love language of the soul; it is the medium between this and the other world, between the natural and supernatural. We shall for all time continue to study this language, for it shall forever help to bring us nearer to God. All men need an ideal world, and all men love to wander therein; religion and music are the portals that open into this world. To deny the ideal and to live only for the real is the same as denying religion and art.

Music cannot do what the ancient Grecians claimed it would do—restore the equilibrium of the soul; no musician with a just appreciation of his art will make such claims for it. Give the art its proper place where Luther has assigned it, namely, next to theology, and rational musicians are satisfied.

The love power speaks out of music, and it is the one force that leads us all. If it is not, pray tell us what it is. Love is the all-ruling principle; without it the true, the just, the beautiful are not possible. The heart is the living power in man, and love is its centre; it is the motor of the world. Music is love; hence its mighty power. Love is the source from which emanate all great art works; they bring down heavenly love, peace on earth to men, and so they lift us up again, for God's revelations shall not be without their results. Often, when listening to good music, my heart becomes sad, for I see my shortcomings, and then there is heard a voice within, saying: Rise and become better. And in a like manner, when I hear good music, I say: Oh, that it may make my pupils better men and women! In view of what has been said of the art, in view of its capabilities and its sanctity, I repeat what I have said before, that I am most happy in my field of labor, and that if I could fill the highest offices on earth I would still say: Let me be what I am, a teacher of music. This love in art softens men's hearts, but it cannot change them, religion alone does this. Hence, an unloving, a selfish musician, a proud, vainglorious and haughty musician, is an inconsistent being, as anomalous as would be a selfish, proud and haughty minister of the Gospel. Read the lives of our great musicians and notice how they loved their art, and how highly they thought of its influences and purposes. They had studied the art; surely they ought to know, in part at least, what its capabilities are. Says Philip Emanuel Bach: "One of the noblest objects of music is the spread of religion and the elevation of the human soul." Glück said: "The object of music is to soften men down without injuring them, and to make them favorable to their surroundings, without lowering them." Hauptman says: "The highest good of art is not for the connoisseur or the artist, but for all mankind." And right here I say, and that in contradiction to what others have claimed, that pure art, like religion, is for the masses, and not for the few. Marx says: "That the tendency of music is to benefit the masses, and that it cannot be without its influence upon their moral and spiritual condition." Berlioz says: "Do you think I listen to music merely to be pleased? The perfect, be it expressed in the strangest sphere, operates toward the perfect." Schumann said: "Does your music come from within? Have you felt it? Be sure it will also affect others." Liszt says: "Everything designed to purify the taste operates upon the heart of man, and the rules of art give us a better understanding of the world's sentiment." Ambros says: "That one is compelled to call music a moral power; it is more than an amusement." Prætorius wrote: "Experience teaches that music does not remain where the devil rules, for the wicked are not worthy of the art."

"Music," says Beethoven, "is the medium between the spiritual and the realistic life." This great master always saw something holy in his art, which he placed above philosophy; hence all musicians of high attainments are opposed to anything rude, commonplace, frivolous and enervating in art. Hoffmann says: "Love and music live in each other as head and heart." Another said: "Where there is no heart there is no music." When Händel was told by his sovereign that the performance of the "Messiah" had afforded him pleasure, the composer replied: "Your majesty, I did not intend to amuse or to afford pleasure; I meant to make the world better." But I must cease giving quotations. There were musicians who did not view the Gospel as you and I view it, although they were not without religious sentiment; they all believed that the essence of music is love. Hence all great musicians were self-sacrificing in their spirit; they cherished an undying devotion to their art; nothing calculated to enhance its progress was too difficult a task for them to undertake. Most great musicians had a religious side to their lives. Look at Haydn, when the ideas ceased to flow, how fervently he prayed. Read Mozart's letters and notice his devotion to religion. On Beethoven's table constantly laid a tablet, and upon it were printed these words, "I am He that is. No one has my veil uplifted." Hear Händel, who tells us that when he wrote "He was Despised and Rejected," he shed tears; and when he wrote the "Hallelujah Chorus," he thought he saw the heavens open, with the angels standing around the throne. Behold the solidity and indestructibility of Bach's religion. Read what Weber wrote under a picture or in an album, saying, "As God wills," and that right under Rossini's words, who said, "As the Public wills." Feel the spirit of genuine piety that fairly streams out of the works of Palestrina, Allegri, Pergolesi, and the older Italian masters. Behold Liszt turning toward religion; notice the religious tendencies of Mendelssohn's pure soul, as it reveals itself in his oratorios. What good has been done in this world by one such work as the "Messiah"? Behold how constantly our art is coupled with works of charity! How many concerts in aid of the suffering have been given! Yet, there are men who smile at the powers of music; they make light of its influence, nor will they recognize the difficulties which the study of the art presents. Music is not a deception, it is not a creature of the imagination, it is not a plaything or an amusement; if it were this and nothing more, then, as has been said, the art would *not* deserve to exist, while those who teach it would lead the most useless lives of any class of persons. Take away its religious basis and it becomes a tinkling bell; what Ambros said with so much irony is true: "Men who divest music of its religious element, and claim to derive pleasure from the art, are like galvanized frog-legs. There is motion but no life. There may be emotions but there is no love. Music is designed to express the inner longing of the soul; it says in tones what the mind fails to utter in words. It is heart-language; it is a heavenly language, and he who banishes heaven from his heart fails also to fully comprehend the tone language." Let me reiterate what has been said: God honors music in His word; it is connected with most important sacred events. The ancient Grecians used it as an educational means, and sought to restore through it the equilibrium of the soul. God inclined the human heart to love music; yes, he placed the animal creation under its sway. There is not found a nation or a tribe without music. All the great poets speak of it in rapturous language; nature itself is full of it; it is to be the language of the great beyond; it is love, and love only can come from God and must lead to him again. In view of these facts, can music be a mere plaything, a mere amusement? If so, all musicians and all lovers of the art are most cruelly deceived by the influence it exercises. All those that study it waste their time as well as their means, and the Koran is right when it forbids the use of it, as weakening and injurious to man. Not only are we all deceived by studying music, if it be not what it claims to be, nay, millions before us have been deceived, and among them some of the loftiest minds and purest of hearts. No! Let us accept music as a gift, a most precious gift of God; let us study it with reverence; let us practice it with humility and diligence, so that we may catch and drink in the spirit of love which it breathes, which is of God, and which leads to God. Let us bear in mind that music is to go with us to heaven, and that there we shall see it in all its glory and beauty.

CHURCH MUSIC.

The history of Christian church music begins with the fourth century. Doubtless, the early Christians used either the songs of Greece or India whenever circumstances permitted them to sing in their worship. Christ left no directions for the musical portion of divine worship, and, indeed, a peculiar Christian church music could develop only in the slow course of time. St. Ambrose, who lived in the fourth century, was the first to establish rules, and St. Gregory, who lived two centuries later, continued the good work. It was he who laid the foundation of the present system of Catholic church music. The masses of the people were musically uneducated. Perhaps the church of Rome found it difficult to teach the people to sing; perhaps she could not supply the teachers needed; perhaps she preferred to exclude the people from all participation in the musical part of divine worship; whatever the reason may have been, it is an historic fact, that only monks, friars and deacons were permitted to join in the singing. In order to establish uniformity in singing, the popes sent teachers throughout Christendom, and whenever disputes arose concerning the authenticity of a method, bishops and monasteries sent teachers to Rome to be instructed. Despite these earnest efforts to establish uniformity, the music of the church from time to time declined. A certain Cardinal, when asked by Pope Nicholas (1447) how he liked the singing then common in churches, said: "Methinks I hear a herd of swine that grunt with might and main, without producing an articulate sound or word." Surely this was severe criticism, and that, too, from one high in authority in the Catholic church.

Observe that Rome established an ecclesiastic church music. She excluded the people not only from the pulpit, but from the choir. More than that, in her desire to keep the art from evil tendencies, she checked its growth, but while thus the art was fettered within the church, it developed without. The people were fond of singing, and while at an earlier period the Minnesingers developed song in castles of knights and palaces of the nobles, the Meistersingers at a later period spread song and poetry among the common people, and made the homes of the plain burghers resound with cheerful music.

This was about the musical condition of Germany when Luther entered upon his work of the Reformation. The great reformer was a musician, and as such appreciated the benign influences of the art. He calls it the fairest and most glorious gift of God, to which Satan is a bitter enemy. He said that music makes people more meek-minded. He advocated the introduction of music into the public schools, and next to theology, he gives the divine art the highest honors. . Luther only gradually loosened those bonds which tied the people to the Roman service. The first reform measure was the introduction of the German language. He translated those Latin hymns which were free from error, and wrote others himself. In order to provide new music for his people he introduced the popular melodies of the day. The whole congregation were invited to join in the songs of the sanctuary. Observe how Protestantism in its earliest development differed from Rome in the rise of religious music. The one had an ecclesiastic music with which the people had nothing to do, the other insisted upon congregational singing.

Music proved to be a powerful agent to help along the work of reformation. In all ages and among all nations great political and religious upheavals have found an expression in song. These outbursts are usually designed to fire the heart and to engender loyalty to a cause. Catholic writers of those days said that the people fairly *sang* themselves into Luther's doctrines, and the Jesuit, Conzen, added that more souls went to destruction through Luther's hymns and tunes, than through his doctrines.

It was but natural that the want of a hymn-book should make itself felt. This want was supplied in 1524, when a little pamphlet appeared containing but eight hymns and five tunes. The next edition, which appeared in 1525, had 16 hymns, and the book, as published in 1545, contained not less than 89 hymns. Luther not only used many popular tunes, but he converted popular songs to religious uses. Aside from this he drew largely upon the Bohemian or Moravian church-music collection. Luther's agents and missionaries traveled all over Germany selling and giving away the new hymn- and tune-books. These often became popular before a Lutheran preacher had addressed the people. Thus song conveyed the seeds of the gospel and spread the spirit of the Reformation. These song-peddlers, as they were called, were often arrested, but where one was put into jail ten others were ready to take his place.

Luther and his co-laborers were nobly aided in their work of providing new hymns and music. These often were mere chance productions. An organist, for instance, took sick, and his pastor wrote a hymn as a word of consolation, and, after the organist had recovered, he set it to music. This is the simple origin of that celebrated hymn and choral, "What God does, that is well done."

Both hymns and tunes of that period are very different from those of modern times. The latter appear weak, yes, often insignificant, when compared with the church music of the reformation time. The tunes and hymns that were produced during Luther's time, and for a century afterward, must be called *heroic;* they have about them a solemn grandeur, like the men and the times from whence they sprang. The Reformation was not only an outburst of thought, but also one of song. God's spirit was moving the masses, the Bible was unchained, the shackles of centuries were loosened, and the days of religious freedom began to dawn,—religious freedom which is the necessary precursor of political freedom. Who could keep from singing at such a time! What poet, what musician was there, who, when breathing the spirit of his times, could fail to produce a new hymn or a new tune? When the heart is full of religious fervor, the lips will overflow with religious song. These hymns and tunes sprang from a genuine religious spirit; hence they live to this day, and if Protestant churches do not admire them, sensible musicians do. Over 2000 hymns and tunes have been collected from the first century after the Reformation. With the sad scenes of the

Thirty Years' War this activity ceased, and as all standing still in moral and religious life generally leads to a retrograde movement, we may well say that the decline of German hymnology dates from that period.

Although I am writing on the subject of Protestant church music, I am, nevertheless, under the necessity of saying a few words about the music of Rome. The Catholic church was friendly to the cultivation of arts, but because the Catholic church is charged with errors, the arts, especially music, need not be suspected of vicious influences.

As Germany's best Protestant church music was written during the century succeeding the Reformation, so also was the best Catholic church music written during the same period. I need but mention one Italian master of the 16th century whom Protestant musicians admire as much as Catholics possibly can— I mean *Palestrina*. But this leads me too far. It has been said that the Catholic church did more for the arts than for religion, just as Cardinal Wolsey did more for his king than for his God. The modern Catholic church music is grand, highly artistic, and often dramatic. It affects the listener as if it were coming from an angelic choir above. It is, therefore, in the main inspiring; it is designed to draw the listener into the presence of God. Protestant church music is plainer, less pretentious, but more vigorous. It has less of an art tinge and more of a popular character. It is not designed to be a means of drawing worshipers into the presence of God, but should call praise from their lips to the throne of grace. The Bible more often bids us praise than pray. Are there any among you who excuse themselves from singing, by saying: "I am musically uneducated, I cannot sing." If so, let me ask whether you would refuse to pray because you are not a scholar, and are not educated enough to use the best language. God hears the humblest prayer of the humblest man that kneels in his cabin to supplicate his Father. Yet that prayer may be far more effective than hundreds of petitions offered by those who know how to use elegant language. So God will hear your songs of praise, be they ever so humble, for God looks to the heart first and then to the voice.

Rome has ever been the centre toward which a world contributed her wealth. She was, therefore, rich and well able to cultivate the arts. Germany, on the other hand, was poor, her climate was rougher, she lacked those refining influences which Italy enjoyed for centuries before Germany became christianized. It was, therefore, but natural that Italy should have been in advance of Germany in the cultivation of the arts. Poor Germany was afflicted with wars and political commotions. Foes from without and within assailed her. Germany is the geographical centre, the heart of Europe, and owing to her peculiar situation she quickly feels the slightest tremor of any part of the continent. She was chosen by God to stand the shock of the Reformation, and bravely she stood it. That music did not flourish during the Thirty Years' War is but natural; but when peace returned, and the poor land ceased to bleed from its many wounds, art began to flourish again. There arose two great men who laid the foundation for all future German musical art, namely, Bach and Händel. They were sturdy Protestants, and thus it may be said that German art rests upon the spirit of Protestantism. Italian church music is found only in Rome. France has really no church music that is deserving of the name; German Protestant music is found everywhere in that country.

During the last century, Lutheran church music underwent a process of modernizing; the chorals were changed from the church modes to the modern major and minor keys; the language of the hymns was softened, but both hymn and tune suffered in their spiritual character. The spirit of rationalism now made its influence felt, both in the pulpit and in the choir; worldly music was heard and purely metaphysical sermons were preached. And again the hand of affliction was laid upon Germany; the land was again invaded by the old enemy; but, when peace was restored, William III, King of Prussia, took vigorous steps toward a revival of religion, and this work was begun with a process of purifying Protestant church music. Germany still adheres to congregational singing.

Despite German rationalism, we may still go to Germany for our best works on Protestant theology. All the English-speaking people of the globe have produced but about 5000 hymns, while Germany alone has enriched sacred literature with 80,000 of them. If it be true that the lips run over with what the heart is filled, no one dare to deny that Germany at one time was eminently a religious country, and if she is no longer that, the sin must be laid to the charge of her ministers, who first forsook the truth.

France.—The Reformers found a rich storehouse of music and hymnology in the Bohemian collection of church music. The Bohemians sang in their native tongue, and practiced congregational singing long before the Reformation. While Lutheran church music was set to harmony, that of the Bohemian book was not. The tunes were to be sung in unison. The Jesuits have had a special dislike to this book, and so persistent have they been in the work of its destruction that but very few original copies are left us. Wherever Moravians sing, be it among the Indians, the Hottentots, or in the snow-covered huts of the Esquimaux, they use to this day the same grand old tunes and hymns. More than once, while traveling in Pennsylvania, have I visited their churches, and have listened with delight to their singing, but I am also sorry to say that the youth of that church are opposed to these jewels, and seek to exchange them for "Sweet-By-and-By," "Hold the Fort," etc. Of this style of church music I shall, however, speak more fully.

The third and fourth styles of church music, namely, the Episcopalian and Calvinistic, I will treat in connection with each other, because in England they developed side by side, and because a great deal of English history is closely connected with the development of English church music. The history of the Calvinistic mode of singing reaches into all countries where Protestantism has gained a foothold; yes, it reaches even into our present time. Lutheran church music was more or less without centralization, that is, different cities and countries had their own hymns and tune-books. The music of the Reformed churches, however, was everywhere the same. The Calvinists at Geneva, at Cassel and Frankfort used the same tunes. Calvin differed more radically from Rome than did Luther, and, inasmuch as the Catholic church was much given to the cultivation of the arts, the early Calvinists were hostile to them. They stripped their churches of everything that reminded them of Rome, and in doing this they at times went to extremes. What if they sang a Psalm before they began the work of destruction in the Cathedral at Antwerp, such work cannot be called sanctified. It is, however, a noteworthy fact, that while pictures and statues were excluded from churches, the most rigid Calvinists finally retained music. Still, the church organ question is now, as it has been in the past, one of dispute in Calvinistic churches, and there is no telling when it will be settled. When speaking of Calvinistic church music, Psalmody deserves our first attention. Psalmody is of German origin—I mean thereby the singing of Psalms in their metrical form. It is claimed that Huss and Wycliffe sang Psalms, but there is no good evidence of this assertion. The Psalms, of course, were chanted in synagogues and in the Catholic church, but the one used them in Hebrew, the other in Latin. Luther translated a number of the Psalms, and sang them in his family worship and at social gatherings, but not in public worship. He often expressed the wish that some one might continue the good work he had begun. Suddenly there appeared a translation of fifty Psalms into French. The work was done by Clement Marot, and the first edition appeared in 1540. The work of translation was afterward completed by Theodore Beza, who five years later, in 1545, caused a complete translation of the Psalms to appear in print. It was first believed that these Psalms would morally revolutionize the realm, for they became at once very popular, so much so that they were heard in the streets of Paris. The king, queen, and, in fact, all his courtiers had their favorite psalms, which they sang to common ballad tunes, and which were heard on all, yes, even the most trivial, occasions. Thus, when the Dauphin went out on the chase, he paused for a moment under the window of his favorite *Diana de Poitiers* and sang, "As the hart panteth after the water-brooks," etc., and when he returned his mistress came to the balcony and welcomed him by singing, "Out of the depths have I cried unto Thee." Of Madame Valentinois it is said that she sang the thirtieth Psalm while she danced. In England the Psalms were roared out at the Lord Mayor's dinner, and that by men heated by wine. How common the singing of Psalms to dance tunes was may be seen from a line in Shakespeare's "Winter Tales," which reads thus: "There is but one Puritan amongst them, and he sings Psalms to hornpipes."

Calvin determined to use these Psalms in his churches, and gave orders that they be sung in unison by the whole congregation.

When it became known that Calvin had adopted the Psalms to be used in the regular service of the reformed churches, Catholics at once abstained from using them, and Psalm-singing henceforth became a synonym of *heresy*.

Let us now turn our attention to England. When King Henry VIII determined to emancipate England from Rome, he aimed quite as much to emancipate himself, and in his reformatory work he was at times guided just as much by passion as by reason. He who defended the faith against Luther now followed in the footsteps of that great reformer, and like him, began by introducing the language of the country into the church service. Henry VIII and Edward and Elizabeth were all great lovers of music, and they did all in their power to make the Episcopal church service brilliant and impressive. Edward VI continued the work of reformation, and during his reign the entire Liturgy of the English Episcopal church, together with the Book of Prayer were perfected (1552). All Catholic missals, breviaries and church music-books were then gathered and destroyed. This took place in 1560. Despite the fact that the English service was sanctioned by law, many were opposed to it, and a struggle ensued which lasted nearly a century. Psalmody was one of the principal points upon which this struggle turned. The oldest translation of the Psalms into English is that by Coverdale. It was followed by another, prepared by Sternhold and Hopkins, 1549. In 1562 these Psalms were supplied with suitable music, which was mostly borrowed from Germany. These Psalms were bound in with the Prayer Book, and, in order to please the Dissenters, were allowed to be sung in public worship. These tunes were set to harmony after the Lutheran and Episcopal style of music. During the reign of Queen Mary, Psalm-singing was not a safe mode of worship; many Christians died bearing witness to their faith, while others fled to Cassel, Frankfort, Geneva and other cities, where they became acquainted with the style of singing practiced in Reformed churches, which style was afterward designated the Geneva style of singing. When Elizabeth ascended the throne, the Episcopal church service was reëstablished in all its splendor. In 1559 she published her sentiments in decrees, and twice during her reign was the church service sanctioned by law. The Dissenters who had to flee during Queen Mary's reign now returned, and at once began the work of agitation against the regular service, and in favor of the Geneva style of singing. They insisted upon it, that plain Psalmody was best adapted to the praise of God. Being men of great persistence, they gave the virgin Queen much trouble, and it required all her firmness to keep these "meddlers," as they were called by Episcopalians, in check.

Now let us hear what critics have to say about this Geneva style of singing. Reports do not agree. One writer says that the Psalms sounded grand; another tells us that they were wretchedly sung. Of course, due allowance must be made in accepting these criticisms, for the Cavaliers hated Psalmody as cordially as the Dissenters hated the regular service. Both sides were determined not to yield, and each did what it could to advance its own views.

During the persecution of the Duke of Alva in Flanders, many reformers had to flee from that country, and they generally turned their faces toward England. These exiles were all Psalm singers, who added greatly to the strength of the Puritans in England. Many of them were weavers; men who were also well skilled in music. They were known all over England, and Shakespeare, in his "Sir John Falstaff," speaks of them in these words: "I would I were a weaver, then I could sing Psalms." It is claimed that the descendants of these weavers are to this day among the best singers in England.

How sad it is that men had to fight for religious liberty! How slow the world was in recognizing the fact that neither powder nor the flames could conquer a man's religious convictions. Men may bow before a hat, or submit to oppressive laws in order to save life and property, but a Christian never yields to what he conceives to be error. Whatever may be said against these men, this much is sure, that their courage deserves our admiration, for they fought out the battles for religious liberty. Through these struggles they established principles, they infused a spirit of independence which can never be crushed; and this is the true spirit of Protestantism, the right to protest, the right of liberty in matters of religion.

The struggle in behalf of Psalmody gradually became general. Sermons were preached and lectures delivered, and even such noted men as Dr. Whitgift,

Archbishop of Canterbury, went so far as to challenge Thomas Cartwright to a public debate. The Puritans became bolder with every success, and finally petitioned Parliament "to put down all cathedrals where the service of God is grievously abused by piping with organs, singing and ringing and drawling of Psalms from one side of the choir to another, with the squeaking of chanting choristers, disguised in white surplices, some in corner caps and filly copes, imitating the fashion and manner of Antichrist the Pope, that man of sin and child of perdition, with his other rabble of miscreants and shavelings." This was indeed bold language to lay before the highest tribunal of the church and the country.

The Episcopal style of singing was then by the Puritans called "curious style of singing, heathenish in its tendency and belonging to Rome." With the accession of strength by the Puritans, Psalm books also increased in number. The most popular one then in use was that published by Ainsworth, 1612. This is the book which the Pilgrim Fathers brought with them to this country. The poetry of this book, if such it deserves to be called, is simply execrable. Let me give you a few specimens :—

> "Why dost withdraw thy hand aback
> And hide it in thy lappe,
> Oh pluck it out, and be not slack
> To give thy foes a rappe."

In another place we read—

> "For why their hearts were nothing bent
> To God nor to his trade."

Further on we read—

> "Nor how he commit their fruit
> Unto the catterpiller,
> And all the labor of their hands
> He gave to the grasshopper."

One more quotation, and I will pass on with my paper :—

> "Confound them all that do apply,
> And seek to work me shame,
> And at my harm do laugh and cry,
> And say, there goes the game."

Playford, in his Psalm book of 1677, says that the piety of these people exceeded their poetry, and he was mild in his criticism.

During the turbulent times of King Charles I, singing degenerated. The clerks, who were appointed by government to take charge of music in the church, became licentious. Says an Episcopal writer : "They are bad company, and yet a society of good fellows. They were deep in the choir and still deeper in taverns. Their pastime and recreation is prayer, but their exercise is drinking. So grievously are they addicted to this vice, that they serve God oftener when drunk." Was it a wonder that Puritans hated the very church service that was sung by such musicians? The English Puritans might eventually have yielded, but when

King Charles I attempted to introduce the Episcopal liturgy in Scotland, he undertook more than he could accomplish. They took up arms and came across the borders. A Scotchman is an unyielding sort of a being. It is said that you cannot break him. Though you roll him, twist him and double him up, yet will he strike an attitude for a fight, when you think you have him completely in your power. King Charles at first attempted to persuade the Scotch to accept peaceably the new order of things. He gave them new tunes which were called after Scottish cities and towns, in order to flatter them, but the good people of Caledonia would not accept of King Charles' new tunes, even if they were called Glasgow, Dundee, etc. They preferred to fight, and being a brave people they at last conquered. When they had the King in their possession, a Scottish minister boldly preached a sermon at him, after which he gave out the 52d Psalm, which begins thus:—

"Why dost thou tyrant boast thyself thy wicked works to praise?"

Such a hint a King of England had never before received. He could not endure such an insult, and therefore demanded that the 56th Psalm be given out, which begins thus:—
"Have mercy, Lord, for me, I pray,
For men would me devour,"

which Psalm the people sang. But I need not relate here the end of this sad struggle, for you all know the fate of King Charles I.

The Dissenters, who had for so many years asked for simpler forms of worship, now took matters into their own hands. In 1644 they passed a law authorizing the destruction of organs, Episcopal music-books, painted windows, in fact of every thing that reminded them of the Episcopacy. Especially severe were they against organs, those "instruments of the devil and the Pope," as they were called. Cromwell, however, had the pretty organ of St. Magdalen's Chapel taken to Hampton Court, where he privately enjoyed its sweet tones. Organists and clerks had to flee, and Psalmody became the established mode of singing.

After the return of Charles II, psalm-singing was again somewhat subdued. This monarch, upon his return to England, at once began to gather the remnants of the cathedral service. There was great need of books and music, great need of organists as well as organs. Old organists had died, others had fled the country, and the few that were still found could not agree as to how the service should be played and sung. In this dilemma Charles II called many musicians from France, for he was fond of the music of that country. This, of course, gave offence to English musicians, and in order to get these foreigners out of the country, English musicians went diligently to work; they studied hard, until at last the old order of things was reëstablished. Since that time the service of the Episcopal Church has remained fixed. New Te Deums and Gloria Patris have been and are being written, but the service is the same to-day that it was in King Charles' times. The two parties have ceased to war and fight, for the Episcopalians allow the Puritans to sing psalms, while the latter are willing that the Established Church should toss the psalms from one side of the church to the other.

A good old Caledonian of the free kirk of Scotland came to this country and settled somewhere in Illinois. The Presbyterians of that place were building a new church, and Sandy took a lively interest in it. One day, while attending a congregational business meeting, the question of procuring chandeliers came up for discussion. Our Scotchman, having but recently come from a little church in the Highlands, knew nothing about chandeliers, for there were no such things known in his church. With genuine Scotch caution he suspected at once that it was some sort of a musical instrument they were talking about, and being bitterly opposed to the "wistling kist," he arose and gravely said: "Well, and what if you do get a chandelier, there is no one in this church who can play on it."

With a few remarks about Calvinistic churches and their music in Scotland and Ireland, I will leave the old country and trace out the history of church music. All churches stand alike before the law. Organs have of late been introduced in Established churches whenever people have desired to use them. I am, however, unable to mention a single instance where an organ has been admitted into a free kirk. Still the law permits them to use organs, if they wish to introduce them. Psalms, paraphrases, and even hymns are used. Throughout Scotch rural districts, however, Psalmody without the use of organs is the general mode of worship; yes, even in larger towns organs are the exception. The Irish church, at the time of the union of the Secession Church and the Synod of Ulster, recognized Rouse's version. Some congregations in the Synod of Ulster had used paraphrases in addition to the Psalms, hence these churches were allowed to continue their use, but none others were to follow their example. Melodeons found their way into Sunday schools, and finally also into churches, which led to much controversy. When the question came before the Assembly, there was a tie vote. The Moderator refused to vote, the matter was dropped, and a resolution was passed that vigorous efforts should be adopted to improve congregational singing.

The English Presbyterian church uses an excellent collection of hymns with Rouse's version. They have chanting in their churches, a mode of singing which the people like very much. Thus we see law and order prevailing everywhere, and so we will leave Europe and come to America.

When speaking of the history of American church music, we must turn our attention to New England. The Pilgrim Fathers naturally enough introduced the customs prevalent in the Independent churches in which they worshiped in England. As has already been stated, they brought with them Ainsworth's collection of music, which they used until 1640, while a few churches retained it until 1682. The reason they gave up their old friend was owing to the fact that in 1640 the first music book ever published in this country left the press. This was called the "Bay Psalm Book," which became a general favorite; so much so that it passed through many editions, and was used in Scotland as late as 1776. The versification of this book is simply horrible. Thus we read :—

"Yah is my strength and song,
And he is my salvation,
He is my God and I'll prepare
For him a habitation."

As a specimen of a spiritual song, I will quote the following:—

> "Jael the Kenite, Heber's wife,
> 'Bove women blessed shall be,
> Above the women in the tent
> A blessed one is she.
> He water asked, she gave him milk;
> In lordly dish she fetched
> Him butter forth; unto the nail
> She forth her left hand stretched,
> Her right hand to the workman's maul,
> And Sisera hammered;
> She pierced and struck his temples through,
> And then cut off his head.
> He at her feet bowed, fell, lay down,
> He at her feet bowed where
> He fell, whereas he bowed down,
> He fell destroyed there."

Comments are needless. A *fac-simile* of this book was published in 1862. It is prefaced by an argument, showing forth the lawfulness of singing Psalms. It deals with the question as to how Psalms ought to be sung, whether in prose or in meter, and who should sing them. This book passed through not less than seventy editions, the last of which appeared three years before the Declaration of Independence. In the ninth edition (1696) there appeared a few tunes, the first music ever printed in this country. These tunes have only the air and the bass, and directions are given as to "how to set them within the compass of the voice, so as to avoid squeaking above or grumbling below."

For sixty years after the formation of the first New England churches only about ten tunes were used, and this small number, at a later period, was even reduced to six. They were Oxford, York, Lichfield, Windsor, St. David's and Martyrs. Every one of these tunes was copied in the worshipers' Bibles; later, as I said, they were printed in song books.

The Pilgrim Fathers appreciated music, not music in our sense, but their church tunes. They were taught in public schools, and children were early trained to reverence them. Whenever they sang in church the congregation arose, and when hearing one of them sung on the street they took off their hats. Though their singing on Sundays often occupied a half hour, old and young would remain standing until that part of divine worship was concluded. The Psalms were sung in regular rotation, without regard to the subject of the preacher's discourse. In consequence of the long-continued use of these tunes they were regarded as inspired; hence, the opposition to the introduction of new ones.

John Cotton, of Boston, in his constitution of the church, published in London in 1642, two years after the "Bay Psalm Book" had appeared, defends congregational singing. Two years later he wrote another book, entitled "Singing of Psalms a Gospel Ordinance." An unsettled state of things had made itself felt, for there were many who had scruples about singing at any time, while others were bitterly opposed to all musical improvements, especially to the introduction of new tunes. Many Nonconformist churches had to meet secretly, and, in order to avoid being detected, they had to dispense with singing. Thus they acquired a habit of worshiping without music, and finally took a dislike to it. An instance is mentioned of a congregation which, after deliberating for years, agreed to sing once on communion day, but not regularly on Sundays. After six years of further deliberation they agreed to sing on Thanksgiving Day. Fourteen years later they arrived at the conclusion that they would not sin by singing once on a Sabbath; but, so as not to give offence to those who were opposed, singing should only be indulged in after the last prayer, when the objecting portion might leave. But, to reach the climax, a portion of this congregation seceded, and worshiped twenty years longer without singing.

Many objections were raised against what was then called regular singing. These may, in part, have sprung from prejudices, but they generally were based upon conscientious convictions. It was the opinion of some that Christians should not sing with their lips, but simply with their hearts. Others considered it sinful to sing Psalms, inasmuch as we had no longer King David's music. Still others claimed that Psalms should be sung in prose, while their opponents were in favor of singing them in meter. Some permitted the use of hymns, others pronounced them as sinful. Many were of the opinion that only one should sing, while the congregation were to join by singing *Amen*. It was also a vexatious question whether men alone or also women should sing in church, and whether only Christians or also *carnal* men might join in this exercise. Surely there were enough questions for debates. Cotton answered all these objections with lengthy arguments and also with much skill. People were at last prepared to allow all to sing who could or would.

The practice of lining out was then general all over New England. In the course of time this practice was attacked, and, of course, also stoutly defended. Many were opposed to it, on the ground that God had not instituted an office for the lining out of Psalms. This practice was strongly rooted. As late as fifty years ago, a New England settler who lived somewhere near Chillicothe, O., was in the habit of singing Psalms on a Sunday afternoon. This was all well enough and praiseworthy; but think of it, there sat our good brother, solitary and alone, lining out the Psalms for his own especial benefit. Cotton also engaged in this struggle. He admitted that the lining out of Psalms was useless, if all had books and could read, or if they knew the Psalm by heart. The same writer argued that, as God had only given us Psalms and not the tunes, we were forced to invent new ones. After this idea was generally accepted, music books gradually increased. The controversy, however, was by no means ended. During the years of disputing over the question, whether or not it is sinful to introduce new tunes, the people neglected their music, until, at last, their singing could no longer be called such. All manner of shakes and twists had crept in, and scarcely any two sang alike. Rev. Thomas Walter, in his book, entitled "Grounds and Rules of Music," 1721, said that he had heard "Oxford" tune sung in three churches with as much difference as there possibly could be between as many different tunes. The church music of that time was mutilated, tortured and twisted, said Walter, and psalm-singing became a mere disorderly noise, left to the mercy of every unskilled throat to chop and alter, twist and change according to his own odd fancy. He further adds that their singing sounded like five hundred tunes roared out at once, and that they dragged so fearfully that he was obliged to take breath twice while singing one note. All this came so gradually that they still deemed their singing good, yes, the most horrid discords seemed to gratify their ears.

Walter's book brought about a great commotion. Many were the struggles in behalf of better singing, and many and bitter were the objections raised against the regular singing, as they called singing by note. They said that singing from notes was an unknown tongue, that it was *not* as good as the old way, that there were too many tunes to be learned, that no one could master them all, that the new way caused disturbances, grieved good men, exasperated them, that it caused them to behave badly, that it was popish, that it would soon bring the organs, that the names of the notes were blasphemous, that this new style of singing was merely a contrivance to get money, that it led to Rome, or at any rate to the Church of England, and, lastly, that it must be bad, because the young people took hold of it so readily.

The war was briskly carried on, and the people were at times so excited that there seemed to be danger of bloodshed. Of course, there were those who defied authority. Thus, we read in an old record that Rev. Samuel Niles, of Baintree, in 1723 suspended eight church members for persisting in singing by note. They were, however, soon restored, and the congregation was allowed to sing by note and rule alternately, so that both parties might be satisfied. This rule, however, gave offence to the Rev. Samuel Niles, and thereafter he held regular service in his own house, leaving the church to the deacons and their new style of singing. At last the controversy came to an end. The people of Charleston voted that "Mr. Stephen Badger, Jun., be desired to read and to set the Psalms, and that he be excused his poll tax as long as he shall officiate in the said work." In 1742 the church in Hanover voted to sing in the new way, and thus church after church followed. This created a desire for musical instruction, and the necessity of singing schools was felt everywhere. This is the origin of the old-fashioned singing school, which soon spread over all New England.

Having gained this much, let us see what the party of progress next demanded. It was but natural that those who took singing lessons should also desire to sit together in church. For many years they occupied the front pews, but were not recognized as organized choirs, an institution not known in this country until after the Revolution. Psalms were still lined out, and not unfrequently the most ludicrous mistakes were made or contradictions were heard, causing the young folks to titter and to behave badly. Thus the old deacon read out:

"The Lord will come and he will not—,"

and after singing this line he continued reading—

"Keep silence, but speak out."

Against this practice of lining out singing schools now declared war. The unfortunate deacons not unfrequently made mistakes by leaving out a line, or by reading another twice, thereby throwing the whole congregation into a state of confusion. It is said that deacons in those days used brass candlesticks for the getting of the pitch. This, of course, is a base slander. It is, however, a fact that the deacons used a large wooden pitch-pipe, said to have looked like a good-sized mousetrap. This was stealthily passed from mouth to mouth as slily, says a writer, as a bottle of brandy in a stage coach. It must have been considered a stupendous task in those days to start a tune, for we are informed that as many as three were appointed to assist in this work. In spite of this fact, they often took the pitch too high, thereby causing the old people to look at each other in a state of consternation, while the young folks chuckled and laughed as one voice after another dropped out, until at last the deacon had only the stout-hearted Ezekiel or the reliable Prudence left to assist him in saving the tune from utter shipwreck. What a relief when the end of that tune was reached! Imagine the deacon as he gravely wiped his face, for, indeed, it was hard work to stretch the neck and to sustain such high tones. But woe to the deacon if he stopped to take the tune lower, for he was sure to go too low.

There was therefore a popular movement set on foot against lining out and against musically uneducated deacons starting the tunes. One parish after another gave music over to the singers, and deacons were forced to struggle for their time-honored rights or retire. It seems strange that a congregation should meekly wait until the words were doled out to them, yet there were many who cried *Popery!* whenever any one proposed to abolish the system. While these discussions were being carried on the singers resorted to all manner of intrigues in order to carry their point. They would start the tune before the deacon had time to do so, and when he stopped for the purpose of lining out they sang right on. Then, again, they would sing fast, leaving the deacon and his followers far behind. If the deacon succeeded in starting his tune before they were ready, they would suddenly start another, thereby bewildering the people. The good old deacons, of course, resented these insults; but then the system had to go. It received its first official blow at Worcester, August 5th, 1779. A public meeting was called to consider whether they should sing in the "usual way or in the rulable way." "It was then decided by a vote that the singers sit in the rear seats, on the men's side, and the mode of singing be without reading the Psalm line by line." The following Sunday Deacon Chamberlain arose in the meeting in order to fulfill his time-honored duty of lining out the Psalms, but the singers made no pause. Still, the deacon read on till overpowered, when he took his hat and, with tears in his eyes, retired. This was the first organization of a choir, and, as you see, it started with a fight. Deacon Chamberlain was censured, and the choir rested on their laurels. Another deacon revenged himself by waiting until the choir had finished, when he gravely arose and said: "Now let the people of God worship by singing such and such a Psalm." At the same time he looked at the choir as much as to say, "Whose people are you?" The struggle went on, but the deacons finally had to surrender.

Having thus gained two great victories, the choirs introduced still greater changes. Now came a multitude of new tunes, and with them the bass viol, commonly called in those days "the Lord's fiddle;" there came also the small violin, that profane instrument the "devil's tunebox," as some churches named it, and all this under the guise of assisting in starting the tune. Deacons and ministers resisted these innovations, and people took sides. Thence churches in those days were distinguished as catgut and anti-catgut churches. A good old deacon, when giving out the Psalm, said, with much irony in his face, "Now let us fiddle and sing in praise of God such and such a Psalm." Still another, when hearing the violins, became very daring; he took his hat, danced a while before the pulpit, and then, as gracefully as he could, skipped down the aisle and out of the church. These deacons were, of course, reprimanded, and the choir chuckled and laughed. Do you ask where and how all this ended? In an old record in Hanover church, 1805, we read that money was voted to repair the bass viol, and to put cushions (?) in the singers' seats. Now came also flute and horn, and all that without further resistance on the part of the people or church authorities.

Strange to say, while the good people of New England churches sanctioned the orchestra, and that poorly played, they still fought against the organ as the instrument of the devil and the Pope. When an attempt was made in 1713 to introduce an organ in Boston, the instrument remained unpacked on the porch of the church for nine months. When the Dean of Berkshire presented an organ to the town in 1735, it was decided not to accept the gift, because the organ, as an instrument of the devil, was designed to entrap men's souls. Since 1830 organs have, however, become more common in New England churches. As new churches were erected galleries were put in for the use of the choirs, where they sat often a hundred strong. Quartette choirs are a modern institution. The choirs were recruited every spring out of the past winter's singing-school, which was kept open two evenings in the week, and that at the expense of the church.

As choirs increased, new books flooded the market; singing-schools and choirs were organized from Maine to Georgia, and so rapid was the progress, that the people could not follow—they surrendered everything, and finally sat in silence. It would be a waste of time to mention all the books that now appeared; it is enough to say that the trade, in connection with compilers of books, dictated what churches were to sing. The pioneers of American church music were Wm. Billings and Oliver Holden, both Boston men, and born in the middle of the last century. Many books became popular, but none perhaps exceeded the sales of Lowell Mason's "Carmina Sacra," of which a million copies were scattered over the country.

But we have not yet overcome the modernizing spirit. Our churches have not yet arrived at any positive rules concerning church music. With the Sunday school came also a new style of music. Children were willing at first to use the regular church tunes; they knew nothing else and asked for nothing else. But soon there was a cry raised against the old church music as being too stiff, too old fogy, too unmelodious for children. The little ones suddenly needed some inducements to draw them into the Sunday-school, and one of these inducements was to be lively tunes. The trade soon supplied the article desired. The first real departure in this direction was made by Bradbury. Before speaking more fully of our modern Sunday-school music, allow me to say, that I shall have no criticisms to make of the texts—read them carefully and judge for yourselves. Neither am I unmindful of the fact that at least some of our so-called Gospel hymns have become a power, and that I speak not indiscriminately against all of them. On certain occasions it is proper to use them—especially is this true of home singing around the fireside.

To sum up all the good points that can be claimed for our Sunday-school music, I would state, that it is easily learned, readily remembered, and, by reason of its popular character, it fosters congregational singing. When, however, this music is weighed, it is found wanting—in what? In dignity, in solidity, in strength—elements which are very essential to good church music.

Rhythm is the most striking trait of secularism in music, and it becomes vulgar in the same proportion as it is crowded into the foreground. Rhythm lends character to a musical composition, and without it music cannot exist. The ancients knew this. Plutarch already raised his voice against voluptuous rhythmical music. If rhythm is essential to music, it is also its lowest element. The ruder a people the more they love rhythmical noises. The beating of a drum excites an Indian to ferocious deeds. The Hindoos never sing without their talaams and tamtams. The Persians accompany their singing with snapping of fingers. The Australians beat sticks together while shouting out their rough songs. The Spaniards dance to the sound of tambourines and castanets, two instruments neither of which produce a melody. The negroes are remarkable for their strong rhythmical feeling.

Rhythm principally touches the sensual element of our natures. If rhythm predominates, melody and harmony usually are the sufferers; just as the spirit suffers when the body largely predominates. Rhythm is the ruling element of the dance; the dance-rhythm touches our nerves, and, as the saying is, it makes our feet move. A dance consists simply of a pleasing melody, with plain harmony and a decided rhythm; and here let me add that these are exactly the ingredients of most of our modern Sunday-school music, and also of many Gospel hymn-tunes. It is but natural that such music should be popular with children and the uneducated.

If the art, however, is an agent for good, the church should only use it in its purest forms, for then religion is to be benefited by it. The question I desire to put to the ministry is this: Can the church afford to use such music which appeals, appealing as it does, to the lower nature of man? Can the church afford to abuse an art, though she aim thereby to improve the condition of man? The art, being a gift of God, ought to be used conscientiously, especially so by those who profess to love and serve God. Surely we could not afford to decorate our church walls with coarsely drawn pictures in order to please the uneducated. Yet in musical matters we do this very thing. Would it be safe to fill our Sunday-school libraries with novels and silly stories in order to please uneducated children? Yet the modern Sunday-school tunes are the silly stories of church music. The rhythmical element is strangly developed in it; hence these tunes are often converted into dances, they are heard played at parades and picnics, minstrels with blackened faces sing and play them. Hilarious young people, coming home from picnics and parties, are known to have sung "Sweet By and By," "Hold the Fort," and tunes like these. Surely such popularity cannot be a credit to any church music. The old and calmer church tunes have never thus been popularized, neither is it desirable that they should be.

The body is a creature of habits. Pleasures of the body are apt to lose their charm—the truth, the spirit alone abideth. It is for this reason that such Sunday-school music soon loses its power, and we hear constantly that children need new music, they have grown tired of their old. In order to continue this interest in the Sabbath school the church is forced to supply from time to time still more rhythmical music, and the question now is, how low shall we sink? The church cannot afford to gratify the carnal man in one thing and oppose him in another. The church should create and satisfy demands of æsthetic emotions, and should not use the art to foster sensualism, for there is danger that musical sensualism may produce its effects upon religion itself. It is alarming to notice how ministers regard these melodies as a power in the church, and how frequently they are used in order to produce that sentimentalism and nervous excitement which many mistake for religious fervor; hence these tunes are used especially when revivals are the object of religious services. The church was blessed with revivals long before these tunes were known. I believe in revivals of religion, but only in such as are preceded by much prayer and humiliation. Alas! the Gospel wagon moves too slow in these days of railroads and electricity. Men seem unwilling to wait patiently on the Lord's coming, so these tunes are used, and though the fact is never stated, it is nevertheless true, that they are used for the purpose of creating sentiment, which is supposed to be religious fervor. The people, especially younger folks, with all their strong emotional natures, are often influenced by these tunes, and when under their influence they decide to join the church. Be it far from me to sit in judgment over any one's religious professions, but, young gentlemen, it will be one of your duties to sit in judgment over those who seek church fellowship. Be careful to ascertain whether the conversion is thorough, or whether it merely seems so. Mere sentimentality does not last long, it needs many props; and a church member whose religious life must be sustained by sentimental food, is usually very unreliable and often troublesome as well. This is the sort of people who supply your stock of backsliders and formal Christians.

Ministers alone are not to blame for this; nay, the church at large is guilty of wrong, for ministerial successes are but too often measured by mere accessions to the church, and not by a high standard of piety. People look too much to the number of sheaves a minister gathers, unmindful of the quality of the grain.

The change for worse began in the Sunday school, and there also must begin the work of reform. The fact was overlooked that children, while singing this flimsy music, acquired bad musical tastes; and was it reasonable to suppose that when these children came to join the church there would also come change of musical taste along with a change of heart? *Certainly not.* The young church members still preferred their own light music, and disliked the hymns and tunes of the sanctuary as old fogy stuff, and too unmelodious. Thus young converts found themselves, in matters of music at least, in antagonism with the older members, who preferred the old tunes.

But, then, the music of to-day, like the music of ten and twenty years ago, must pass away, and the question is still unanswered as to where we shall stop. Where and when will the church call a halt! But how shall this evil—for such I call it—be overcome? Surely its eradication will not be accomplished as long as the ministry fails to see the evil. The beginning of the reform should be to use at least some of the regular hymns and tunes in the Sabbath school. Teach the child to love that which is good, and when it has grown up to manhood and womanhood, it will continue to love it.

Church music which is revered, and which children hear from their youth up, is sure to become a power in the sanctuary. As it is, however, our music is unstable as a reed in the wind, hence it cannot become that power which it is designed to be. The evil is long-standing, and so, likewise, will the cure be slow and tedious. But no matter how difficult the cure may be, nothing is gained by delay. It certainly was easier to step down to the sensational and the flippant, than it will be to step up to the good, the true and the solid.

Much has been said and written on the subject of church music; men, however, differ widely in their views concerning its mission. What, then, is the mission of church music? There are those who view it as a pastime, a mere means of destroying the monotony of the services. Others view it as a sort of a concert, designed to entertain and to attract people to church. Still others regard it as a concession to the people, who would otherwise take no active part outwardly in the devotional exercises on Sunday. Some look upon church music as a means of arousing emotions and of opening the heart for the reception of the Word. There are still others who claim that it is the object of church music to raise worshipers to a higher religious sentiment, to refine their feelings, and to dispel worldly thoughts. Much of all this is true and correct, but church music is more than all this. It ought to be the purest praise which intelligent creatures can offer to their Creator and Benefactor. This is, indeed, a most serious act, the first characteristics of which ought to be heartiness and sincerity. He who sings in such a frame of mind will not likely indulge in criticism about the singing of others, no matter how plain their voices may be.

Religion does not instill boldness, it does not make us over-confident, neither does it give us over to despair. Church music should, therefore, be favorable to calm reflection; it should be purely spiritual, never appealing to the sensual man; it should subdue passion, and not arouse it. The less prominent its rhythm is, the better for it.

World and church are opposites, so should worldly music and church music be opposites. When visiting one of the cathedrals of Europe, we are impressed with its grandeur, and although there may be no worship held within its ancient walls at the time of our visit, one feels a holy awe, scarcely a whisper escapes our lips, for we feel as if God were very near. So, when hearing church music, we should at once recognize the fact that it is not worldly music we hear.

There are many ways of worshiping and praising God,—by singing hymns or Psalms, by using organs or by singing without them : but whatever your mode of worship *may* be, try always to perfect it, remembering that God loves the perfect better than the imperfect. Do not despise art. As God is all-wise and all-merciful, so is He also the concentration of all that is beautiful. Art is a manifestation of the all-beautiful; hence, it is a revelation of God. Let your choirs, then, cultivate art, let them sing the grandest and best our masters have produced, but never surrender congregational singing. Do not yield it under any circumstances, for it is not only your privilege but also your solemn duty to praise your Maker with your own lips. Let there be progress in all things, in your singing not less than in your moral life. Good singing tunes the heart and makes it ready for the reception of the Word. Good singing inspires the minister, it unites the people, it impresses the mind deeply with lessons and Scriptural truths. Good singing makes you happier and better, thus the very praise which God commands you to offer is turned into a rich, never-ceasing fountain of blessings. Allow me to add a few practical "Hints for Ministers," after which I will close my discourse.

In many churches people rush their hymns through as if they were impatient to be done with this exercise. I fear many people sing hymns merely as music, and not as an act of worship; hence, the subject of singing praise ought to be explained to the people. Hasty songs, like hasty prayers, do not amount to much. On the other hand, you must guard against dragging, which also is injurious to the dignity of divine worship. The organist must regulate this largely, and unless he appreciates the sentiment of the hymns, unless he is in sympathy with the act of worship, you will be apt to have defective congregational singing. From this it follows that the organist should be *more* than master of his instrument. He should be a good player and a true Christian. This leads me also to say a few words about employing singers who lack religious sentiment. If the singing of praise is an act of worship, then the heart, and the *whole heart*, as well as the voice, should be employed in this act. As well might we employ an eloquent Ingersoll to preach for us, provided he would abstain from that which is heterodox. Yet all thinking persons would call him a hypocrite, and his words would be without effect, no matter how we might have admired his oratorical powers. The same is true of singers. They may sing with great skill, but it is the heart only that gives weight to the act in the sight of God. This is the central idea of worship in all its forms. Said a soprano singer one rainy Sunday morning, "I suppose we will not sing our anthem to-day, for there is scarcely anybody here." My answer was as quick, as it was emphatic, "We shall sing this anthem if there be nobody here but the preacher; for we sing not for the people, we sing in praise of Him whose Spirit is ever present. Let me enjoin it upon you, always to realize this fact."

Another point I desire to touch upon is this: many ministers, when selecting their hymns, pay attention *only* to the words and not to the music. They are satisfied if the hymn suits the subject of their sermon, forgetting, at the same time, that the people are expected to sing the tune. This lack of judgment often disturbs a service that might otherwise have been called perfect. The poor singing of a hymn puts everybody ill at ease; yes, it often tones down the fervor and zeal of the minister, while, if the mistake occurs at the close of the service, it is apt to wipe away many good impressions. If you wish the people to sing, give them music which they *can* sing. There are many tunes in our hymnals that are not fit for the people's use, and why they were admitted into that book I cannot tell. Moreover, we have too many hymns and tunes as it is; as a people, we cannot become familiar with them all. There is a disposition on the part of hymn-book compilers to reach out for chips from operas, oratorios, popular music of any kind, which is usually presented in a garbled and mangled condition, neither fit for the choir nor the congregation. There are in every church plenty of poor singers, and this is all the more a reason why only plain and easy music should be used. Let churches hold praise-meetings from time to time; see to it that you have a leader who knows how to present his lessons both from a religious and a musical standpoint; let the people begin with plain familiar tunes, and aim first at perfection in the singing of these, before you take in hand new tunes. If the people learn once to sing certain tunes well, the act of praise will become more and more a source of delight. Let a people once be put on the road of improvement, and they will take pleasure in walking therein. The American people love song, Christian people love to sing. The problem is what means should we use in order that we may have good singing. If our youth were properly instructed in the Sabbath school our congregational singing would rapidly improve as well. Alas! the church hymns and tunes are denounced as unfit for children, they are excluded from the Sabbath-school exercises, and, as has been said, it is unreasonable to expect young worshippers to like at eleven o'clock what was denounced or ignored at nine.

Now only a few words about the relations of the Pastor to the choir. There are many and varied opinions on this subject; of course, these relations must somewhat differ among the various denominations, but in their essentials they are the same. If the minister is placed over the house of God as a spiritual guide, he should, also, rule choirs; he should watch over the music of the sanctuary. But if he would rule intelligently he should also know something about music, and no doubt the time is coming when a course of musical lectures will be regarded by theological seminaries as a necessity. There is no minister living who has resting upon his shoulders as many heavy burdens and perplexing duties as had Martin Luther, yet in the midst of his arduous duties he found time to practice and to study music. Why should not as much be expected of the theological students? Ministerial ignorance in musical matters often is the cause of much mischief, it is often the first cause of disturbances in choirs. Says Mr. A.: Why should the preacher presume to dictate to us what we shall sing or how we shall sing it, when he knows nothing about the art? It is for this reason that many organists and choir-leaders say, let the preacher attend to his end of the church and we will attend to ours. Pray, where is the line that divides the two ends? Such a spirit is wrong, and is sure to be productive of hurtful results. This ignorance in musical matters causes many ministers to step very lightly when they approach their choirs, for they see danger, and feel their helplessness. No matter how prudent a preacher may be when making suggestions to choirs, there is danger of an explosion. There are found choirs, made up of Christian people, that get along peaceably, because of their character and interest in the church as well as their love for their pastor. So one finds even here and there a choir made up of non-Christian people, that do their duty as they are asked to do it by the minister, but in such cases it is usually found that either the great personal influence, or perchance the musical culture of the minister, keeps the singers in the line of duty. Such choirs, however, are few and far between. Let ministers guard their rights of supervision over choirs, let them not surrender the least of them, for there is no telling what the outcome will be if preachers fail to keep watch over the music of the church. Alas! many preachers fall asleep, or pretend to see nothing, whenever a question arises with which the choir is connected. Of course, young gentlemen, be prudent, use judgment and skill, when you handle these musical bombs, but rather than yield to that which you deem wrong, I advise you to burst that bomb, even if it costs you your position. The next pastor, at least, has the benefit of your courage. Some churches, like some cities, never seem to learn true lessons of good government and moderation until a bomb or two has been exploded. The kind-hearted minister, the gentle, loving and long-suffering servant of God, who has the heart of his people, who, to use a vulgar phrase, is backed by his people, as a rule, may safely walk in and out of these musical powder magazines, yet I have known even such inadvertently to step on a Lucifer match and blow up everything. Let me urge it upon you to post yourselves on musical matters, acquire some musical knowledge, so that you may be true leaders, in fact as well as in name. To give you some information on the subject of musical history, to arouse you to action with regard to our Sabbath-school music, to point out a few of the sharp corners on which you may hurt yourselves when in active life, was the object of my lecture. If I have done you the least service, I shall feel amply repaid for my trouble. With the words of the Psalmist I will close my discourse:—

"Praise ye the Lord. Praise God in his sanctuary. Praise him in the firmament of his power. Praise him for his mighty acts. Praise him according to his excellent greatness. Praise him with the sound of the trumpet. Praise him with psaltery and harp. Praise him with the timbrel and dance. Praise him with stringed instruments and organs. Praise him upon the loud cymbals. Praise him upon the high-sounding cymbals. Let everything that has breath praise the Lord. Praise ye the Lord."

HINTS TO PUPILS.

1. You are a student of the University. Observe all the rules of the institution.
2. To master an art requires much time and close application. Be diligent.
3. Do not constantly look to the end of your studies; look more to the daily steps you take. Do your daily duty as well as you can, for then you will, at the end of the year, have cause to feel satisfied with your progress.
4. To attempt to do in one day what should be done in two, crowds your work and over-taxes your strength. This is sure to lead to bad results. Neglect, therefore, none of your daily duties.
5. There is no short-cut in mastering an art; there are no jumps!
6. No matter how gifted your teacher may be, remember that you yourself must labor hard in order to attain success.
7. You have no right to expect your teacher to take a deep interest in your progress if you yourself are not interested in your studies.
8. Remember your parents spend their money, while your teacher spends his time, in order to advance you. Use these means conscientiously.
9. If you do not mean to be a good student, do not enter this department.
10. Have regular practice hours, and never deviate from your plan of work unless there is a good cause for it.
11. Never practice listlessly; always have your whole mind and heart in your work. Know *what* you do and *why* you do it. Always hear yourself while practicing. Watch the tones you produce.
12. Practice slowly, for thus alone will you secure a correct impression of a composition.
13. When practicing by yourself, count loud and regularly.
14. He who uses bad tools is almost sure to do poor work. The pianist who fails to play technical studies will play with a stiff hand; he will do poor work. Playing technical studies is for the pianist what the sharpening of the tools is for the mechanic.
15. Do not play a piece over ten or twelve times—try to master the difficult places.
16. When tired or nervous, cease practicing. Take care of your health.
17. Watch your fingering. Good fingering is for the pianist what a good road is for the traveler; it facilitates motion.
18. Always phrase correctly.
19. Remember it is easy to acquire bad habits, but it is difficult to correct them. The correction of bad habits in playing or singing consumes much precious time. Always do your work so that you may not have to undo it.

20. Strive to enter into the spirit of the composition you study. By playing the notes merely, your playing is not artistic. Let music awaken in you sympathy and love. Unless it produces these results your studies are in vain. It is the object of your musical education both to awaken and refine sentiment.

21. Study your lesson until you have mastered it. Then review the past work. He who neglects the pieces learned, is like the laborer, who, after earning the money by hard toil, places it in pockets with holes in them. After *reviewing* you may also try your skill on new things and practice sight reading.

22. Measure not your progress by the number of pieces you play, but by the manner in which you play them, as well as by the character of the music that you study.

23. Do not imagine that you are making progress in attempting to play a difficult piece. Only what you can play well and what you know, is your own; not what you choose to put into your portfolio.

24. The playing of a concerto or the singing of a great aria, represents as much brain labor, and surely as much patient toil, as does the mastery of a language or a science.

25. In your intercourse with fellow-students as well as with musicians in general, indulge neither in jealousy nor envy. Always put art before yourself; never yourself before art. The jealous and envious musician has not true music in his heart, for music is love.

26. Strive to reach perfection. After tasting the pleasures of perfection in one piece, you will be sure to aim at it in all your work.

27. Have confidence in yourself, but keep vanity out of the heart.

28. Carelessness in forming habits, negligence in doing your work, indulgence in vanity or in envy while engaged in your musical studies, are sure to affect your whole character.

29. Keep your music and piano in good order. The piano-lid reveals your character. Have your piano tuned whenever it is needed.

30. Be punctual in coming for your lesson.

31. Feel sure of a hearty welcome. Never be afraid to ask questions.

32. Be cheerful while being corrected.

33. Be grateful to all your teachers, for they are good friends of yours.

34. Study harmony and musical history. Without the mastery of these studies, you will always be a one-sided musician.

35. Read good books on music, and musical journals. Read also good books on other subjects than music.

36. Hear good players and singers whenever you can.

37. Mingle among musicians, converse with them about your art. Seek the instruction of more than one teacher, for every good teacher has his or her points of superiority. Never belittle another teacher or his work.

38. Be more than a mere player or singer. Be an intelligent, many-sided musician; a thinking and fine-feeling musician.

39. View your art as a precious gift. See to it that you use it properly, and do not neglect to thank the Giver:

THE PHILOSOPHY OF THE BEAUTIFUL.

When I appear before you as the advocate of the Beautiful and of Æsthetic culture, I am not unmindful of the fact that this subject has, of late years, suffered in public estimation through the efforts of that apostle of æstheticism, Oscar Wilde. But say what we will about him, we must give him credit for this virtue, that the end at which he aimed was a good one. Had he been a manly man, had he dressed like sensible people, had he cut his hair short—for in these days long-haired men and short-haired women are, as a rule, looked upon with suspicion—he would no doubt have spoken to more willing ears. As it is, his influence seems to have spent itself in one direction mainly. Instead of planting sun-flowers in the rear of our garden patches, and giving the seeds to the chickens as feed, we now plant them in the front yard, and many maidens wear the big yellow flowers in their belts.

I therefore invite your attention to the question, What is the Beautiful? without promising, however, that I will answer it, and for the simple reason that the Beautiful, being concentrated in God, is infinite and cannot be fully understood by the finite mind.

Wieland said, "the Beautiful can only be felt, but cannot be expressed." Nevertheless, throughout all ages men have endeavored to do what Wieland said could not be done. The greatest minds of all ages have busied themselves speculating about the Beautiful, yet very few among the philosophers that have written on this subject, have advanced new theories.

It is at any time difficult to give a correct definition of an abstract term, and this difficulty makes itself felt in a special manner when attempting to say in words what the Beautiful means. Writers have said that all things which are pleasing to the eye and to the ear are beautiful. It is true, the Beautiful is pleasing to the eye and the ear, but, for all this, the definition is exceedingly vague, for not all things that please the eye and the ear are necessarily beautiful. Let me illustrate. I have heard hungry German students go into ecstacy over the beauty of sausage! No matter how pleasing a sight it may be when nicely browned, it is after all a very prosaic sort of an object. The hungry man is apt to see beauty in everything calculated to satisfy his cravings. I have heard men sing praises of their meerschaums, and no doubt they were things of beauty in their sight; to others they were mere loud-smelling objects. I have heard ladies go into ecstacy over what they called a bonnet. Who doubts the fact that to them it was a thing of beauty? To men it was an object of ridicule. I have heard ladies speak with rapture of the lover's language, as it was whispered into their ears. I doubt not the words of my fair friends, but while love's language is beautiful to them, to disinterested persons it sounds absurd and far-fetched, and often deserves to be denounced as a pack of exaggerations.

When speaking of things that are pleasing to the eye and the ear, the question arises: Whose eyes and ears are pleased? And then comes the second question: Whose eyes and ears are to be regarded as the standard for all others? Human eyes do not see alike, nor do human ears hear alike. They are mere agencies that lead impressions to the brain, and in this operation they are often very defective and delusive. But granted we all were to see and hear alike, are our minds not so constituted that they differ widely in their operations, in their power of receiving and assimilating impressions? But granted all minds were alike gifted in this respect, would we not still discover a vast diversity in our emotions and in the training produced by early impressions and surroundings? Even if we felt alike and enjoyed the same opportunities for culture, men would still differ in the operations of their imaginations, for this gives a thousand colorings to objects and situations, to thoughts and sentiments, and these colorings must be peculiar to the individual. The true human standard lies in the recognition of the best minds, a recognition which must endure for all ages; for that which is really beautiful cannot become ugly, no matter how tastes may change and how far art may progress. The art-works of the ancient Grecians are beautiful to-day; indeed, I am inclined to believe that we are better qualified to appreciate their beauty than were the Grecian people themselves. Palestrina lived centuries ago, Bach and Handel were born two hundred years ago; and although there is an almost immeasurable distance between these men and Wagner, their works are still considered beautiful.

When I speak of a human tribunal concerning the Beautiful, I mean one which is infallibly sure, instantaneous to perceive and to appreciate that which is beautiful in art. Least of all, is there to be found a tribunal which is qualified to comprehend fully the essence of the Beautiful, and to lay down infallible laws for the artist. When men measure the depth of the sea they sink lines with lead attached to them. So, says a writer, our intellects fathom the depths of the arts and literature. But what a difference there is in the length of the mental strings! All human beings no doubt derive more or less pleasure from the Beautiful; indeed, the power of enjoying it is inborn; it is a gift of God; it is an evidence of our divine nature. But, for all that, we differ widely in the degree of our enjoyment of the beautiful. Some have strings only a few inches long, while others have only chips attached to them, which cannot sink. Yet persons of this class are most ready in the expression of their views; they are the most hasty and the severest critics. No matter how long the lines may be, it must be accepted as a truism that none have as yet reached the bottom of the art sea, and no matter how far we shall progress, none will ever reach it. No one can see the All-Beautiful, no one can conceive of it; and for this reason there can be no positive human standard either for the eye or the ear, or for the brain, the emotions or the imagination. Art is unlimited, and it is as free as it is unlimited. The human race is progressive, and I conceive it to be our great mission ever to progress toward the perfectly Beautiful, which is concentrated in the Deity.

The definition, therefore, that that which is pleasing to the eye and the ear is or constitutes the Beautiful, is not a good one. The same is true of Webster's definition. He says the Beautiful is an assemblage of graces or of properties which please the eye or the ear, or the other senses of the mind. Let me put by the side of this the diversity of human tastes and styles of beauty as admired by different nations as well as by individuals. Allow me to quote Voltaire, whose opinion I give merely in connection with this subject, not because I endorse either his religious or social views. Said he: "To the toad, a yellow throat, two round eyes and a big mouth are objects of beauty; to the Hottentot it is a black skin, thick lips and a flat nose." What a distance from such an ideal of the beautiful to that represented by an Apollo Belvedere or a Venus de Medici. Again, look at the pleasure the uneducated derive from a French harp, and how far above them stand those who admire Beethoven's symphonies, Händel's oratorios, etc. We will therefore accept it as a fact that the term Beautiful can no more be defined than we can define the sensation of seeing, hearing or feeling. "Beauty," says a writer, "is a sense of the soul, and everything that touches this sense is beautiful." Indefinite as this is, it is far better than either of the other definitions I have quoted. In order to excite this sense God has made this world beautiful, and he has given us this sense, evidently meaning thereby that we shall cultivate it, and that it shall be made one of the avenues which shall lead us to Him, who is the All-Beautiful.

The Beautiful was a favorite subject of speculation among the ancient Grecians. Though they had no correct idea of God they sought the Deity for the source of the Beautiful. Thales, who lived toward the close of the seventh century, B. C., one of the seven wise men, and by many considered the first who speculated on the constitution of the universe, said that "the Cosmos, as the art-work of the gods, is the Beautiful." In other words, that the Beautiful, as concentrated in the Deity, is expressed and manifested in the creation. This is the foundation-stone upon which rest all ancient as well as modern speculations on this subject. Pythagoras, who lived 570, B. C., and who is called the founder of what is known as the Italic School of Philosophy, teaches that as God Himself is the All-Good, the Harmony of liberty and necessity, so are all His works impressed with the principles of harmony. Nature has her contrasts, but these are blended in harmony. This unity in multiplicity, this harmony in contrasts, Pythagoras defines to be the Beautiful. His teachings are also based upon the idea that in the Deity we find the source of the Beautiful in its perfection.

Heraclitus assumes a similar theory. He said that the world consists of contrasts, but that the Deity brings harmony out of these contrasts. This harmony, he teaches, is also found in the arts. There is contrast but also unity in the colors of a painting; there are high and low, long and short tones in music, yet all make sweet melody.

An American writer said that "Plato was the first who speculated upon the Beautiful." This, as I have already shown, is an error. Plato's name is, however, closely connected with this subject. While he has said much that is interesting, we must bear in mind these two facts: First, he never gave a system of his own. Second, he never separated the Beautiful from the Good. The sum and substance of what he has said may be expressed in these words: The foundation of the Beautiful is a reasonable order addressed to the imagination through the senses; that is, symmetry in form, harmony in sound, the principles of which are certain as the laws of logic, mathematics and morals, all equally necessary products of the Eternal Intellect, whom we call God. Thus Plato, like his predecessors, ascribed the Beautiful to that source of all force, the Creator of the universe, the sum of whose exalted attributes he calls "*to Agathon,*" the Good. Plato refers to this subject in detached sentences, and it would be difficult to formulate a complete system out of his discourses. He distinctly says that "God is the All-Wise, the All-Good and the All-Beautiful." Of these three ideas Plato regards the All-Good as the highest, for it approaches nearest to the Deity. Out of this spring the other two ideas, those of the All-Wise and the All-Beautiful. The boundary line between these two, he claims, is difficult to draw; for the Good plays over into the Beautiful, so that persons are often misled. Everything good, true and beautiful has its foundation in harmony. Virtue is the health and beauty of the soul, vice is sickness and deformity. Plato makes distinctions in the grades of beauty. First, he regards the beauty of the body; second, the beauty of soul; third, beauty of wisdom and knowledge; fourth, the beauty of the Divine Idea. Everything earthly, he teaches, is in so far beautiful, as it partakes of the beauty of God. He who has the most perfect body and purest soul is, according to Plato, the best representative of the Beautiful. The effects of the Beautiful are joy, happiness and love. The Beautiful, therefore, be it represented in colors, in tones or in words, is productive of pleasant sensations and an agreeable state of satisfaction. This he explains through the theory of pre-existence, according to which every soul had, before its birth, while it was yet with God, also Godlike ideas of the Beautiful. Hence, when the soul sees anything beautiful, it is instantly affected by it, for it is suddenly seized by the recollection of its original home, for every earthly beauty is but a reflection of heavenly beauty. Thus Plato tries to explain why we are so powerfully moved when seeing fine art works, when hearing beautiful music or when reading grand poetry, and why they so often make us sad; for they produce in us a longing for our former home of joy or a state of perfect bliss. In other words, art makes us homesick for Heaven, our real abiding-place.

Aristotle thought that the Beautiful was created with the good and the true, and that its main characteristics are order and limit. According to his theory the Beautiful consists of definite quality and quantity, of correct arrangement and perfect symmetry of parts. Hence neither a very small nor a very large animal, according to Aristotle, can be beautiful. Small things are only pretty and well-proportioned. The idea that the Beautiful calls forth love, was so self-evident to him, that when he was asked for an explanation, he said that this was the question of a blind man.

Aristotle's theories were for several centuries accepted as the only correct ones; here and there only, an idea from Plato and Pythagoras was mixed in with them. The only philosopher after Aristotle who wrote with authority and originality on this subject was Plotinus, who lived 250 B. C. He was the most important philosopher of the new Platonic school, and his system in the main was based upon Plato's theories. "Usually," says he, "we imagine the Beautiful to be something recognizable through the aid of the eye or the ear, but does not the Beautiful exist more in the spiritual than in the bodily? Is there not beauty in noble deeds, and in virtues? What then is beautiful? The usual answer is that symmetry is beautiful; but according to this idea only the complicated things can be beautiful. Hence, sunlight, lightning and the ocean cannot be beautiful. "This theory," he argues, "is not correct, for we know that sunlight, lightning and the sea are beautiful in themselves." "Our soul," he says further, "is a part of the higher and better world, and when we behold anything relating to it, we are happy." This is, as you will observe, a revival of Plato's theory of pre-existence.

Says Plotinus, a thing can be beautiful only as it is related to eternal things, only so far as it is connected with divine beauty. Our soul compares its inward idea of the Beautiful with the beauty of the things seen, and if they harmonize, a thing is beautiful. This is, in substance, the same theory with which we started out, namely, that that which pleases the eye and the ear is beautiful. The falsity of this theory has been shown, and I shall not, therefore, stop to repeat. But there is a conclusion to be drawn from it, namely, that while tastes and intellects differ, while we have no general standard whereby to measure the Beautiful, it may safely be accepted as a fact that every soul has its own standard of beauty. It is, therefore, perfectly proper for a person to say, I consider this object beautiful, while it might be presumptuous to say, it is beautiful. Therefore, when finding an object of beauty which fills our souls and draws forth all our admiration, we may say that we have found *our* ideal of the Beautiful, but we have no right to say that we have found *the* ideal.

As long as the soul is imprisoned in the body, mixed with clay, says the philosopher, it cannot be beautiful. When the soul, however, is freed from this tabernacle it regains its beauty. The soul through eternity becomes better and purer; more like its divine source. Hence it becomes more Godlike, for God is the source of all that is beautiful. All those who seek the Deity are beautiful. Blessed are those that hear and see His beauty; miserable are those that hear and see it not. We love the beautiful, furthermore says the philosopher, as something that reminds us of our former existence, and he continues by urging his readers to cleanse their eyes, so that they may see the Spirit-World, for we shall never see the Beautiful until we ourselves have become beautiful.

Plotinus regards the Beautiful as something immaterial. Symmetry and proportion are to him the foundation of the Beautiful, but not beauty itself. The Beautiful is that which we perceive in the symmetric and well proportioned. In order to make clear his idea he draws a comparison between a face of a live person and that of one who is dead. The symmetry, he claims, is the same in both, yet there is a beauty in the live face which does not exist in that which is dead. This comparison is penetrable from the fact that there is no beauty in a dead face, unless means have been used to keep it in a condition resembling the live face. If a person dies, the muscles relax, the chin drops, the eyes stare, etc.

Plotinus says further, that beauty is spiritual, not material. True, divine beauty never appears upon earth. Yes, it is according to his ideas sacrilegious to suppose that divine beauty ever descends upon earth to dwell in vile clay, in filthy, sickly bodies, where it would ever be marred and soiled. Yet Christianity teaches that the divine beauty has dwelt in this "*sickly, filthy human body.*"

"Let him," says he, "who would speak slightingly of art, bear in mind this fact, that nature is but an imitation of the divine idea, and in order to make nature appear more perfect the artist draws upon the resources of his own mind." Yes, the philosopher goes so far as to claim that art is far more perfect than nature, but being without life and therefore soulless, it cannot be perfect.

I have already said that the heathen philosophers have advanced the theory that the Beautiful is found only in the Deity. Modern learning has added nothing to this. To the contrary, some writers who enjoy the light of Christianity endeavor to fix the idea of the Beautiful far lower than did the Grecian writers already quoted. It was but natural that the ideas of the Beautiful as taught by them should be perpetuated by the church Fathers, who were good Greek scholars. The claim, therefore, on their part, that all beauty is divine in its origin and that all created things are beautiful because their Creator is such, is simply a reiteration of the ancient Grecian philosophy; and when they further say that God, the Father of all spirits, endows men with the powers of imagination and ideals of beauty, they are not far, if any, in advance of these ancient Grecian teachers.

Before reviewing German philosophy let us hear what English and French writers of modern times have to say on the theory of the Beautiful.

English writers have in the main speculated on the Beautiful in form and color. That they felt unable to dive into the mysteries of the tone-world was but natural, for while music was loved in England, it never prospered there extensively as an art. Moreover, the English even to this day regard vocal music as the highest and only true form of art. They always subordinated the tone to the word, and speculated whenever saying anything tending that way, from the one to the other. The English sought more to find the Beautiful itself, and not so much the idea of it, as the Germans did. "English philosophy is an answer," says a writer, "to the question, What is it that makes a thing beautiful? Is the Beautiful inherent or is it based upon association?"

Shaftesbury entertained Platonic views, but his own peculiar theories are denounced as unintelligible. It was he who believed in a sixth sense, for which he was severely criticised by Jeffrey.

Sir William Hamilton distinguished absolute and relative beauty. "Both the imagination and the understanding find occupation, and the pleasure an object gives us is in proportion to the gratification these faculties derive from it."

Addison speaks on this topic in his immortal "Spectator," and does so very ingeniously, but without producing anything new. Burke teaches that beauty consists merely in the relaxation of the muscular fibre, but his theory was demolished with one sentence from Jeffrey's pen, namely, by directing him to a warm bath, if he wished to realize the Beautiful. An able critic when speaking of this author said, that "No work on the Beautiful is as worthless as Burke's, and that none is read as widely as it." Jeffrey no doubt said a smart and crushing word. But there is more in Burke's theory of relaxation than his contemporary was able to see. I shall refer to this theory again.

Sir Joshua Reynolds advanced the idea that beauty consists in mediocrity, or in conformity to that which is most usual. *Vox Populi* may be *Vox Dei* in morals, but it is not so in art. This is a low view of the Beautiful, for it robs it of its own superiority. Let me add, however, to the credit of Sir Joshua, that his theory is of French and not of English origin.

Allison attributes beauty to association, in which he leans on Diderot's idea of realism. "If beauty consists merely in association," says a thinker, "then the same is true of deformity, for association is capable of awakening either." The most powerful exposition of this theory of association is that given by Jeffrey. He claims that the emotions seemingly produced by art and objects are the result of association of recollection, but not of art-work themselves. There is some truth in the theory, but it does not hold good for a thorough system. Ruskin and Blakie gave it its death-blow and there is scarcely any one holding it now.

Ruskin says the term Beauty signifies two things. First the external quality of bodies, which he calls the typical beauty; and secondly, the appearance of felicitous fulfillment of function in living things, more especially a perfect life in man. This kind of beauty he calls vital Beauty. He further holds that the application of the term Beauty to any other appearance or quality is false. Thus Ruskin recognizes a Beauty of Body and a Beauty of Spirit. Undoubtedly the ideal Beauty, that which constituted the Beautiful, must be the same in both. The great writer denies that the Beautiful is the Useful. He denies that it is dependent on custom or on association. Ruskin is also Platonic in his theories in so far that he seeks the ideal of Beauty in God.

Spencer teaches that all the æsthetic activity is essentially caused by the play of the mind. He regards the æsthetic pleasure in degree according to the number of powers called into activity. The mere pleasure of sensation derived from tone or color he considers the lowest. A step higher follows the pleasure of perceptions derived from a combination of colors and symmetry of form; the highest are the æsthetic pleasures proper, derived from the varied emotions existing in the mind through association. The idea of association has been rejected by Ruskin, as has just been stated. It also will be noticed that Spencer places the pleasurable sensation of tone and color lowest, while Schopenhauer in his philosophy of music, which is regarded as the best thus far produced, places music above all the other arts.

But, to go a step further, there were philosophers who denied the existence of the Beautiful, simply because it cannot be proven like a geometrical problem; because mathematics cannot measure and calculate it. Because the Beautiful must have a source they would rather deny the principle, so as not to be compelled to acknowledge its divine origin. This applies to Voltaire, who belongs to this class of negative spirits. He says: "Ask a toad what is beautiful and he will tell you, two round eyes, a big mouth and a yellow throat. Ask a Hottentot and he will tell you that beauty is a black skin, thick lips and a flat nose. Ask the Devil," continues he, "and he will say a pair of horns, four claws and a tail. Inquire of the philosophers and they will answer you in a jargon." Voltaire would rather ask the Devil, a Hottentot or a toad, than to acknowledge a divine Beauty. But if France has left us the doubtful legacy of Voltaire, she has also left us other writers whose words we must not overlook.

Diderot declared that beauty was an inherent quality of things, that it was a power to excite sentiments in the mind. Thus far he was Platonic and correct, but he spoiled matters by declaring finally that beauty depends upon relation only.

Hear what Victor Cousin, another French writer, says: In his "Du Vrai, Du Beau et Du Bien," or the True, the Beautiful and the Good, he declares that "the ideal beauty is found in God."

And now let us turn our attention to Germany, and hear the opinions of at least a few of her great metaphysical speculators.

Kant, one of the foremost, if not the most noted philosopher even to this day, says that the sublime cannot be contained in form; that it can dwell only in the soul of man. He teaches that the Beautiful is of one substance with the Good and True. Accompanying the will and intelligence there is a mysterious factor within us, commonly called the imagination, or, perhaps better, the phantasy, in and through which the Beautiful comes to be recognized. Here, however, the idea is not uttered in action or in thought, but is enshrined in some sensuous form out of which it looks directly upon the soul. There is, therefore, accompanying the ethical and intelligent worlds an art-work, which challenges our attention as a part of the heritage of man.

The first in Germany who speculated on the science of the Beautiful, and who invented the word æstheticism, was Baumgarten, a professor at Frankfort-on-the-Oder. With him, the Beautiful is the result of the highest æsthetic perceptions to the realization of which our finer natures aspire.

Wieland follows in Kant's footsteps, and claims, as has already been stated, that the Beautiful can only be felt, but can never be explained. Schelling holds to Platonic theories. He teaches that the Beautiful is the eternal, bodily represented, and that the highest beauty is concentrated in God and expressed in the harmony of the universe. Hegel claims that the Beautiful is an idea, bodily represented and realizing itself. There is a ceaseless approximation, a continued attempting to realize it, but no full realization can be attained. He might have gone further without destroying his theory or himself, by saying that this absolute idea exists in God and cannot be realized, because the finite mind cannot comprehend the infinite.

Schiller is very lucid. He does not admit that the Beautiful is the result of mere limited experience, but pure abstract reflection. It originates in the perfect union of matter and mind, and cannot be mere life or mere form. Schiller sought a path of his own while speculating on the Beautiful, but he could not free himself from Kant's influence. He says that "the source of all æsthetic pleasure is suitableness. The touching and sublime elicit this feeling, implying the existence of unsuitableness." He further says that "Beauty is the work of free contemplation, and we enter with it into the world of ideas, but without leaving the world of sense."

Vischer seeks the Beautiful in history, but be this history sacred or profane, there is much in it that cannot be called beautiful.

I might here quote also the principles of Winckelmann and others, but this would make my paper too lengthy.

Hand, who views this subject more from a musical standpoint, says that "if the speculators on the Beautiful had taken painting and music more into consideration, they would have avoided many errors, for many theories advanced by able writers are utterly inapplicable to music. Indeed, many philosophers regarded the Divine art as mere play, totally devoid of a science. Every human being has an idea of the Beautiful," says he, "and an object which reaches this idea, which moves within us the sense of admiration, that is beautiful." He acknowledges, however, that this does by no means define the meaning of the Beautiful. He declares that it is only perceptible through feeling and not through thought, and that it exists only for its own sake and for no other purpose. "The utilitarian principle," he asserts, "has nothing to do with it."

Schopenhauer is partially Platonic in his theories, but his original propositions are of such vast importance that I shall give a few of his leading ideas. He starts out by saying that "An object affords us pleasure only in so far as it relates to our wills and purpose. But," continues he, "the Beautiful affords us pleasure without affecting our will or purpose. The operations of the will disappear in the enjoyment of an art work. The will is the cause of our misery in life. When looking at an art work we forget the will; the will is silenced for a time, and we are therefore in a state of pure will-less, painless, timeless contemplation. The will is the source of our desires and emotions; it is the source of our wants and suffering. But no gratification here can completely satisfy us, and thus we are on the wheel of Ixion; we pour water into the sieve of the Danites, we are like suffering Tantalus. By looking at an art work or listening to a piece of fine music, we are suddenly, and of course only temporarily, removed from this endless stream of wants; rest and quiet is established, the wheel of Ixion stands still and we are happy—happy whether the light of the sun shines upon us in a prison or in a palace." This, no doubt, is in part at least, what Burke meant when speaking of the relaxation of the fibres.

A thing is beautiful only when it does not concern us, for, says our author, and here we meet with his pessimism, "Life is never beautiful, while the picture of it, when idealized and represented in the mirror of art, is." Schopenhauer considers light the greatest diamond in the cluster of the Beautiful, and it is of decided influence upon the cognition of the Beautiful itself.

While Schopenhauer regards sunlight as the diadem among the objects of the Beautiful, I will go a step farther and point to Him that made the beautiful sunlight. Nature as the creation of God is greater than art, which is the product of man's mind and imagination. Nature is superior to art, and as the real thing is always superior to its silent representation, so God's work must be superior to that of man. There are writers who claim that man is the ideal of the Beautiful, who according to Scripture is the Temple of God. It must be acknowledged that all human activity is but a reflection of the power of God, hence the true scholar is not satisfied in his reflections to stop with the art work, but turns from it to the mind that produces it, and finally ascribing all honors to Him that has made all things, including so fearful and mysterious a power as the human intellect. As God created the world, so, in a limited sense, He permits man to create art work, so that by his representation of the Beautiful he may show forth his Divine origin, thereby honoring the Great Creator from whom came all good things and to whom all good things must lead. God is the All-Beautiful, as He is the All-Good, the All-Wise, the All-Just and the All-Merciful. All beauty is concentrated in Him, and both art and nature are made beautiful so that we may see God in His beauty. The artist, therefore, who produces a fine work, draws his inspirations, whether knowingly or not, from the

Eternal source of the Beautiful, he brings a part of the Eternal Beauty down to man, which like a magnet draws us up again to the source from whence it came. We cannot come in contact with anything of a Divine nature without being made better thereby. Art has a Divine nature and to teach its beauty from this standpoint I consider one of the noblest occupations man or woman can be engaged in. Heart culture coupled with a love for the Beautiful is a blessing to any people, for the Beautiful and the Good always walk hand in hand; religion and pure art are akin; they came from the same source and must lead to the same end.

To be æsthetic means to perceive and to enjoy the beautiful in art and nature. "As logic applies to thought, aiming ultimately at truth," says a writer, "as Ethics sets forth the laws of morality, referring to action, so Æsthetics appertains to the Beautiful, which appeals primarily to sentiment."

Nature is a wonderful texture, interwoven as it is by innumerable objects of beauty. Who can name them all? To study and to love the beauties in nature tends to produce in us reverence; they soften us down and make us more attractive. Virtue is virtue, but it may be lovely and again it may be very homely. Knowledge is knowledge, but it may sparkle as a thing of beauty, or it may lie dull and inert like an uncut diamond. Without æsthetic culture the best man lacks something. He may be learned, he may be honest and temperate, but he is not what he might be, had he developed within him a love for the Beautiful.

And now that I have come to the end of my discourse, I would remind you of the fact that the Holy Book points us to the beauty of Holiness; it speaks often of the beauty of God's Holiness; it portrays to us the beauty of the character, and it says that this world shall be made beautiful as it shall be made good. Have faith then in the final victory of the Beautiful, as you have faith in the final victory of the good. If God loves goodness, he also loves beauty. If He is mighty, He is also lovely. The millenium will not come until this earth shall have been made beautiful, until the desert shall rejoice and blossom as the rose, "and it shall blossom abundantly and rejoice with joy and singing."

A PLEA FOR MUSIC.

Music! What a theme! As the guardian angel is said to follow us through life, so music seems to be ever with us on our journey from the cradle to the grave! The little infant is lulled to sleep by its mother's song, and scarcely is its tongue loosened, when it chimes in, trying to sing in unison with the voice it loves so well. After entering the school-room and the Sabbath school, the little one takes renewed delight in vocal exercises. Notice how, forgetful of self, children will follow a hand-organ through the streets, while the sounds of a military band arouse wild enthusiasm. The songs of childhood, the songs which our mothers sang, who can ever be forgetful of their charms? When love's gentle impulses for the first time take possession of the heart, the maiden gives expression to them in song, while the youthful lover delights in a serenade. Oh, how great is the spell, when love's young dream is telling its story through the medium of melody. We scarcely know, then, which is the mightier—music or love! In the sanctuary we hear the peals of the organ, the strains of the choir, and the mighty song of the congregation. When listening with a believing mind and a feeling heart, our souls are wafted upward on the wings of song, until in the imagination we are in the blessed realm above. Watch the soldier when he hears the bugle call. Notice how the sound enters his innermost nature! Ask him what it is that stirs him, and he will tell you that those strains speak alternately of security and danger, of quiet camp-life and of terrible strife. Sing the old war songs before our veterans, and notice the effect. The one becomes excited and chimes in, while the other settles down into quiet reflection, the tears streaming down his cheeks. On how many weary marches have these songs been a means of cheer? How often have they inspired the fighting soldier, when almost ready to give up in the face of overpowering forces? How sad, when a dirge is played over the grave of a departed comrade, and how full of meaning was that short bugle call which was sounded after Gen. Grant's remains had been committed to their last resting place. The brief signal said "Lights out," and no doubt it conveyed a more forcible meaning to the soldier's heart than words could have conveyed. I have witnessed a revolution in Europe, and from personal observation can testify to the power of music in swaying an excited crowd of people. It was song that imparted to the timorous populace the courage to resist the strong arm of the militia. Even when the light of reason has gone out, music follows man into this darkest period of his existence. Music is one of the chief joys of those unfortunates who are confined within the walls of insane asylums, and it is a fact but little known, and far too little appreciated by our medical profession, that many a shattered mind has been restored to reason through the soothing influence of our art. Who can imagine a Fourth of July celebration without music? When far away from home and the loved ones, what language is so powerful to keep alive affections and pleasant remembrances of our birthplace, as that of music? The strongest heart, that has endured many trials and braved many dangers, the heart that has learned to govern its emotions, yields to the few notes that make up the little tune "Home, sweet Home;" and this simple strain has been the means of bringing many a wayward wanderer home again. When a young couple is about to take upon themselves the solemn marriage vow, the brilliant wedding march is almost certain to be a part of the ceremonies, and when they have advanced in life until their hair is frosty and their steps are tottering, they still listen with indescribable emotions to the songs of old. Though they stand on the brink of the grave, these songs carry them back to childhood's years, and with a fond smile they view once more the scenes of their youth.

Ah, the old tunes, the dear old songs, how easily they lead us along the whole of life's path; they cause us to stop at the places where we plucked the fragrant flowers, where we whiled away our leisure hours, enjoying the sweets of tender, youthful love. The eye may refuse at such a moment to shed a tear, but the heart throbs and beats wildly. Even when our voices have lost their former fullness, when we lie stretched feebly on the last couch of sickness, when night is about to break in upon our earthly career, when kind friends stand by our side, waiting with sorrow for our departure, when we say farewell to the things of this life and wait patiently for our removal, music is still with us, and in faith we sing a hymn of praise, only to take up the unfinished strain in the great beyond, where saints stand around the throne, praising Him who has bid us exchange mortality for immortality, and who has called us to dwell in that great mysterious realm, from which music comes as a divine inspiration.

Doubtless the fact that the love for music as well as its cultivation among the people is so general, leads many to view it from their own standpoint, which is generally one of limited knowledge, for, say they, is it not natural to sing, is it not easy to catch a tune? Many believe this to be most of what there is of music. It is, however, a fact worthy of notice, that while learned philosophers and scientists have successfully grappled with many great topics, they have failed, as yet, to discover the true inward nature of music. Earth is not its nativity, hence it is not likely that we shall ever fully penetrate its mysteries. Yet it is so simple to our minds and hearts, so easily understood and so readily felt, that to speak in its favor is like holding a candle out of doors at night, in order that we might see the moon or behold the stars in all their beauty.

In the estimation of many persons, and even of learned men, our beloved art is merely a pleasurable sensation and nothing more. This is the lowest influence of music, but let us bear in mind that even in the production of pleasurable sensations it is a great power. It may not have occurred to these persons that these influences are always pure and refining, provided we use the art aright. Music cannot be impure, and if it becomes at all degrading in its influence, as no doubt it sometimes does, it is not so by its own nature, but through its connection with improper acts and words. Music has a higher mission than merely to please the ear. It is the art which appeals most powerfully to the heart, and through this affects our characters. The idea that music has no higher influences than simply to produce, for the time being, pleasant sensations, has done much harm to the progress of the art, in schools as well as among the people, for it has caused many thinking men to regard music with a good portion of suspicion. It has always been a great disadvantage to our beloved art, that among those who feel its powers most, there were but few well qualified to set forth its benign influence and inward operations. Being preëminently emotional in their natures, they failed to view, and hence to teach, the art from an intellectual as well as from an emotional standpoint. On the other hand, philosophers, who are preëminently brain-men, could not enter into the emotional powers of the art, and these are, after all, its true key. Relying upon mere speculations of the reasoning faculties, the real powers of the art remained a mystery. 'Tis easy to yield to emotions, but it is difficult to analyze them; it is difficult to reduce them to thought, for just as soon as the mind steps into the arena, the emotional fire wanes. The fact that music deals with our emotional natures first, leads men of brain to snub the art; they look down upon it as a mere pleasant pastime. Yes, they go so far as to charge that music tends to weaken character, while directly the opposite is the case, as I hope to show. I am aware of the fact that in claiming refining powers for music, I have many weak spots to meet and to explain, but this can be done. Says a writer, refinement of mind may be defined as an act or process of putting the faculties into the condition in which they can do the best work, appreciate the nicest distinctions, value properly the highest ideals, and grasp the loftiest conceptions. The term refinement, says the same writer, is generally applied to work done upon valuable material. We do not refine iron, but only gold and silver; we endeavor to instruct the ignorant and the degraded, but we speak of refinement only in connection with those who are educated. There are learned men and women who lack the very first traces of refinement, while there are musicians who lack a good education and a correct moral training. But I shall speak on this point in another place.

The mere emotional influences of the art alone will never refine. If we aim to impart culture, we must do it through subjects that are worthy of the human mind as well as the heart. Music is such a subject, if it is properly presented and rightly taught. Whatever we search for in a subject, that we are apt to find. He who seeks in music mere pleasurable sensations, will find what he seeks, and he who searches in it for discipline both for the mind and heart, will no doubt find that also. He who seeks but shallow reading, can find it in the domain of literature; he who delights in crude pictures will invest no money in works of the masters. So he who loves the shallow in music, he who uses it merely as a pastime or as a means of show, may find the kind of music that responds to his tastes. For the student, however, who strives higher in art, there is much in the great storehouse of musical literature that is worthy of his closest study. If our tastes point in the direction of music, let us see to it that its study becomes a means of refinement, and with this purpose in view, let us pursue our work with our best emotions and our clearest thought.

We must aim to be intelligent students; we must strive to see more in music than mere pleasurable sensations; we should study it as an art, hence we must become artists; that is, we must be imbued with the highest love for and the best understanding of what we study. To make it a refining, elevating medium, we must not merely be players and singers, but also art students. Strive, then, to become thinking as well as feeling musicians. Believe what has been said by those who know most about our art, that its refining, its humanizing influences deserve our closest attention.

A taste for brutal noise, for coarse sounds, goes hand in hand with a taste for brutal conduct. A taste for shallow music indicates a shallow mind, as far as musical culture is concerned. Cultivate the inborn love for the beautiful in any form thoroughly, and it is sure to lead to a love of the beautiful in all things; and again, this love produces a dislike for ugliness, in morals as well as in our surroundings. Let the influence of your studies be a chastening and softening of the spirit. Good music never fails to enter our inner natures, and if at all rightly used, it cannot fail to exercise an influence for good. This influence I claim is eternal. The little snowflake, which, in all its purity and beauty, falls into the ocean, is melted instantly, and, as far as our eye is concerned, it has forever vanished. Yet the little drop of sweet water it contained has helped to sweeten and to increase the immense body of water, in which it disappeared. So the honest hearing of a good piece of music cannot be without *some* lasting influence, be it ever so feeble or ever so completely hidden. Every beautiful idea, be it expressed in marble, in colors, in words or in tone, comes of necessity from the one source of the beautiful above, and is it at all reasonable to suppose that such repeated influences should be merely transitory in their character? It cannot be!

No doubt God had a great and wise purpose when he gave us music, and that it was given to us with a purpose is manifested by the love for music that lies in the hearts of all right-feeling people. Is not the same true of that religious sense which pervades the breasts of all men, let them be ever so low in the scale of civilization?

It is the testimony of learned musicians everywhere, that the art is inspiring, that it arouses our inner natures, that it awakens powerful emotions, and that the higher we soar in its realm, for the time being, at least, the less we care for the empty things of this world. This enthusiasm is not what some characterize it, a selfish indulgence, but it is a pure gratification. This enthusiasm and inspiration arises from our coming into contact with works of beauty, and through them with some of the best and loftiest minds that ever existed here on earth. This enthusiasm is akin to religious zeal and devotion, and this zeal forever forces us onward and upward, in search of greater beauty and perfection. As religious devotion produces the spirit of missions, so the lover of art knows no greater pleasure than to unfold its beauty before others, that they too may enjoy its benign influences. When viewing the music teacher's work from this standpoint, does it not deserve to be called a noble work?

In common with all musicians who have studied their art and its effects, I claim for it refining influences. No doubt you will accept this as a truth, yet you cannot fail to say, behold the passions of musicians, the petty rivalry and jealousy that are displayed among them; are not these also the effects of music? No, they are not. They are the outcome of defects in character, they are the result of a defective education. Having given themselves too exclusively to music, having enjoyed and studied the art only from its emotional side, they neglected the cultivation of the mind and development of character, hence those defects among little as well as great musicians, which are so offensive in our sight.

Moreover, musicians of prominence are too often flattered, and that to such an extent, that what little strength of character they possess is almost entirely destroyed. Let us also bear in mind that great musicians are as shining lights, and in our foolish adoration, we often fail to condemn them for improper acts. There is no reason why genius should be allowed to overstep the boundaries of good breeding, and if public condemnation were to follow swiftly, even the most eccentric of musicians would be more careful about his public behavior. The more prominent men and women are, the more we notice their public lives. Bad behavior in common mortals hardly produces more than a local excitement; the misstep and degradation of a prominent musician becomes the gossip of a nation.

A father and his daughter once visited me, the object of their call being a consultation with regard to the latter's course of education. There was a radical difference of opinion between the two, and I was evidently chosen as arbiter because the daughter, being fond of music, expected me to decide in her favor. She desired to devote herself exclusively to music, though her common school education was deficient. My advice was for the father to give his daughter a thorough literary education, allowing her at the same time to study music. Turning to the young lady I said, "If one of the two must be delayed or neglected, let me beg you to delay or neglect music." The arts are educational means, but, like all other branches of study, they are merely so many spokes of the great educational wheel. A musical education alone must produce one-sided results, and so a complete education which has included art studies, is more perfect than one that lacks such culture.

Man is a social being. Says a writer: "Unselfish society is the harmony of humanity," and so it may also be said, that kind words and pleasant interchange of courtesies are the music of social life, which is designed to enhance human love. Music should be made a part of our home life, of our school life, and without fail it will in the course of time also become a living part of our national existence. Music is a social art; it fills many hearts with the same emotions, it sets many minds to work, and like no other art, oratory perhaps excepted, it arouses large bodies of men to almost superhuman action. We scarcely ever meet for any great object but that music is drawn in and is made to serve a purpose. Is it simply to pass time? No, it is introduced in order to lend additional charms to the proceedings and exercises, in order to arouse pure sentiment, to strengthen enthusiasm for a good cause, to unite those who meet in the assembly; and thus the art is often ignorantly used for good purposes, even by men who have but a low opinion of it. As a people we need every good agent to help along the cause of culture and refinement. Wherever art plants its foot, the tendency is to tone down and to moderate our well-known national self-assertion, our aggressiveness, our youthful boisterous roughness, which many mistake for independence of character. Americans delight in boasting of their liberties, but they are often slaves to business and speculation. This is our national failing. We need more restfulness, more reserve, and art studies are among the best means to bring about such a result, for meditation about art and the looking at fine art works causes us to lose sight of the world without. Rough people take no delight in art, yet it is created for them, just as religion exists for the benefit of the unconverted. Many persons lack all culture and refinement, they even lack good breeding and polite manners. They prefer noise, loud talking and rough sports to the gentler influences of art and literature. You can scarcely arouse them to enthusiasm, except it be in the gratification of their lower natures. Young people quickly show by their outward appearance, by the choice of their amusements and social preferences, what their true inwardness is. Alas! people say, boys must be boys, and under this plea much rudeness and offensive conduct is tolerated. We need social agents designed to lift us out of our daily routine life, to turn boys from the ways of boisterous roughness; we need agents to awaken sentiment, agents that shall prove sweet harmonizers between the outer and inner man. Music is such an agent, and while as a people we love it and take readily to it, we fail to cultivate it sufficiently as an art, and for this reason we fail as yet to derive the fullest benefit from it. Our art efforts, like our church enterprises, must be individual efforts, for our government, unlike those of European countries, can do nothing directly for the advancement of art culture. The unsupervised and ill-directed effort of individuals unfitted to teach music, retards its growth. But its slow development is no argument against its ennobling mission, nor against its final success. Look at the immense machinery that is set to work to christianize and to educate mankind, and notice its slow progress. Music is the youngest art; it is only now in its highest state of development; let us give it as much time as we have accorded to religion, to education, before we indict it as being without lasting and ennobling influences. Only of late years is our musical profession rising to a higher level, and the most surprising results already have been attained. That music is making rapid strides in this direction, the most short-sighted should be willing to acknowledge. Notice the increase of cheap popular concerts in our cities; notice the numerous bands which play in public parks; observe how deeply music is striking root in our public school system, and then say whether or not we are on a fair way toward becoming a musical people. And right here let me repeat what I said in the *Musical World* recently: "It is undeniably true that our public school education falls short in the development of the child's emotional and imaginative faculties. Music is one of the best means at our command to awaken sentiment, yet there are teachers who make great pretensions as educators, who speak boastingly of training the whole child, but who would not lift a finger in behalf of music as a branch of public school education. How short-sighted and inconsistent!"

But look still closer at our national musical progress. Concert programmes are multiplying and improving, and likewise the standard of public performances is rising. More copies of standard musical works are sold, musical literature is improving, the taste is better and purer than at any previous time, music schools are increasing and charlatans are driven into the backwoods. If you as future teachers would be useful and stand in the ranks of the profession, you must study the masters. With light music you will hardly get along any more, for where you least expect it, you will be asked to use these great works. Prepare yourselves, therefore, that you may be up to the standard of the profession.

It has been said that Music is a great art; it binds together rational natures; hence it has a high moral influence in the family, and for this reason all thinking people love to foster it at home. A musical home is a happy home. Ill-natured, cross-grained people rarely love music; why they would hardly whistle a tune.

But then music, if it once permeates the heart's feelings, drives out ugliness; ill-nature and music cannot exist together, for the heart that comes under the spell of good music is thereby made ready for good deeds. Parents who fail to cultivate the musical gifts of their children deprive them, and through them the coming generations, of that moral and intellectual legacy which is due them. And just as music is a power in the family, so it is in the world at large. The Reformation came a little later than printing, but it came with the first artistic development of music. Says a writer: "Had the Reformation occurred among a people less musical than the Germans, it is a doubtful problem whether it would have succeeded as well as it did." Music is a means to refine and to elevate social solitude. But if music is a social art, if it inspires numbers, it is also a true friend. In fact, it is best felt when alone, just as the most fervent prayers are offered in private. It is good for us to seek solitude, it is beneficial to meditate. Go in the evening to the doors of musicians' rooms and listen, and there you will hear their hearts' best emotions poured out upon their instruments. I can conceive of no greater pleasure than to express my emotions upon my instrument, unheard by man. When in the twilight hours there comes a feeling of yearning, a feeling of loneliness, I find no words to express my emotions; but through the medium of music I can tell all I feel, and in this expression of my inmost emotions, I find relief. We are so constituted that we must give vent to our feelings, and because there are sentiments the words cannot convey, music was appointed to serve man. When I am thus alone with my art, the masters come and go; they visit me in spirit, and the air is as full of music as it would be full of fragrance, had the room been filled with flowers.

And then at such an hour the soul often rises on the pinions of song to the very footstool of grace, for music being a divine language, the language of the heart, is well understood by our heavenly Father. Yet there are those who say that music is only a plaything, a recreation, a very agreeable pastime. Music, say some, is good enough for girls, but is illy suited to boys. In Europe, boys as well as girls study music; hence, everywhere in that country will you find statesmen, generals, priests and bishops, professors as well as students, bankers as well as merchants, practice the art. Some of these amateurs, such as Thibault, Ambros, Hauslick, and others, became famous in the world of music. The much lamented Emperor Frederic was a good pianist, while the celebrated Moltke, the general whose wars are beyond comparison on account of their brilliancy, played the piano. Yet his musical knowledge did not detract anything from him in the fields of his profession; he was as brave a fighter as ever lived. Would that American boys could be more thoroughly imbued with an art spirit; would they could be divested of that destructiveness and loudness that is displayed by some. Their better natures would be called forth through the aid of music; the hidden springs of their affections would be unearthed, so that they could flow more freely. Oh, let us open the windows of our souls, so that the light of love may shine in freely, for love should be our soul's normal condition. How often, when hearing or when playing good music, do I say, God be praised for such precious gifts, and my heart then, methinks, is large enough to love a universe.

'Tis pleasant to express one's sentiments; all good people delight in that which appeals to their better natures; the heart seems ready for it, as a niche is ready for the statue, or the vase is ready for the flowers. No one is contented with the actual; it is the nature of all intelligent beings to aim at the beyond, the supernatural, and music is one of the most pleasant roads that leads that way. Our consciences tell us what is right, says a philosopher, but they never would lead us in the path of the beautiful. To strive after the beautiful is, in a measure, equal to striving for the good, for both come from and lead to the same source. The beautiful surely leads to some sort of progress; it cannot be otherwise. It comes from heaven and it brings heaven down to us; not a heaven too great for our comprehension, but a heaven just fitted for our human needs, for our hearts and homes.

Music is a language. Without language we would not be the human beings we are. Language gives expression to thoughts, and because men are differently constituted, we have a great diversity of dialects. Language is of a people; it expresses a people's thought, and he who learns it, enters into another nation's spirit; he who masters a language, so to speak, multiplies himself.

The emotional world, also, needs a language. All human hearts are akin in their feelings, all humanity feels alike. Music is preëminently the language of the emotions, it is the language of the heart. When comparing the language of words to that of music, Thomas Moore says:—

> "Music, oh, how faint, how weak;
> Language fades before thy spell;
> Why should Feeling ever speak
> When thou canst breathe her soul so well?"

If this language of the heart had not been needed, God would not have given it to us, neither would he have given us the power of understanding it. This language of the heart, this music, brings all humanity into one household; it is the language of the brotherhood of man, while literature brings us only together in the republic of letters. Which is the greater, the head or the heart? Let me answer by saying that God asks for our hearts, not for our brains. Are these not reasons why we should study this universal language? Through its medium, we can speak to and reach the hearts of those whose words we cannot understand. The characters of this language are substantially the same the world over. In studying our beloved art, we learn to speak a world's language, and that the *only* world's language we know of. Its spirit unites, permeates and controls humanity. Music expresses more than the word, in fact, all musical writers agree that where the word fails, the full meaning of Music only begins. Says Wagner: "The tone language is the beginning and the end of the word language, just as sentiment is the beginning and the end of the intellect, just as the Myth is the beginning and the end of history, and the Lyre the beginning and end of poetry." Schumann says: "That would, indeed be a small art that only gives us sounds and no language, no expressions for the conditions of the soul." Music tells us far more than the heart can take in, hence the art is inexhaustible; the deeper we study the more music reveals to us.

Pure art music is but little understood, even by many of our best educated men. The masses lack as yet the depth of sentiment, as well as the mental capacity, to understand the full meaning of the works of the masters. To appreciate the heart language of a Beethoven, presupposes a good degree of culture. The mental strain required to understand it is too great for the uncultivated, hence they cannot understand it as well as he who has spoken this language for many years; yet the charge is that music is a mere plaything, a pastime. Despite the depth of good music, it is never listened to, by the uninitiated even, without some profound expressions. Good music properly played never fails to touch us. Yet there are many who, after listening to the works of the masters, are much in the same position as was the Western editor who, after listening to a lecture by Emerson, turned to his neighbor and said: "What does he mean?" A grand musical composition expresses the composer's inner life far better than would the best biography. To draw near to the feeling hearts and the powerful minds of our great masters is indeed a privilege to be highly valued. Through their works we are made partakers of their greatest joys and deepest sorrows, and on the pinions of their inspirations we rise to heights we never reached before. If the unmusical could but read in words what these master minds have said in tones, how much they would enjoy such literature, and to what a high place they would assign these works.

Man uses human language to express vileness and deceit; men swear and blaspheme in the language of words, but no one can swear, no one can blaspheme in music; it cannot revile. It is the language of heaven, for it seems to be the only one admitted there. All art is pure, all art is sacred, and the works of our masters, as far as they are not coupled with objectionable words or actions, are all sacred music; they are the profoundest utterances of human hearts. Who would dare to play with such an art? who would dare to play with the works of such masters? who would use such an art for selfish purposes, for the low purpose of flattering one's own vanity? Such an art must be carefully and sincerely studied: alas, rather than do this, young people prefer musical small talk, and rather than to train the masses to rise to a comprehension of the pure and good in art, many teachers are satisfied to teach this small talk, and to train pupils to repeat it, as birds are trained to sing. Much of such small talk is often heard in our homes, in schools, and in concerts, yet the question may well be asked, What must be the effect of great and pure works, if even this musical small talk is so pleasing to the ear and the heart?

But say some, music is emotional and not intellectual, hence it deserves no place by the side of other studies in the curriculum. Stupid talk! As a study, music is highly intellectual. He who would learn it, must read new signs, more varied in their character than are those in the Greek language or in chemistry. The study of music implies at least some mathematics, and he who wishes to enter the mysteries of acoustics must have mastered the science of numbers. The study of music implies a knowledge of rhythms more varied than are those in Greek, Latin, or English poetry. It implies correct time and correct phrasing. The student must grasp the melody as well as the harmony, he must read many notes at once, and not only that, he must produce them instantaneously upon his instrument. Not only must he touch many keys at once; he must strike them with the proper degree of strength, rapidity and feeling, and while his eye reads, while his hands play, his feet must properly manage the pedals. To drink in, and to reproduce quickly the spirit of a composition is in itself difficult, yet this is done in connection with such a multiplicity of mental actions, that it is surprising how the human mind can perform them all at once. Music undoubtedly develops the mind in many directions, and yet it is said that the art is not intellectual. But let us go still further and enter the composer's laboratory. The poet or prose writer has his manuscript before him, and he may alter and change it until it expresses his ideas. The painter constantly watches the effect of his colors on canvas as he puts them on, but the composer must write a complicated score of instruments and voices, without hearing a sound. All these artists quietly exhibit their work after it is finished, but the player or singer steps before the public and there executes his art work. Surely a musical performance is a marvel in itself. How many keys does a Sherwood or a Mrs. King strike during an evening, and yet each must be struck at the proper time and in the proper manner. Notice how these artists perform whole programmes from memory, and this they do with the utmost accuracy and dexterity. Some great singers know as many as forty operas by heart, each of which requires hours for a hearing. Where are the orators that remember forty lectures? And yet there are some who say music is not intellectual. Look at the study of harmony, counterpoint and fugue, examine the mysteries of orchestration in all its wonderful tone colorings, look at the study of musical history and biography, take a glance at musical philosophy and æsthetics, and then answer the question whether or not the study of music requires thought. Languages and sciences may be mastered in far shorter time than it requires to fully master music in all its branches. Educational history tells us that for centuries our art has held its place in the universities of England. It is now taught in all German universities, and this, no doubt, is also a testimony in favor of the intellectuality of music. Even the ancient Grecians had a musical system that requires the acutest mind to understand, and this is also true of many Persian and Arabian musical works. But let us take another interpretation of the term intellectual; let us regard it as meaning a natural constant preference for higher thoughts over lower, and according to this definition, music will have to be regarded as an intellectual study.

The performance of a piece of music may not arouse or call into activity the faculty of reason, but then, let me ask, does poetry or does a prayer do so? Are we reasoning when looking at a pretty picture or a fine statue? Of course we begin to reason as soon as we begin to criticise and analyze a work of art, and this holds true, also, with reference to music. Having viewed the artist's work so far, let us now measure, if we can, the flight of his imagination when composing or performing an art work, let us listen to the wild beatings of his heart, and the artistic work becomes still more intellectual. Everything that calls into activity our spiritual natures is intellectual; and who dares to deny that music does this to a high degree? Why such an art should be regarded as a mere plaything, why it should be treated as stepmotherly, as it is treated in many schools and by many learned men, I cannot comprehend.

The normal sentiment of the human heart is, or ought to be, love. Music is love in its purest essence. Berlioz said somewhere, "Which one of the two powers may lift man to the highest plane, love or music? That is a problem. But it seems one might say, love cannot give us an idea of music, while music expresses love." And then he bursts out by saying, "But why separate the one from the other? Are they not the two wings of the soul?" Weber said, What love is to man, that music is to the arts, for it is love itself. It is the most aesthetic language of the passions. Love also is the essence of religion, hence they are closely allied. Every good piece of music therefore is religious, for it expresses love, and to take into our hearts this love, to express it again in tones, that is and always must be one of the most edifying acts we can engage in. Oh! that we might see the art in all its grandeur, purity and loveliness! Luther fairly bubbled over with powerful sayings when speaking of it, and in one of his table talks, he places the art next to theology. If the art you study is a social, emotional, intellectual and religious agent, if it is a blessing, let us use it, study and enjoy it as a blessing. Be impressed with the fact that your studies are worthy of your most serious attention. View your art always from its sacred side, aim to rise as high as you can, and you will be happy in your work—nay, more, you will be fitted to use your attainments as a blessing to others as well as yourselves.

THE VALUE OF A MUSICAL EDUCATION.

It is not to be expected that all should study music as a science or as an art, but it is expected that people of culture should know something about it. Place yourselves under the benign influences of the divine art, and you will not regret it. Learn to love good music; cultivate your taste as much as possible.

When I first entered this pleasant field of usefulness, I perceived the necessity of meeting music pupils collectively at least once in a week. Would that we could meet oftener, for there is much to be said, and there is always inspiration in larger gatherings. The student who plods along on the road of learning without associates, the student who never meets those that are engaged with him in the same work, is apt to become self-sufficient and conceited, or perchance he become independent. At any rate, he fails to develop a spirit of competition and a wholesome emulation. Students should meet students at proper places and at proper times; they should hear and see what others do. There is always a great deal of good coming from class-work, for in the class-room the student may realize his own standing, his degree of proficiency and growth, and in the class-room the sluggard is often stirred up to greater activity. Private instruction is absolutely necessary for those who aim to master an art, but class instruction should not be neglected on this account. That there is more in music than mere playing and singing, that there is something objective, something absolute, spiritual, elevating, eternal, yes, that there is something divine in our art, I desire you to realize; that music, as an art, does not depend upon the frail criticism of the uninitiated. It is necessary that you should be made to believe, at the very outset of your career as students, that there is something higher in music than that which the masses see or hear in it; those who know nothing about æsthetic or artistic enjoyments; those who assert that there is no more in art than they themselves realize and recognize. It is my duty to lift you up; to give you higher ideas of art and artists. It is my duty to lead you onward and upward on that golden path of beauty, as it is revealed in art, feeling certain that you will also learn to love and to adore the source from whence cometh all this beauty. In order to accomplish this, I must give you weekly instructions, for these lessons will never come to you through mere playing or hearing music. A good technique is not sufficient; nay, there must be understanding as well as execution. So, in the reverse order, musical instruction, without hearing good music, avails but little. Hearing, without understanding, is as the top of the tree without life-sustaining roots, and so understanding without hearing good music, is all root and trunk, without flowers, leaves and fruits. You see, therefore, the necessity of both lectures and recitals; they supplement each other, for the lecture prepares the mind to hear aright. In order that you may become well-rounded and intelligent teachers and musicians, you must be educated as thinking and feeling men

THE VALUE OF A MUSICAL EDUCATION.

and women. The lecture sets you to thinking, while the recital arouses and cultivates your feelings as well as your art-taste. In order to enjoy an art, you must understand it; the more you think about it, the deeper will become your emotions, and the more you thus study your art from its twofold sides, the more effectively thought and sentiment will harmonize and develop within you. Sentiment is the top-soil in which grows our art, but let us see to it that our emotions are pure, so that the thoughts arising from them may also be pure. These plants must be carefully nurtured, for they never develop well without fostering care. You perceive from this that both lectures and recitals are needful for your musical growth. They help to surround you with a musical atmosphere, which is sure to be conducive to a healthy musical growth. I therefore commend such exercises to you, and it is to be hoped that no music student will absent himself from them without good cause.

Let me ask you to remember that our life's journey is divided into smaller portions by certain events. These events appear as huge milestones, and are rarely ever lost sight of. Your entrance into an institution of learning is one of these milestones, for no matter how old you may become, you will always look back upon your stay there as one of the most important events of your lives. It is in accordance with our natures, that, when entering upon certain new phases in life, our minds and hearts are more receptive than usual, and to be permitted to make impressions upon hearts and minds in this condition is one of the greatest privileges a teacher can enjoy. Some of you are for the first time entering college life; others are merely continuing the work begun in former years. It may be a sad fact to realize, but it is nevertheless true, that you have left the parental home, never again to dwell for any great length of time under its sheltering roof. You enter college to prepare yourselves for life, and you expect to enter upon its duties as soon as this work of preparation is completed. Be this as it may, all of you are beginning a new year of mental activity. A college is a small world in itself; within its limits you have every opportunity to exercise your faculties, to develop your minds and to cultivate your hearts; here you have all necessary means at your command to fit yourselves for your future duties. One part of your life is closed and lies behind you, and you enter college to prepare yourselves for that portion of it which lies before you. Your state here is that of preparation for an unknown future, exactly as our existence here on earth is a state of preparation for eternity. Bear in mind that he who loses the chances and fails to embrace the opportunities offered here on earth, is, so the Bible says, a sufferer throughout eternity. So he who fails to improve his opportunities in college is the sufferer, at least throughout life. Mistakes made there, habits formed there, avenge themselves throughout life. Allow me then to say a few words as to your life and work, hoping that what I offer may not be spoken in vain.

He who wishes to live right must strive to know this world of ours, with all its hardships and joys, with all its certainties and uncertainties. Realize, then, this fact, that we are not all made alike, neither in size, looks, gifts nor characters. We differ widely, and this difference among creatures of the same species is noticeable everywhere in the world; it is God's intention that so it should be. If we differ widely, it becomes our second duty to study others as well as ourselves.

In a word, our success in life depends largely upon a correct knowledge of the world in which we act, a knowledge of the men with whom and for whom we act, and especially does it depend upon a knowledge of ourselves, who must forever act, and who are destined to rise and fall by our own actions.

This created world is the same everywhere; it is fashioned after God's plan, and he pronounced it good. Although it is the same in goodness, it makes many kinds of impressions, it is viewed in many ways, and all this for the simple reason that we are differently constituted. Most people see the world as through colored glass, only few learn to see it with the naked eye, and as water often partakes of the taste of the soil through which it runs, so the world in its appearance partakes of our own natures.

You think you deal with the world, and so you do, but you deal every time first with yourselves. You cannot get out of, nor can you get away from, yourselves—it is you that is living your own life, it is you that is writing your own life's history every day. You cannot escape from this world and its responsibilities, do what you will, least of all can you escape from yourselves; you must forever live and act, and while here on earth, you must once in every twenty-four hours fill a page of your life's history. Every human being has his or her own peculiar experience, hence, a peculiar history of his own, different from that of others, and that is owing to the fact already stated, that every individual differs from all others. From the foregoing statement, it follows that the appearance of this world, our views of life, its duties, its pleasures and cares, depend not upon our surroundings, but altogether upon our own conception of them. As the man sees the world, says a philosopher, so it appears to him. If he is stupid or vulgar, the world likewise appears stupid and vulgar, and naturally he delights in the company of the stupid and the vulgar. If he is bright, happy and contented, if he is cultured and refined, this world will be the same to him. Start out then with this idea, that God made a good world, and that, if all men were alike gifted and alike good, all would see this world in the same light of beauty and goodness. Man, however, fell; man is imperfect, he has necessarily an imperfect view of self and the world, and as men are differently constituted, they must differ even in their imperfect views. The higher we rise in culture, in refinement, the more this life and world must become to us. The lower we sink in degradation, the lower must also be our views of this world, of man, and of life itself. Having thus thrown some light on your relations to life and to the world, let me draw from it this lesson, which I beg of you never to forget, that, inasmuch as our views of life and men depend upon our own inward condition, our happiness lies not without, but within; that we are made happy, not by what we have, but only by what we are. A great mind sees great things in this world and life, a petty thinker, a small-minded man, finds fault and quarrels with everything. To him, men and things appear small and defective. A bright-thinking and quick-observing mind sees a thousand things which afford it pleasure and also pain, all of which escape the notice of the dull and unobserving. The intellectual and charitable man has a high and noble purpose in life, the selfish and sensual man always lives for low purposes, yet both live and exist in the same world, all chances and opportunities for good are alike open to both. From this it follows that the world is not to blame, but man is. It follows, also, that no matter how our condition may be changed, no matter how rich we may be made, even if we were to live in luxury, or to enjoy all the honors this earth can bestow, we ourselves would still be the same, hence, we would in reality not be happier than we were before. In order, then, to improve ourselves and others, we must lay hold of the inner man; we must educate both the head and the heart, for the mere bestowal of riches and honors would not be bestowing real happiness. If we were to give men all the honors, all the wealth they desired, it would be found true that the drunkard would still drink, the blasphemer would still blaspheme; nay, their conditions might possibly be worse, for great material prosperity without correct mental and moral training often fosters all the greater evils.

As this world appears to us either good or bad, according to our own goodness or badness, according to our own understanding, it must be plain that the highest gift a man can attain is understanding, or in other words the one thing most needed is education, which, in the full meaning of the word, includes religious and moral training. Education, therefore, is of more value than money and precious stones. An ignorant millionaire cannot be as happy as a poorly paid but well educated preacher or college professor. An ignorant lord or king is far more miserable than is the poorest paid and least recognized country school teacher. Many a rich land owner sees less pleasures in life than does his hard-working tenant.

Life is like a kaleidoscope; it changes with every rising and setting sun; but while life constantly changes in its situations and scenes, man changes but slowly. It has been said that the man of a clear brain and a good heart sees the world as it is; the man of mediocre mind sees it through the lens of his own desires and passions. The man of clear mind and good education understands events; he sees their effects; he seizes upon them and uses them, and thus he advances his own interests. The ignoramus, the uneducated, is not qualified to do this. The ability to seize circumstances and to use them for one's own good, or the inability to do so is by many called good and bad luck. In reality it is good and bad training, good and bad education; it is ignorance versus wisdom, quickness of mind versus dulness of mind. Men embrace their chances because they have education sufficient to see them, and they fail to see them because they lack education. Shun the idea of fatalism, it is hurtful. Dismiss the foolish notion that some are born to succeed, while others are doomed to failure. Every man is, in a sense, the maker of his own destiny; if it were otherwise, we would be mere puppets on the stage of life, pulled here and there by that invisible force called Fate. This idea is repugnant, yet many clutch and cling to it, probably as an excuse for their own stupidity or laziness. Some people act in life as if they were hoodwinked—whatever they obtain is caught by chance; whatever they do seems to be done by chance. While this is a fact much to be deplored, it must be acknowledged that the fault is not with the world, it lies with men. The good things lie about them all the same, but they cannot see them, and that because of a lack of education. He, however, who is educated, has the scale of ignorance cut from his eyes; he sees things and situations in their true light, and he therefore acts wisely, using this world without abusing it. To obtain an education is a great privilege, for the proper use of which you will be held responsible.

Therefore use your opportunities, for you will need, in active life, all the information you can possibly obtain.

Impress upon your minds this lesson, that religion, character and learning are three precious gifts worth striving for; they are permanent gifts; they do us good; they lift us up, while money and honors fail to do so. Through education you are enabled to draw pleasures from this world which are denied to the rich ignoramus, for the only true and lasting pleasures come from within; all outward pleasures are necessarily followed by renewed wants and often, also, by bitter results.

Some young students seem to think that college life is or ought to be, in part at least, a period of pleasure-seeking. There are peculiar pleasures connected with student-life, and every rational person loves to see students merry and lively, but remember it is a sad mistake in students as well as others to seek pleasure first and all the time, for to him who does so, amusements will be as the Loreley rock. They will surely wreck his life's barge. It has been said that our lives unravel themselves like balls of twine. When watching students in schools, it will be noticed that many sincerely endeavor to weave this twine into some design, into some useful articles; there are, however, others who simply drop it as it unravels itself, thus wasting their days and opportunities. Many students are unmindful of the fact that, as has been stated, they must fill every day a new page of life's volume. Alas, how much foolishness is noted down day after day, how many bad deeds and idle words are recorded which can never be blotted out. No matter how successful you may be in after life, no matter how useful you may become in after years as men and women, you will find that in your quiet moments of reflection, this book of your life's history will be thrust before your eyes, and whether you will or not, you must read. Memory and conscience are two great accusers; they will bring back foolish actions and idle words, and this will necessarily give you much pain. It is wicked to palliate young people's indiscretions by saying that they must sow their wild oats. No one has a right to sow wild oats; no one has a right to claim that young people must do so. Sow good seeds; sow them now, that in after years you may enjoy fragrant flowers and luscious fruits. Sow seeds of morality, for they spring up to be heavenly plants in the life to come. Sow seeds of pure thought, for they lead to pure action. Sow the seeds of pure action, so that you may form good habits, and thus you will establish character. Look not too much to the future, for it often deceives; look more to the present; look to every day, for every day unravels your life's twine, every day a new page is turned over for you to write upon.

Many young people start out in life with the idea that happiness consists more in having than in being. Of course they aim first at riches, for they care more for what they have than for what they are; true happiness, however, is found only in moral and mental progress. A good conscience, a clear head, and good health, are the true sources of happiness, for the loss of which neither money nor honors can compensate you. You may be poor, and no doubt many of you have to struggle for your education; you may have to stint and deny yourselves in many ways, but from this it does not follow that you must be unhappy or humiliated; it does not follow that he who has all the good things imaginable is necessarily happy. We look too much to what we lack, and not enough to what we have. Having nine things and lacking one, many foolish people fret over the one and forget to enjoy the nine. Remember to look first to what you are, and aim at that alone which is truly worth having, namely, character and learning. Money may be taken from you; at best it entails many cares and is apt to prove a chain that ties men to the things below, but character and learning remain forever with you; they are cords that draw you to the world above. It has been said that we cannot get away from ourselves; we are forever with ourselves, we remain ourselves throughout eternity—we are, therefore, "forever our own company," and is it not sensible to improve this company, so that it may be worth enjoying? The bad man has always bad company, the ignorant man is always in company with an ignorant man, and that, too, every day of his life. What lives such people must lead! Happiness produces outward cheerfulness, and never lose sight of the fact that cheerfulness is always welcomed. It makes you strong and gives you influence among pupils, both old and young; it is welcomed in the sick-room, in the store, in church, on the street, in fact, everywhere. Cheerfulness is always useful, no matter what sphere of life you may enter. Young students sometimes allow moroseness, jealousy, envy and other unwelcome guests to enter their hearts. At first they come as brief callers, as momentary guests, but there comes a time when these guests will stay, and so there comes a time when they will rule you in your own household, driving out every good caller. These guests will prove to be cruel landlords, hard taskmasters and tyrannical, and they will become more and more so until your dying day. Would you be your own masters, your own landlords and kings, watch your hearts and minds now; see to it that you allow no bad roomers to come in. Says a writer, "Bad habits are masters; the slave has only one, but how many have we?" And so it might be added that the turnkey puts the law breaker behind only one or two locks, but your habits are as a thousand locks, almost closing every avenue of escape. Let me beg of you, to remain free, to keep bad company out of the heart, to avoid forming bad habits.

As students, be social with each other, seek all proper sources of enjoyment, but, bear in mind that while the pleasures of society are often agreeable, they also consume much time, they lead often to temptations and entail many burdens. Therefore be sparing with them. When you are alone, you are yourself; in society, said a philosopher, you sometimes must be somebody else, at least you are tempted or even forced to be somebody else. Fashionable society does not often recognize real worth, for wealth and beauty generally take its place. Social conversation often leads to trouble, and these troubles you may safely avoid by staying at home, where your tongue keeps quiet. Never indulge much in talking, for often will you be sorry for words spoken thoughtlessly. We are often innocently led into making statements which, when once made, are like stones that have left the hand, they belong no more to us, neither can we stop them in their course. Said a great man, when speaking of having attended social parties, "I often came home less of a man than I was when I went." We are constantly tempted to talk freely; most people love to hear themselves talk; but free talkers often destroy their own peace and that of others. Select not your friends among such, for you are apt to regret it. Young students are often dazzled by those who have glib tongues, and thus they form friendships hastily and inconsiderately; friendships which lead to no good. Grow slowly into your friendships; see who it is upon whom you bestow this boon, and if you find you were mistaken in selecting a companion, cut him off! Be sparing in your friendships, be friendly to all, but let your bosom friends be few. Friends sometimes turn out to be "robbers of our time and invaders of our privacy." Make it a rule not to make too much of any fellow student, lest you might be compelled to make too little of him. He who goes with persons afflicted with contagious diseases, is apt to catch the ailment; he who goes with students addicted to immoral or ungentlemanly habits, can scarcely escape catching immorality and rudeness. Lively fellows, men given to the same evil habits and inclinations, like sparrows and blackbirds, always go in flocks, for birds of a feather flock together, but, says a thinker, eagles fly alone.

There are many young people, and older ones too, who cannot bear to be alone, for they are poor, miserable company for themselves. Hence they seek society; they visit every theatre and opera house where anything can be seen or heard; they indulge in all manner of games; they love to gossip, and all this because they are but poor, miserable company for themselves, because time hangs heavy on their hands. Time is one of the most precious gifts, yet how wasteful we are with it. When Queen Elizabeth was about to die, she offered all her possessions for a little time, an article which you have now in abundance. Oh, use it carefully and wisely; for though your ball of twine seems to be large, though it seems to unravel slowly, believe it, there is an end to this string, and there is a day known to God now which must be your last. Ministers who have visited death-beds testify to the fact, that selfishness, wordliness and waste of time are among the chief causes of unhappy death-beds. Oh, that I might cause you to realize now what you are sure to realize in later years, namely, the preciousness and the shortness of time. Oh, that you might do every day your duty toward yourselves and others, for this is the only ladder that leads to fame and distinction. Said a young musician to me, "How can I best secure fame? What must I do to have reputation?" My answer was, "Do every day's duty as well as you can. No other road leads that way." It is sad to think that there are so many who leave this world pretty much as they found it, having done nothing toward the progress of self or others. Employ your time well, for sometimes the busiest people waste most of this precious article. Learn to find contentment within yourselves, and thus time will never hang heavy upon your hands. By improving yourselves, you will be able to dispense with the amusement world, which robs you of much valuable time, and which is apt to lead you into trouble. You deprive yourself thereby of certain pleasures, it is true, but you avoid also much pain, and, as an old philosopher says, "There is more true happiness found in avoiding trouble than there is in actual indulgence." Says another philosopher: "The man who feels constantly the need of company and pleasures, is like a State which imports everything, but produces nothing." He is sure to remain poor in the end. Amusement seekers have no peace; they are forever on the alert for new pleasures; they are apt to get into bad company; they are somewhat like the giddy fly, which gayly and thoughtlessly roams around until suddenly it is caught in the spider's web. Amusement seekers always are poor students; they are nearly always poor thinkers. Do some thinking for yourself; do not import exclusively; raise a crop of home pleasures, for these you may have at any time.

Take the best care of your health. Health depends upon steady and judicious employment, and upon a rational, regular, moderate style of living. Be systematic and moderate in your work, in your rest, in your social intercourse, and also in your eating and drinking. I attribute my good health to the systematic living and working which I have followed for twenty-five years. You may feel the power within you to do great labors, but be sure that you do not overtax the body, for thus you live no longer on the interest of your money, but you are actually using up the capital. Reduce your needs and wants to the minimum, for thus will you stand the least chance of disappointment and privation in life. He who needs a big house for his happiness, has much expense in furnishing it and much labor in keeping it in order. But do not go to the other extreme of denying yourself the necessities of life. Students who endeavor to deprive themselves of necessities, will find to their sorrow, that when they have nearly accomplished their task, they have also ruined their health.

Healthy students are usually happy students, for happiness, says a writer, is necessary to health; but health does not always produce happiness. In the end, happiness, like many other states and conditions, is in part, at least, a matter of habit. Happiness is not apt to allow those other roomers, already mentioned, to take possession of your own house and home. Happiness, in a sense, means freedom and enjoyment of labor and of one's own existence. Cultivate it now, and believe it, that in later years, it will prove to be a big shade tree under which you may rest securely. Happiness desires to see others happy, and, says Sydney Smith, "If you send one person, only one, happily through each day, that makes 365 in the course of a year. And suppose you live only forty years after you commence that course of medicine, you have made 14,600 beings happy, at all events, for a time." Be happy and diligent students and you are pretty sure to meet happy teachers. What a trial it is to instruct soured, ill-natured, fault-finding pupils, and what a delight it is to see sunny faces about you. Verily the latter always have my best efforts. He who does no good, rarely ever gets much good; he who cares not for others, soon finds that others care not for him. Be mindful of the wants of others, for thereby others will also be mindful of your needs. The student who shirks duty is not happy. Never shirk duty, never put off till to-morrow what ought to be done to-day. Every day has its own duty; do it with all your energy, for to-morrow brings new responsibilities, and, if you would make good the neglect of to-day, you must, on to-morrow, overtax, or at least double, your energies. If your life is a journey, remember you never go twice over the same portion of it. If your life is as a book, with as many leaves as you may live days, you never write twice on the same page. You never live a single day twice over. A day seems but a little span of time, it is only morn, noon and night, yet poets like Pope, Young and others have deemed it one of the greatest sayings of the Emperor Titus, that he bemoaned the loss of a day. Every day brings you nearer to that line which divides the known from the unknown, and the devout Lawrence Scutari correctly said, "Spend it always as if it were your last."

Many music pupils err in constantly looking toward the end of the year or the term. They wish to know positively what they shall have accomplished by that time, and when telling them what others have accomplished, they are continually on a strain trying to do as much as others did. Avoid this, for it is hurtful. Do every day's duty, and let to-morrow take care of itself. Whatever you may have accomplished at the end of the term, if you were faithful, that is all you can do, and with a good conscience you may rest, feeling assured that you have gone as far on the road of improvement as lay in your power.

Avoid all half-way work. It is one of our national failings to be sometimes contented with outward appearances, but be assured, this sin is fast vanishing from our national character, and with every succeeding generation, Americans look more and more to real merit in learning as well as in character. Many young music pupils measure their progress by the number of pieces they have in their portfolios. This also is a great error, for only what you know is your own, not what you have. I have had pupils who in their great eagerness for progress practiced too much. Bear this in mind, that your work will benefit you only as long as the MIND is fresh and active. Whenever you work beyond this limit, you begin to consume your capital, you shorten your days. Aside from this, such work avails but little. Set aside regular hours for practice and also for rest and for the reading of good books. I am a friend of newspapers, but remember that mere newspaper reading is sure to lead to shallowness of mind. Strive to cultivate your minds; store them with good knowledge, for the mere singer and player is in these days regarded as a machine that simply grinds out music. There is more demanded of you than the mere ability to sing or play, for a musical education consists of more than a high degree of execution.

Take daily exercise. Your body is a piece of machinery, says a doctor, the interior of which is constantly in motion; give the frame also a chance to move and to exercise. Breathe plenty of fresh air, for this is the food for your blood. Open windows and doors and let in fresh air and sunlight, for both are needful for the student. That our health is of the utmost importance is plain from the fact, that when we meet friends we first ask, "How do you do?" When answering this question, stop a moment and think whether you do well with yourself. Many young people fail to appreciate the value of health, and never realize the greatness of this blessing until it is lost. Value your health; for it is a bank account, which you draw upon every day, and which may at any time run out. Do not overdraw it, for there is no borrowing of health, no matter what interest you offer.

The healthy and clear-headed man usually sees the world as it is; he sees it as if it were reflected in a clear mirror; the sick man sees it through a glass that is blurred and untrue. How can he act prudently and wisely? It is worse than foolishness to trifle with one's health; it is wicked; for its loss robs you of your usefulness and happiness. In your intercourse with students, and, indeed, under all circumstances, guard your honor. Seek not your honor merely in the opinions of others, but be the honor itself, clear to the core of the heart. You may be regarded as a good student, and at the same time be a consummate scamp. You may be looked upon with suspicion, and yet have honor. This inward knowledge of being on the side of right is honor. Honor is of more worth than gold. It may be quickly lost, but it requires years to restore it, if indeed it can ever be fully restored. To have one's honor questioned, wounds our feelings; be therefore slow to doubt that of others. It is better that you were deceived twenty times, than that you should suspect or accuse one person unjustly. While public opinion is unable to create or to destroy your honor, it is nevertheless of importance to you that you should be well spoken of. Never be indifferent toward public opinion, but never seek to turn it into your favor by sacrificing principles. Always see to it that you are right, and then fear no one. Have some positive influence. Act so that when in after years your name is mentioned and your influence is measured, it shall not merely be said of you that you were good pupils, that you never failed, that you never were known to do a wrong thing, but rather strive to have it said that you exerted a decided influence for good.

Be assured your true standard will be ascertained, your mental and moral calibre will be tested and measured by teachers and fellow students. He who thinks that among students he can appear as something else than what he is, is much mistaken. Your and my character will be read without fail, and is it not the wisest plan to be open, frank and candid; is it not the wisest to appear exactly as we are?

While I would not have you be over-sensitive, for this fault brings much trouble to our hearts, yet would I urge you to look well to your right and left. I would have you open your ears for criticism, for, from those who uncover our faults, we learn more than from those who bestow fulsome flattery. It is customary to compliment those who sing or play well, and flattery is an exceedingly pleasant dish for the average musician. You may do well and be deserving of praise, yet you should not forget that perfect performances are as rare as perfect bodies and souls. Remember also, that while you have done well, others have done better, and there is room for improvement clear around the circle of your art attainments. Of all faults that make young people most frequently disagreeable and unhappy, jealousy and conceit are two of the commonest.

Jealousy is one of the meanest of human faults, for it envies others their own possessions. The jealous person attempts to obtain for himself the praise and honors due others; at least, he would withhold that which is due. Often he speaks in an unfriendly tone of others, and secretly he wishes evil and ill success to the one envied, and thus becomes malicious. What if a fellow student has attained higher perfection than you; would you have this perfection, attained through much labor, destroyed or belittled, simply because you are a lesser light? Ought you not rather rejoice, that so high a degree of perfection has been attained by human effort, and ought we not to esteem those who through diligence have attained it? How mean, then, to be jealous, how mean to belittle the efforts of others. Would you not feel grieved to hear others belittle your own efforts? Endeavor to establish an atmosphere of generosity; listen not to those who try to destroy the reputation of others; give credit honestly for what is due others, remembering what Carlyle said: "It is one of the noblest traits of human character to recognize the worth of others." Not to do so is a mean trait, which I hope never to encounter here.

It is claimed that we musicians are especially afflicted with jealousy and conceit, but this is a false charge, for both faults blossom and often come to ripe fruit in other professions. Conceit, like the measles, is a disease which breaks out more or less among all young people. All that is needful is to watch that the disease does not strike in, for if it does, there is scarcely any hope for recovery. There is a period in every one's life, when, in order to see either the smartest or the handsomest young person, the young man steps before his own mirror. There are people so conceited that they imagine the west end of the town is sure to tip up whenever they step toward the east. Conceit is always a way-bill of an empty head. The cranium must be filled with something, and the room which is not occupied by solid learning, is usually given over to conceit. He who knows much, realizes the vastness of the fields of learning, and comparing with it, his own limited stock of knowledge, is apt to proclaim: How little we know, after all. Conceited people are an innocent sort of beings. Conceit, therefore, is a harmless sort of a malady, harmless in its effects upon others, when compared with jealousy. How silly to think too much of oneself, for it is the sheerest self-deception. What if you think yourself twelve feet tall, there is sure to be some one who considers himself still taller than you. Conceit, however, often provokes us, for the conceited man not only overestimates himself, but also undervalues us. Be assured, young friends, that the conceited student is cordially disliked among his classmates. Often this ailing disease is brought in from other places, for it does not easily take root in a large school. Generally the conceited one comes from some small academy, where he stood at the head of his class, on account of which he has become an object of praise and admiration. Of course, he becomes inflated, like a football, and when at last he enters the university, he is apt to be treated like one. 'Tis hard that it should be so, but then young people often are inconsiderate; they have their strong likes and dislikes, and they especially dislike a conceited fellow student. There is always a disposition to let the wind out of the innocent little balloon, and this operation often is apt to be painful and vexatious. Usually the knife of ridicule is used, for this seems to be the only instrument sharp enough to penetrate the rhinoceros hide of the conceited one. There is danger, however, that the operation of letting the wind out of the balloon may be too sudden, for in that case there is apt to be a great fall, from which there may be no rising. Look about you, and you will find everywhere young men who, in their own estimation, are Adonises, Ciceroes, Napoleons or Shakespeares, and so we find some who imagine themselves to be Liszts, Beethovens, Pattis and Nillsons.

When the Scotch pray that they might be blessed with a canty conceit o' themselves, they mean not to pray for the power of over-estimation, but rather that they might have a proper appreciation of themselves, that they might "see themselves as others see them." Self-knowledge is apt to produce self-confidence, and self-confidence is not to be confounded with conceit. The conceited man overrates his powers and has nothing wherewith to sustain his high opinions of self; the self-confident man knows his powers; he trusts in them, uses them judiciously and effectively, and for this reason generally succeeds. The self-confident man dares to aim at the prize and often he gains it, while he who hesitates, seldom wins anything. Self-confidence is needful in all stations of life; he who lacks it, is an humble sort of a fellow, better designed to follow and to serve, than to lead. He needs constant advice and encouragement, and people usually weary in bestowing it.

Keep your imagination in check. 'Tis a useful article to the artist, but it is often a very untrustworthy mirror of life. Do not waste time and strength in building castles in the air, for you can't live in them; they won't keep you warm, and in the end they will be pulled down either by yourself or others. Build on solid facts; build solid houses, resting on genuine attainments. Visionary people are driven to and fro; they are unstable. They are apt to be optimists or gloomy pessimists.

Be prudent about the display of your knowledge and wisdom. Do not press your ideas too much forward. Talk only about those subjects with which you are familiar, for knowledge, like timber, says a writer, should be well seasoned before it is used. Be a ready listener, and a reluctant talker. Never be ashamed to confess your ignorance of a subject; hesitate not to ask questions. Most people will be generous toward you when confessing a lack of information, but they can hardly be expected to be generous toward the pretender.

Be polite to all. Cultivate politeness as a habit, for it cannot be put on and off at pleasure. Politeness endears you to everybody; as future teachers, preachers, physicians and lawyers you need it every hour in the day. Cultivate it now, so that it may become a part of yourselves.

Cultivate patience. Be patient under reproof, patient in the discharge of duty, patient in waiting for results. 'Tis foolish for pupils to be impatient under reproof, if kindly administered. You come here for the purpose of being reproved; you need your teachers' corrections; how foolish, then, to feel unduly sensitive and restless, or even offended, when corrected. Impatience makes your work all the harder, while your restlessness eventually becomes a serious impediment to happiness in life. Write these lines as a golden lesson in your mind; wait patiently on the world and its opportunities, but never keep the world waiting on you. Wait patiently until the world shall recognize your merits. Be patient in bearing with the peculiarities of others; do not hastily and rashly attempt to correct or reprove what you see amiss in others. Do not press your own individuality too forcibly upon others, but miss no chance to place yourselves under the influence of great and good men. He who builds a house by the wayside must be satisfied to let people passing by criticise his plan; so if you play and sing in public you must expect people to criticise your efforts. Be patient under criticism.

Compare yourself with others, but look not exclusively up or down—measure yourself with those above as well as with those beneath you. Be severe in your judgment of yourself, but be lenient toward others; be not easily satisfied with your own attainments; seek to see the faults of your own work; but when criticising the work of others, seek first to see that which is good. Seek not after distinction, but do everything well, because this is the right way to act, feeling contented with having done your full duty. It was Rückert, the poet, who said, that the rose which ornaments the bush also ornaments the garden. What if your merits are not recognized by others, you are surely not the sufferer, for you are still what you are, and more than that you cannot be. I love the spirit of emulation and competition; I like to see men strive for front places and honors, but those who recite best, those who obtain first honors, are not always the greatest men. Who then is the greatest? Not he or she who recites, or plays, or sings best, but, says a good man, he who chooses right with invincible resolution, he who resists the sorest temptations from without and within, he who bears the heaviest burdens cheerfully, he who is the calmest in storms and whose reliance on truth and virtue, on God, is the mos.. unfaltering.

It only remains for me to speak on the subject of your musical studies. There is a truth in music as there is a truth in religion, in the sciences, and in politics. The question which I wish to put to you now is this. Is it wise to spend one's time in following error when the truth lies right at our feet? Surely not. Is it right to read dime novels when there are so many good books to be had, and that almost for the mere asking for them? Is it right to live on the husks when there is so much good corn growing? Surely not. Is it right for you to use the divine art as a thing of fashion or selfish gratification when it may do your souls good? Surely not. We use only the purest gold of music in this workshop. But say some, there are many people who pass brass for gold, or who even prefer it to gold. Let me say that if the people, the world over, were to take brass for gold, it is your duty to expose the fraud. If all people were to run after Baal, would you join the crowd and deny your God? No, you would stand by the truth; and the same you should do in your musical studies. The truth comes from God; to stand by the truth means to stand on God's side, and this makes you strong. But say some, my friends do not like such music. In reply, let me say that you do not study music to please your friends, but to elevate yourself and others. Every lover of truth can afford to wait until those for whom he labors see the truth also. That good music must win the victory, is as sure as the fact that the Gospel must win the victory. Let us help, then, to hasten the good time coming, by doing our share toward the spread of good music.

And now in closing, only a few words in behalf of those good parents you leave when you go to college. There are, to-day, many anxious fathers and mothers whose children are before me. There may be those among them who do not pray, but there are none among them who do not wish their children to do well, none who wish you to forget their parental instructions. Never, therefore, undertake anything of importance without asking yourself in your heart, whether your parents would sanction your action. You may, and you may not, be children of the church; but even if you are not, remember the old Sabbath-school lessons which you received. Do not cut loose from the old moorings of home instruction. And now success to you and to your endeavors. May our efforts be crowned, and may we all feel that it was good for us to have met; may we realize our expectations, and may you accomplish that which you seek.

MEMORY.

The ability to play music from memory is justly regarded as an accomplishment. Of late, however, an *undue* importance has been attached to it, for pianists seem to vie with each other in the exhibition of the power of memory, even more so than in the art of playing itself. That the power of playing from memory is of great value, both to teacher and pupil, cannot be denied, and it is therefore a proper, yes, even a very profitable subject for consideration.

Memory is that power which enables us to store away in that great, unseen safe of ours—the mind—the many ideas that have presented themselves to it. Memory retains all past ideas and perceptions of the mind; recollection, however, as the word indicates—meaning to recollect—is the faculty which enables us to recall them. Recollection is usually spontaneous; it is *not* as much subject to the will as appears to the general observer. Yet it must be said, that *the will* often is of great assistance to us in the exercise of this faculty. Memory is the safe, it is the storehouse for thought; without it, we would gain no knowledge. But, says a writer, memory is not like a post-office box, or like a pigeon hole, in which all information may be stored like so many letters or memoranda; to the contrary, it ought to be like a well edited periodical, which prints nothing that does not harmonize with its intellectual life. This implies that the mind should not be mindful of anything that does not benefit it, or that does not come up to our moral and intellectual standard. Memory is absolutely necessary for our existence; for without it, there could be no personal identity. Haven says: "Memory is our only voucher for the fact that we existed at all at any previous moment."

Nature never bestows her gifts equally. To some she gives great power, while others are left almost empty handed. The power of memory also is unequally distributed. It must, however, be borne in mind, that the power of memory is to a great degree the result of cultivation. Some persons, as we shall presently see, have attained an unusual degree of perfection of memory; their mental safes seem to be both larger and more secure than those of others. It must be acknowledged that the power of retaining and recalling facts, dates, incidents, faces, ideas, locations and so forth, is certainly a most remarkable gift; for all, it is true, that this power is not by any means the highest faculty of the human mind. The mere memorizer is, at best, but a mechanical being, his mind is simply stuffed with other people's ideas. Or, if we would make another comparison, the mind that thrives only by memorizing, is but as a cistern. It must be filled from the roofs, while the mind of the original thinker is as the well, that supplies itself. Pump out the facts of a "memorizing man," and like a cistern he eventually becomes empty; but try to pump the ideas out of a thinking mind, and you will never strike bottom, for, like a well, it supplies itself. One idea leads to another, one thought produces another. The memorizer's mind is as a storehouse in which so much merchandise is put away; the thinking man's mind is as a factory that produces this merchandise. As the merchant must go to the manufacturer to replenish his stock, so the memorizer must go to the thinker for his ideas.

The power of memory has been the subject of much investigation and many curious theories have been advanced with regard to it. Thus it is said, that the memory of the lower classes of human beings is superior to that of the more civilized races, because the primitive people must rely more upon their memories for the preservation of facts, while educated people may refresh their memories at any time by referring to books and manuscripts. It has also been observed, that idiots and otherwise weak-minded people had remarkable memories. This is a flat contradiction of the idea entertained by many, that those who are possessed of good memories, are also great people. In the "Memoirs" of Mrs. Summerville, we read of an idiot, who lived in Edinburgh, Scotland. He could repeat the entire sermon he heard on a Sabbath; yes, more than that, he could tell where the preacher coughed and where he wiped his nose. The same writer speaks of another idiot, who knew the Bible so well, that he could, without hesitation, tell where any verse was to be found. Archdeacon Fearon speaks of a man who, though a complete fool, could remember the day when every person had been buried in the parish for thirty-five years, and that he could recall the name and age of the deceased, as well as the names of the mourners that attended the funeral. Aside from these facts, he could not give an intelligent reply to a single question.

It has been said that memory, as a rule, is stronger among the uneducated. Let me give a few illustrations. Hone, in his "*Table Book*," speaks of a Sussex farm laborer named George Watson. Upon being asked what day of the week a given day of the month occurred, he immediately named it, and also mentioned where he had been and what the state of the weather was. A gentleman who had kept a record put many questions to him, and his answers were invariably correct. Daniel McCarthney, a native of this country, who had no higher employment than turning the wheels of a printing press, had a prodigious memory. He declared, says Mr. Henkle, in the *Journal of Speculative Philosophy*, that he could remember all the dates and the days of the week, from 1827 to 1869; that is, from the time he was nine years old up to his forty-second year. He also could tell where he had spent each of these 15,000 days and what he did. He was employed in the office of the *Salem Republican*, and, says the Hon. T. K. Ruckenbrod, upon turning to the files of the Journal, the man was always found to be correct. This man's memory, however, was not confined to dates alone. He could give the cube-root of such figures as 59,319 or 571,787. He could also repeat 250 hymns and sing 200 tunes. With all this singular power of memory, however, he was not a man whose general grasp of mind was in any way noteworthy.

Reid, in his "Intellectual Powers," gives an instance of an ignorant woman, who in a fever recited page after page of good Greek, Latin and Hebrew, which were identified as passages she had heard by chance many years ago. This, says the writer, is an instance showing the permanence of simple impressions. It is no doubt a fact, that the mind keeps all impressions it receives. This, however, by no means implies the power of recollecting or recalling them at any time.

Sometimes when sitting quietly at rest, memory seems to delight in opening its safe, and the power of recollection, as if it were playing with me, repeats names of persons of whom I had not thought for twenty-five years. Incidents, which I am sure have never been recalled by my memory since I came to this country, suddenly recur and dance before me, as if to tantalize me. It is said, Our power of recollection is not our power of memory. We remember what we cannot recall, but the time will come when we can recall all that the mind has remembered; in other words, all that the mind has been mindful of. The idea that what has once been put into the mind will remain there forever, is one that ought to make us cautious as teachers and parents. It is a most serious idea, and should make us careful in our intercourse with others. A trifling remark upon a serious topic may escape the mind of him who uttered it, but it often makes an indelible impression upon the mind of him who hears it.

Observation goes to show that the memory is most tenacious; that under certain circumstances, it suddenly and infallibly recalls impressions made years ago. Doubtless through some imperfections of the mind, we are prevented from recalling all we saw and heard. Insignificant incidents are often hidden away in the mind, as little slips of paper are hidden among an immense mass of manuscripts which fill an author's drawer. Let a favorable opportunity arise and these insignificant ideas and almost forgotten facts turn up, as do the little slips of paper just alluded to.

An educational journal speaks of a lady in the last stages of a chronic disease, who was carried from her London home to a friend's country residence. While there, her infant daughter was brought to visit her, and after a short interview was carried back to town. The lady died a few days later, and the daughter grew up without any recollection of her mother. When she had reached a mature age, she happened to be taken to the room in which her mother died, without knowing of the occurrence. Upon entering she became agitated, and when asked for the cause, she replied: "I have a distinct impresssion of having been in this room before, and that a lady, who seemed very ill, lay in this corner, bending over me in tears." Other and equally remarkable instances showing the tenacity of memory might be given, but it is, perhaps, unnecessary.

It is claimed by prompters on the stage, and also by professors of elocution, that the memory of women, as a rule, is superior to that of men. This accords with my own observation. It is a fact generally acknowledged, that the memory of youth is more vigorous than that of more advanced years. It is most vigorous in childhood, and seems to be strongest about the age of fifteen, from which period it generally begins to decline. It must, however, not be inferred from this statement that the decline of memory implies also a decline of mental activity. Memory, as has been stated, is to a great degree the result of training. During the years when the boy or girl is at school, memory is constantly exercised and thereby strengthened, while in later years this practice is somewhat neglected; at least, memory is not trusted to a very great extent. While professional men must rely upon memory, while merchants and mechanics will never forget certain facts, it will be generally found true that in later years men trust more to pen and pencil than to memory. As the mind grows older, it necessarily gathers more learning; at the same time it is also burdened with greater cares, and is distracted by the more serious affairs of life. Hence men in advanced years are not very apt to repeat pretty poetry or interesting quotations. This perhaps explains why men are sometimes forgetful of love's vows, and the many tender promises they made when engaged in that interesting and delightful occupation of making love. Ladies, as has been stated, have better memories, especially in this particular direction. Great tact and wisdom is required in recalling these facts to men's minds, and right here let me say that many ladies err and cause themselves much unnecessary trouble. A physician of prominence claims that the memory of feeble-bodied people, as a rule, is superior to that of robust persons; and, as a proof, he adds that by examining the condition of students in colleges, it will be found true that those who are the greatest memorizers, are generally those that are lightly built. It is also claimed that the memory of farmers and of country people is, as a rule, better than that of townspeople. We all know that memory is freshest and easiest impressed in the morning, hence Germans say :—

"Die Morgenstunde
Hat Gold im Munde."

It has also been asserted that people living in warm climates have superior powers of memory, as compared with those living in northern countries. Memories excel in different directions. Some easily remember faces, others remember names, while still others never forget dates. Some are easily lost in the woods, or in the streets of a city, while others quickly find the right road. Some children easily remember poems, others can readily commit whole chapters of the Bible, a gift entitling them to the appellation of good children and enabling them to carry off prizes, while those who lack this gift are often—and that very unjustly—called lazy, or even bad. Because they lack strong memories, it is charged that their minds run away from *good things*. I do most heartily sympathize with such children, for I, too, belonged to that unfortunate class who found it difficult to commit the catechism.

The illustrations thus far given referred to the idiotic and to children. Allow me now to give a few instances calculated to show that great and powerful minds may also display unusually strong memories. Before doing so, however, let me briefly allude to the statement made by Sir Arthur Help, who claims that the memory in past centuries, but especially among the ancients, was more powerful than is the exhibition of this faculty among students of to-day. This is equivalent to saying that the power of memory has universally declined, especially since the art of writing and printing has become so widespread. This is not accepted as a fact by physicians. While in these days of scientific investigations and discoveries we cannot exclusively rely upon the memory, we nevertheless use this faculty very extensively—more so than did our forefathers. We necessarily use the memory more, because the lines of our horizon of knowledge have been removed far beyond that of our ancestors.

A good, active memory is in these days absolutely necessary for success. We need memory to retain facts of science and mechanical appliances; memory to retain languages; memory to retain data and facts in political life, and a very good memory to grasp the lessons of life. Doubtless the ancient Grecian rhapsodists had remarkable memories, but they are equaled, if not excelled, by the modern Shanama-Khans of Persia, singers who recite poetry by the hour from memory, without even stammering. The bards of the Calmucks also repeat songs and poems from memory, the recitation of which sometimes lasts whole days.

There were Grecians who knew their Homer by heart; but then, what is this compared with Justice Scaliger's memory, who committed the whole of Homer in twenty-one days, and all the Greek poets in three months. There have been hundreds that knew their Homer by heart. Isaac Walton tells us that Bishop Sanderson could repeat all the odes of Horace, all of Tully's offices, and the best part of Juvenal. We are told of one Porson who knew by heart the writings of Horace, Virgil, Homer, Cicero, and Livy, and all that, before he went to school at Eton, England. A classmate once played a joke on him by slipping a wrong book into his hands just as he was about to read and to translate. But the boy was not at all disconcerted. He simply recited the lesson from memory. In later years he could recite all the Greek poets and prose writers. He could give whole plays from Shakespeare; he could recite complete books from "Paradise Lost," and many other works.

Archdeacon Fearon, in a pamphlet, tells us of a boy fourteen years old who repeated 14,000 lines in Homer, Horace and Virgil. But I must not pass the ancients, for among them we also find men endowed with remarkable powers of memory. We are told that Cyrus remembered the name of every soldier in his army. Lucius Scipio is said to have known the name of every citizen in Rome, when that city could furnish 200,000 able-bodied fighting men. Pontius Latro could repeat *verbatim* every speech he ever had heard in the Roman Senate. Crassus, when he was prætor in Asia, was familiar with all the Greek dialects; and Mithridates, king of twenty-two nations, administered their laws in as many languages. But then we also know that Sir William Jones could speak thirteen languages and could read in thirty others.

A few years ago England could boast of two men, Borrows and Palmer, who, as a writer says, might have traveled from the hills of Wales to the Ural Mountains, or from Lisbon to Algiers and Delhi, without meeting a language in which they could not converse.

Sir William Hamilton tells of a Corsican who had a most remarkable memory, which he tried thoroughly. Words were dictated to him which were selected from the Greek and Latin, and were so arranged that they conveyed no idea. This was continued until everybody was tired. The Corsican then repeated every word, and having done so he recited them backward without missing one. Then he named every third, then every fourth word, etc., without making a mistake. But what is more remarkable, after a year's time he could still repeat the same words.

An incident is mentioned of a Polish forester who had been located in Germany, and who had neither heard nor spoken his native language for forty years. While under the influence of chloroform, he spoke, prayed and scolded in Polish.

Mr. von B———, envoy to Petersburg, was about to make a visit, but he could not tell the servant his own name. Turning to a gentleman that was with him, he said: "Do tell me who I am." The question excited laughter, but upon explanation he was told who he was, and he finished his visit.

Who among my hearers has not experienced that uncertainty of memory, when suddenly we fail to remember how a familiar word is spelled? If grown men are so forgetful, how much more patient should we be with children. In hospitals one meets quite frequently with patients that are deprived of the use of certain words. They cannot, for instance, remember the words knife or tumbler, but speak of the thing that cuts, or the thing we drink out of. Yet such persons have been known to play games that require close observation and much calculation.

Speaking of the loss of memory, I must recall the case of Rev. Ormond. He met with some financial reverses, took sick, and during that illness he lost his memory. He had forgotten how to read and write; he could not name any one, not even his wife and children. I knew the man, and testify to the correctness of this statement. Strange to say, one evening he engaged in prayer, when suddenly his powers of memory returned. In his devotions he mentioned every one of his family by name, and could even recall facts. That night he died.

In some people the memory is on certain days a blank; nothing can be recalled or remembered. Dr. Azam describes a woman who lived two distinct lives. In one she was serious, in the other gay and coquettish. She had no memory that extended to both conditions. When she was gay, she remembered nothing about her serious spell, and *vice versa*. Indications of such a double life, one sometimes notices among children. Often teachers are forced to ask themselves the question, how it is possible that a child, which a week ago recited such excellent lessons, should to-day be so stupid and thoughtless. Children sometimes seem to be bereft of the powers of memory, for when asking them questions, which at ordinary times they answered readily, they give us simply a vacant stare. Unless the teacher is a student of the human mind, especially of the minds of children, unless he observes the operations of his own mind in order that he may know something of those minds he is called upon to instruct, he is doomed to meet with many enigmas in the schoolroom, the solution of which will be beyond his ability.

Such irregularities in children's minds often lead to sickness and premature decay. Many instances are on record in medical works of children who suddenly forgot all they knew. It has been said that impressions once made upon the mind can never be fully effaced. How then do we explain the failing memory of old age? It can only be explained on the ground that aged people fail to exercise this faculty, and that therefore it fails to act readily.

Men who are remarkable for strong memories are not necessarily remarkable for superior thinking powers. Memory must be cultivated and should receive proper attention in early youth. Yet we must bear in mind this fact, that the development of memory is entirely distinct from the development of the thinking and reasoning faculties. It is a fact much to be deplored that the memory is allowed to become too important a factor in the educational work. Pupils are not only allowed, but often forced to rely upon it, at the cost of clear thought and sound reasoning. There are teachers who are either unwilling or unable to see this. I detest any system of education that relies chiefly upon memory, for by *it* the true inwardness of the lesson is lost sight of. Such pupils must become lifeless, as no doubt their teachers are. We have met pupils who could repeat rule after rule, but who never learned how to apply *one*. I have met pupils who could recite page after page in Butler's Analogy or in mental philosophy, but who understood but very little of what they said. And so many young people recite verses from the Bible, but after all know very little of true religion. There are many who can recite poem after poem and can spell a whole class down, who are, after all, utterly unable to express one solid thought. Many parents and teachers are foolish enough to pride themselves upon the memories of their children and pupils. They cram facts, dates, poems, mathematical rules and what not, into the children's minds, overlooking altogether the fact that they are training mere machines; that by their mistaken course they often undermine the children's health, and perhaps cripple them for life.

Aside from the formation of character, the most important part of the educational work is to teach the pupil *to think*—that is, to set his mental faculties to work to enable him to use that great and powerful tool, the brain. What matters it if we know ever so many facts, but cannot use them? We are then, and always will remain, mere one-story people. Great originality appears to be incompatible with dependence on memory. Those who repeat only what others have said, rarely will say anything worthy of themselves. They fill their minds with other people's ideas. They soak in thoughts, so to speak, but never think.

Memory, says a writer, must be viewed somewhat like a stomach. Only so much of the food becomes nourishment as is assimilated by the body, through the process of digestion. A stomach that fails to digest the food it receives is a dyspeptic stomach; so the mind which fails to assimilate the lesson committed by memory, fails to digest it and is a dyspeptic mind. Only those lessons which the mind assimilates will be of service to the future man or woman. Memorizers can tell many things, but they rarely ever say anything very original or profound. Their minds are soaked in other people's ideas, and thereby they have lost the flow and flavor of their own thoughts. They put other people's ideas into their heads, as bald men put other people's hair upon *the top* of their heads. They cover their baldness, and so far so good, but usually they try to make us believe that the luxuriant crop of hair which they carry about is of their own growth. When examining the article, one readily sees that it is false, and the fact quickly becomes known, beyond a doubt, that the wearer of it is bald. In like manner we soon discover, in the course of conversation, the baldness of the memorizer's brain. He can tell only what he has read, and, like a sponge, as a writer says, he is never very particular as to what he draws in. Squeeze it, says the same writer, and you will be sure to see dirty water.

It is of the utmost importance that pupils be early trained to think and to express their own thoughts in words. One idea coming direct from a pupil's mind, is of more value to him than the reading of twenty pages of Shakespeare. The idea may have no value to the world at large, but to the person that uttered the same it is of the utmost importance. Education consists not only in putting things into the mind, but also in drawing them out, in setting the mind to work in order that it may reach conclusions through its own activity. I never or very rarely give facts which can be drawn out of the pupil's mind by judicious questioning. Many teachers view the child's mind as if it were a mere barrel or a cistern to be filled, while in reality the teacher ought to regard it more in the light of a valuable spring, which he is called upon to open, so that the precious clear water may have free flow.

Education does not consist entirely in putting the seed into the ground, but also in preparing the soil, in caring for the plants that have sprung up. Mere telling is not teaching, mere committing to memory is not learning. He who raises memorizers has nothing else to do than to follow the text-book. He who would be called a teacher, must aim in every conceivable way to set the mind to work, he must put fire into the mental furnace that moves the brain, and like a good machinist he must know the engine he handles, and watch over it with care. Some pupils' minds are like old rusty machines. They require a great deal of heat and oil to start them. This operation is sometimes painful, and the teacher is in danger of being suspected of severity; in the end, however, he is sure to reap his reward. The mental engine must, as a rule, be moved by electric and magnetic forces, and the giving out of these powers is what wears out the teacher's energies. It is this that weakens him, yet this fact is but very little seen or understood by the masses, nor by pupils themselves.

Ours is a time which demands thinking teachers, thinking preachers, thinking mechanics and scientists, and for this reason the teacher should do all in his power to force his pupils to think for themselves and to express their own thoughts in their own language. Said a pupil: "I know the answer to your question, but I can't tell it." "No," said I, "you do not know it, for only that which we can tell or write down in clear comprehensive language, we know. Only that and nothing more."

Let us now speak more particularly of the musical memory. When Hans von Bülow at one time played five of the later sonatas by Beethoven from memory, it was regarded as an unheard-of event, and the fact was mentioned by musical journals the country over. It doubtless required tremendous powers of memory to do this. Since then my friend Henry Bonawitz has done the same thing, while another pianist, whose name I cannot recall, played all of Mendelssohn's "Songs without Words" from memory, and did this remarkable feat at one sitting. But if the present boasts of remarkable memories, the past is not in the least behind. When the blind Irish harpist Carolan heard one of Viotti's violin concertos, he instantly repeated it upon his harp, although he had never heard it before. When Mozart was in Rome during the Easterweek (1790), he heard Allegri's Miserere. He begged the Pope for a copy of this beautiful composition, but this request was positively refused. While attending the rehearsal, Mozart paid close attention, and upon his return home he wrote down the whole composition from memory. To note down from memory such a complicated choral work indicates a prodigious power of memory. Another instance is mentioned showing the power of the same master's memory. He had promised to write a piano and violin sonata for Mad. Schlick, the great violinist. Instead of attending to his promise, he went to work on other things, and postponed the sonata until a few days before the concert, when the new work was to be played. Mozart then composed the sonata in B flat major, and had the entire work ready in his mind, but still delayed the odious task of writing it down. A day before the concert the lady was terrified, having not yet received the manuscript from the composer.

She at once sent a servant to remind him of his duty, whereupon Mozart hastily wrote out the violin part and sent it to the lady. In the concert, however, he played his own part from memory, having never played it before. Instead of being proud of such an achievement, the modest Mozart, fearing to attract attention to himself and his gifts, laid a sheet of music on the instrument. He was absolutely afraid lest the Emperor might discover the fact that he was playing from memory. There are musicians who remember as many as twenty, thirty, and even forty operas, each of which would fill an evening. The blind flutist Dullon knew 125 concertos by heart, and distinguished each by a certain number. Other remarkable facts might be given, but I must pass on.

The mind readily remembers melodies, yes, certain tunes have haunted us for weeks, or have gone with us through life. Tunes usually are connected with incidents, and the one produces the other on memory's page. Tunes open the floodgates of memory, and cause scenes of other days to pass vividly before us. Though the leaves of our life's tree may have been frosted by the approaching winter, we still love to dwell upon the warm days of our spring and summer.

"When through life unblest we rove,
  Losing all that made life dear,
Should some notes we used to love
  In days of boyhood meet our ear,
Oh how welcome breathes the strain,
  Wakening thoughts that long have slept,
Kindling former smiles again
  In faded eyes that long have wept.

"Like the gale that sighs along
  Beds of oriental flowers,
Is the grateful breath of song,
  That once was heard in happier hours:
Filled with balm the gale sighs on,
  Though the flowers have sunk in death;
So, when pleasure's dream is gone,
  Its memory lives in music's breath."

Deep, deep into the heart goes the song that takes us out of our every day life and guides us, as it were, up to a mountain, from whence we behold the distant landscape through which we wandered. Oh how strong is the yearning to tread once more those paths so wrought with youthful pleasures, and how stern the irrevocable command, to pass on to the silent grave! Ah, the imagination *may* take us there, the gale sweeping over these pleasure grounds may fan our weary brow, but it fails to bring us the fragrance it once did. Yet who would not be willing to be led again and again by the gentle hand of song, to see once more the lawns where we played as children, the bowers where we whiled away our time with those we loved best? As the sun's warm rays of the Indian summer plays in vain around the tree, it being unable to bring forth new life, the sap having waned at the approach of winter, so does the recollection of the past come to us through the medium of song, sweet in itself, but unable to give us the pleasures belonging to it, or the power of enjoying them. Well did a writer say, that there is no joy in the true memory of music, but a sadness made sweet and holy, because it is inspired by the purest spiritual sympathy, and has its birth and death in melody.

A strong retentive memory is very useful to a musician. Not only does it enable him to afford pleasures to willing listeners at any time or place, but by playing or singing without the aid of notes, he is free, and is thereby enabled to perform with more liberty and sentiment. The close musical reader is fettered, a good share of his mental activity is expended upon reading the notes, upon observing expression marks, while, if he were free from this bondage, he could throw his whole soul into the performance. The musician who sings or plays from memory is a second-hand improviser, he forgets self, he lives in the music and not in the notes or in his surroundings. This is the reason why musicians prefer to play from memory, and it is the lack of this faculty that keeps so many respectable players from soaring aloft on the wings of their imaginations. The musician who plays from memory is as the bird that flies unfettered ; the musician, however, who is tied to his notes, is as the bird that is tied to a string.

A good memory is something to be admired and to be worked for. The masses, however, are very apt to overrate it, hence Bülow's performance of five of Beethoven's later sonatas from memory was by many considered a greater feat than the performance itself. Such people extol the artist at the expense of art. No matter how we may admire the memorizer, let us not be unmindful of the fact that the memory is, after all, as has been said, but one of the lower faculties of the human mind.

While the strength of the memory depends upon training, it is a power that cannot be forced. Not all are gifted alike. If a powerful memory is to the musician as a portfolio in which he carries his music, the portfolios of some contain *many*, those of others contain but *few* pieces, if any at all. Most of them might be better filled than they are. Parents and teachers often err in discouraging young pupils, when playing from memory. Rather encourage them, but see to it that what they play from memory is correctly played. Slovenly, careless playing from memory, leaving parts out or changing others, ought to be discouraged, and in this particular the teacher cannot be too careful. If a little one catches a tune and plays it on the piano, the teacher should be pleased, but he should guard against this practice, whenever it absorbs too much time and crowds the regular lesson into the background.

It must be said that he who remembers many dance tunes, has not as good a memory as he who plays but one sonata by Beethoven, or a fugue by Bach. Some persons have very incorrect and treacherous memories. When attempting to play without notes, they fare like the Western legislator who was ambitious to make a speech. Said he: "Mr. Speaker, when I reflect upon the character of George Washington—", and here he stopped. Beginning a second time, he said : "Mr. Speaker, when I reflect on the character of George Washington—", and again his memory failed him, and he stopped. He started for a third time, but ended with the same result. At last a waggish member rose and said : "Mr. Speaker, I rise to a point of order: it is not proper for a member of this house to cast reflections on the character of George Washington :"

and amidst shouts of laughter, the man whose memory betrayed him had to subside. Let this be a lesson to all of us.

If you attempt to play from memory, in public, be very sure that you are the master of your faculties. A failure under such circumstances is sure to bring ridicule upon you, because of your unsuccessful pretense.

Many players never get a correct impression of a piece upon the tablet of their memory; others succeed in this direction, but are very easily disturbed and misled. Some take in a piece quickly and forget it in a few days; others must hammer and hammer until the notes remain fast, and these usually are the persons who retain an impression for a long time.

As a rule the blind have the strongest memories. It is nature's plan, that when one sense is denied us, other faculties are strengthened in order to compensate for the loss sustained. In our asylums, the blind sing whole oratorios, and play complete symphonies; rarely do they ever forget what is once committed. When considering the difficulties presented by such works to those *gifted* with eyesight, we may comprehend what it means for the blind to sing or play them from memory. It might be said, that the memory easily grasps the melody, yet even this is difficult in such large compositions, for they modulate much, and often change in other respects. But what shall be said of those who remember the altos and tenors, or the inner voices of an orchestral score? This requires memory pure and simple.

Having said so much on this subject, it will become plain that the cultivation of musical memory should receive a pupil's attention. In this work, as in all other educational processes, we should be systematic; that is, our plan for reaching a given end, should be based on good reasoning. How then should you proceed? Before answering this question let me remark, that a lack of memory does not imply a lack of musical talent. Great musicians have been known to be poor memorizers, while most of them are forgetful in matters of every day life.

He who would use the mind, should know the mind. He should know its operations as well as its capacities. It would be worse than cruel to require of a child's memory what it cannot perform, yet the experiment is daily made, simply because teachers know but little of the mind. Let teachers watch their own memories, and ascertain what may be asked of pupils. Many musicians seem hardly conscious of the fact that they have minds. Let music teachers study that which comes from within, the *subjective*, as well as that which comes from without, the *objective*. Let them strive to be thinking players and singers, for thinking leads to correct teaching, to good judgment, and to correct performances.

In training a pupil's memory, begin with phrases, with easy melodies and chord combinations, then proceed gradually. First commit parts of pieces, then endeavor to play the whole. But, as has been said, whatever you commit should be a perfect performance. Impress all runs, and chord combinations specially upon your mind, in order that you may have a correct impression of them. Once a piece is incorrectly learned and memorized, it is difficult ever to correct the mistakes. Some musicians when playing from memory, play as if they had the notes before them, they simply read the notes from a copy which they see before them. Others play according to phrases, and by rules of harmony. The latter course is the better. Every singer and player has his own methods of playing or singing from memory. But whatever that method may be, the memory should not be disturbed by trying to commit many things at once; in other words, give the ideas time to settle. He whose mind turns to many things in quick succession, he who attempts many things, rarely ever will succeed in memorizing anything well; nay, he will impair the powers of his memory. Concentrate your powers on one piece. I have known musicians who, in order to memorize a composition, copied it repeatedly.

In closing, let me warn you not to bestow too much praise upon the exhibition of musical memory. Do not be dazzled by it, but judge of the performance independently of the display of memory. No musician of high-art ideas will endeavor to astonish by a display of his powers of memory. By all means train the memory, but do not allow it to become the main attraction of your or your pupils' performances.

WOMAN IN MUSIC.

It may well be said that woman is the mainstay of the church and the cause of missions, without casting any reflection upon the many excellent men who are workers in Christ's vineyard. Yes, take woman out of the church, deprive missions of her aid, and see what the condition of these causes would be. In a like manner, woman in this country has been the supporter of music and art in general, and without woman's aid, music would never have become what it now is.

Man is more a creature of the head, woman of the heart. It is, therefore, but natural that woman should delight in music, the language of the heart's emotions. Through her ministering spirit the art has been domiciled in our homes; she has carried it triumphantly into our concert rooms and opera houses; she has kept it fresh in the sanctuary, and, what is still more, she has been a faithful and devoted teacher of the art. Would that American boys could be persuaded to practice the divine art to some degree at least, for it would prove to be a means of culture, tending to remove that self-asserting spirit so prominent among our youths. More than that, it would be a delightful recreation and a great source of pleasure.

My object is to show woman's influence in the fields of musical art. That woman practiced the art in ancient times is plain, from the fact that Miriam and her maids sang and played after the destruction of the Egyptians in the Red Sea, and other instances might be mentioned. That the art was also practiced by the women of other nations is evident from the bas-reliefs found in Egypt, Assyria and other countries, on which women are seen playing instruments. The Grecians had their nine muses; they had their sirens and other female musicians, priestesses, and so forth.

But for my purpose there is no necessity to explore [the writings of the ancient authors, for music is a Christian art. Both music and woman existed before Christ, but our Saviour's birth was the period from which music really began to develop, and from which woman began to be elevated in the social scale. Thus we see that both music and woman have much to be thankful for to Christianity, and it is quite natural that woman should readily take to it. There can be no doubt that woman sang in the earlier churches. She was admitted to worship, and she probably joined in singing the Psalms and hymns. Strange that in the light of Christianity, woman should rise so slowly, and that it required so many years to raise her from her inferior place to the position she occupies now. Behold the torture poor woman endured during the dark ages, and even later, under the charges of witchcraft. Only when the great book is opened shall we learn what poor woman suffered during thousands of years, but especially during the tyranny of the dark ages. She was friendless; not even the church defended her or condemned the superstitious belief in witches.

That woman during such a period should neither study nor practice the art of music is easily believed. Yes, she was even deprived of the privilege of singing in the house of God, for choirs in those times were made up of priests, friars and monks. Yet, no doubt, many a home resounded with gentle lullabies, which flowed from mothers' lips ; no doubt many a hymn was heard within the narrow home, and so also were heard the old folk-songs, those popular airs which come and go like the summer birds. As they make their nests under our roofs without asking for permission, so these songs irresistibly take lodgings in our minds and hearts ; we love them, but we never ask whence they came or who produced them. These airs no doubt made up what may be called the house-music of those times; but who can doubt that this house-music also resounded in the fields, whenever and wherever woman had to labor? It is possible that some of these old songs were produced by women ; especially is this claim made with regard to lullabies that have come down to us in Germany, France and other countries. It is far more reasonable to believe that these little ditties came from the heads and hearts of mothers than from the rougher natures of workingmen, or from warlike cavaliers and barons.

As in olden times, when Christ dwelt upon earth, and in the middle ages, women were often employed as singers and mourners at funerals. Mrs. Ritter says that many of the folk-songs, which, because of their great love power, live so long and exert such a strong influence, were composed by women. There is, however, no evidence of this statement. But if woman has not composed them, she no doubt was the means of spreading them by teaching them to her children. Bear in mind that women were uneducated in those times ; they could neither read nor write. The system of writing music was very imperfect and difficult to learn, hence these songs had to be perpetuated by committing them to memory. All nations have such old airs, while Germany probably has the largest number stored away in that grand old collection by Von Arnim and Brentano, entitled "The Boys' Wonderhorn." Not only was this style of music cultivated among European nations, away in Persia, in Arabia, in Hindoo, we find many and most beautiful specimens of popular songs. May we not also believe that many nuns, leading secluded lives in their convents, having very little communication with the outer world, and especially at a time when the means of communication were very deficient, produced their own songs of praise for their worship. It is also reasonable to believe that the ladies in castles, who waited fondly for the return of husbands and brothers from long and far-off wars, gave vent to their loneliness through the medium of song, and when the sad and ever startling news of death came, music must have been to them a solace. Where else could they get the songs through which they poured out their feelings except in their own hearts and minds?

During the time when the troubadours and the minnesingers flourished, a higher and a better style of music came into use. We learn that these singers were accompanied by female musicians known as the trouveresses. The names of some of these are still known. It is claimed that they produced many original songs, but this is denied by some writers. What has been said with regard to the troubadours is also true of the minstrels who came later.

It is a most remarkable fact that in the sixteenth century, when woman was excluded from church choirs, a woman, St. Cecilia, was proclaimed to be the patron saint of our beloved art. We do not know whether she was a musician, but so much is sure, she was a godly woman and died a martyr's death. There are many legends told concerning her, according to which, she is said to have resided in Rome, and then again in Sicily. But be this as it may, it is a remarkable fact that a woman was selected as patron saint of the divine art.

The Reformation was a necessity, for the work of civilization through the gospel had been retarded in many ways, and a new impulse was needed. With the Reformation began the real growth of our art, and from that time also dates the onward movement of woman's elevation. The Reformation at once admitted woman into choirs; in fact, congregational singing is one of the first outgrowths of this movement. The church had fettered the art, and as it is a growing plant, it sought a new outlet, and this led to the invention of the opera. On the stage, woman quickly proved that she was possessed of great capabilities, and not until she had displayed her powers in this new field was she admitted to Catholic choirs. The invention of the opera took place about the year 1600, and in looking over the history of music since that time, one must acknowledge that woman has indeed accomplished great things. Her musical progress and her advancement in social influence have always kept pace with each other. What a great number of lady singers and players grace musical history during these 300 years! How many books have been written about them; how many operas and sacred songs have been written for them; what vast floral and poetic offerings have been laid at their feet, and how richly they have been paid by kings and princes. With what ovations have they been met, and how many of them have been decorated by governments! You may have heard of the great *Mara*, of whom Goethe says so much, of Gabrieli, who moved the masses to tears and frenzy by her singing.

Catalani's name reaches into our times; she had a most wonderful voice. The sum of $1200 was paid her in England for singing "God Save the King," and $12,000 was paid her for singing at one festival. Malibran was a most fascinating singer; Schroeder Devrient was the idol of all great musicians; Sontag was beloved the world over, and when she died all lovers of art mourned over the loss. Lind, the pure and intellectual, the charitable Jenny Lind, will never be forgotten. In New York, she gave in one week $50,000 to the poor. Then there is Nillson, and, last, Patti, who received greater pay and was longer on the stage than any other singer. She was paid from $5000 to $6000 for one concert performance. As to our own country, we have during the past twenty-five years produced quite a number of great singers. There are Kellogg, Cary, Albani, Nikita, Hauk, Thursby, and many others who are known the world over.

The work these women had to do, the privations they often had to endure in order to fit themselves for their chosen calling, and the good they did through their performances cannot be told in words. They came usually from humble homes, and, rising on the wings of music, they reached positions of honor and gained at times great wealth. They gave the world untold pleasure by their artistic interpretations of art works; they added largely to our culture and refinement. But we must not forget the many women who excelled as pianists, at the head of whom stands Clara Schumann, a nobler musician than whom never graced art history. Though nearly seventy years old, she still plays in European concerts, never failing to arouse great enthusiasm. Then there is Essipoff, Mehlig, Schiller, Krebs, Menter, and our own King, Carreno and Stevens. But we must also mention the celebrated lady violinists that shed lustre on woman's name and fame. In the fore rank of these stand the sisters Millanollo, who set the world nearly wild with their performances; Mme. Neruda, who was a true artist; Camilla Urso, who has almost become Americanized, and Theresa Tua, who now astonishes the artistic circles in Europe with her skill.

In the line of musical literature several names deserve mention. Perhaps foremost in the ranks of those who have wielded the pen in behalf of music is Madame Raymond Ritter, of Poughkeepsie, who has written excellent essays, in which she displays much learning. Then there is Elsa Polko, who has written many pretty stories; Anna Morsh, who has also written very excellent sketches; while our own Amy Fay has made herself famous through her letters. Though they contain but little that is of value to the practical musician, these letters have been widely read and have afforded much pleasure.

We have seen what woman has done in the fields of music, and now it becomes my duty to draw your attention to the fact that in the line of musical composition, woman does not stand as high as in the fields of executive art. We have a Rosa Bonheur who stands high in the line of painting. There are a few women who use the chisel with truly artistic skill; in poetry we have many illustrious names, only one of which I shall mention, Mrs. Browning. In the fields of fiction woman has excelled, and the one name, George Eliot, is sufficient to prove that woman has deep thinking and close reasoning faculties. But while woman has done much that is grand in the fields of literature and art, in the field of musical composition she has never reached an eminent position. We have women composers that are mentioned in our encyclopædias, but they are few—only four in the seventeenth century, twenty-seven in the eighteenth century, and seventeen in the nineteenth. Let me mention a few names: Amelia, sister of Frederick the Great, composed operas and cantatas. Leopoldina Blahatka, of Vienna, published seventy pieces, some of which were admired by Beethoven. Josephina Long, Mendelssohn's friend, composed charming songs. Fanny Hensel, Mendelssohn's sister, wrote many pretty things. Louisa Rugat composed songs which enjoyed great popularity in France. Madame Schumann, the wife of the famous composer, produced many fine numbers. Madame Garcia wrote but few songs, but they were excellent pieces. Virginia Gabriel, the English ballader, wrote songs that were popular wherever the English tongue is spoken.

Why is it that woman does not excel in the fields of musical composition? Many reasons have been assigned, but none of them are satisfactory. When considering woman's emotional nature, it would seem as if the field of musical composition would be best suited for her activity, for music is the language of emotions. Why is it, then, that woman failed to enter this field with more success? An organism as sensitive to the influences of the beautiful, and as responsive to religious ideas, an organism as imaginative and emotional as is that of woman, should have given us the best of works. Some claim that woman lacks the necessary reasoning powers, and that she does everything intuitively. The latter statement is true in part, but the former, namely, that the thinking powers of man are superior, I cannot subscribe to unqualifiedly. True, women have excelled in the study of languages; they have become good scientists, astronomers, mathematicians, lawyers and physicians; they have successfully entered the lecture field, they have filled editorial chairs, they have been popular novelists, all of which goes to prove that woman has fine thinking powers. Yet why does she not excel as a musical composer? In painting, in sculpture, in poetry, as has been said, woman has reached high positions; as singers and players women have excelled, why not as composers? Not one musical work from woman's pen has ever held itself in the world's repertoire. Says Mr. Upton, "Man has been the creative representative." Beethoven has shown the depth of music, its majesty, its immortality, Mendelssohn its elegance of form, Händel its solemnity and grandeur, Mozart its wondrous grace and sweetness, Haydn its purity, freshness and simplicity, Schumann its romance, Chopin its poetry and tender melancholy, Schubert its richness in melody, Bach its massive foundations, Berlioz its grotesqueness and supernaturalism, Liszt and Wagner its poetical idealism; but in the fields of higher art-music woman has been silent, or, if she has been productive, her works have had but an ephemeral existence. The only answer that has the shadow of reasonableness about it is this, that music, being the language of emotions, and woman being preëminently an emotional creature, she cannot project herself outward, any more than she can outwardly express the other mysteries of her nature. Woman lives and acts in emotion, but she does not behold the results of her actions as man sees them. Woman is governed by intuition, man is governed more by cool reasoning. Hence it is that woman comes more quickly to conclusions than man, but she is not always able to assign a reason for those conclusions. It is a great mistake to suppose that men and women are made alike. They differ in their aspirations, their traits and dispositions. Their natures manifest themselves differently. The two characters are complementary; what is lacking in the one the other has, hence the two together make the whole human being. The one is preëminently a head power, the other more preëminently a heart power. The mind must control the emotions; it discerns them; man can watch his emotional nature better than a woman can watch and analyze hers. She is preëminently a creature of heart; she follows her emotions and will power, and herein she is usually right, because hers is a higher moral nature; she comes into the world with purer emotions and higher aspirations. Says a writer, to confine woman's emotions to the expression in music, would be about as difficult a task for her as it would be for her to express her religion in thoughts. Woman expresses emotions in music as if they were her own, but to deal with them like mathematical problems, to measure and to express them through the voice or through instruments, is a cold-blooded operation, unsuited to woman's peculiar faculties.

Mr. Upton claims that when woman advances in years her emotional nature ceases to operate with its former intensity, hence she often loses interest in music, while, as a rule, men continue in their devotion to it. Another writer goes so far as to say that a mother's love for her children undergoes a change when these have reached the years of self-support, while man's love, though it was not as intense as that of the mother, remains the same till the end. I cannot agree with these writers, for there are too many living illustrations to the contrary. Look at Mrs. Schumann, now far over sixty years of age, and yet she is as devoted to her art as she ever was. I have played for aged ladies who were more violently aroused by the power of music than younger women. I believe that women give up music so easily when entering active family life because they never studied it as an art. They know not what good music is; they are fed on light, trashy diet; they studied and used the art merely as a personal attraction, as a means to rule in society. When other duties and pleasures cross the path of such women, naturally enough they drop their music; it ceases to have attractions for them, for it served its purpose; it never had entered the innermost recesses of their hearts and minds. What else could be expected of such a shallow education, if this word is at all applicable here. Give woman a solid musical education, and she will remain true to the art. It is also claimed that woman could never endure the hardships which are incident to great composers' lives. She is not fitted to endure the abuse, the severity of criticism, which is heaped upon them. No doubt man can endure such trials better than woman, still, if woman had been designed for the work of musical composition, this power of endurance would have been given to her also. No doubt she is a finer feeling mortal than man, hence more sensitive to criticism. Strange to say, however, woman is not deterred by fear of criticism from entering other fields of art and those of literature, and even of politics. If she can face it in one field, she surely can face it in another.

Music is purely an abstract art. It has nothing tangible about it. The painter and sculptor see their work, the poet reads his, the musician only hears his. Perhaps, if the art were more tangible, women would more readily become productive musicians. Or, perhaps, if it were merely an art without a positive science underlying it, she would do better. As it is, the field of musical composition does not seem to be open to her. There may be hidden reasons for this state of things which we have not as yet discerned in woman's intellectual and emotional make-up; but it may also be that the fault lies in a lack of education, in the neglect of former years. Music is a most delicate plant; it seems to grow only under favorable circumstances. The development of music was most effectively checked in England during the reign of Cromwell. Up to his time England had produced good musicians, excellent composers; but nearly two hundred years were required to overcome this check of musical growth, and it is only during the past twenty-five years that England may point to productive musicians of note. During these two hundred years England fostered the art, she held festivals, but she failed to produce eminent composers. May it not be that woman, having for ages been neglected, having been denied the boon of a higher education, will after many years of study excel also in this only field of art productiveness? It is only of late years that women as a sex enter more seriously into their musical studies, and we have at least the right to hope that in years to come this one shortcoming will be corrected. There was a time when it was said that women could not do this or that; but behold what they have done, and what they are doing! Let all women study with seriousness, with diligence; let them train their minds and develop their emotions; let them absorb the very essence of art, hoping that continued culture and training will also open to them this one field of human activity, so eminently attractive to their nature.

As men have attained higher views of woman's sphere and power, they have lent a helping hand; they have assisted her in attaining to a better education. It may require long years of labor and study for woman to become a successful musical composer; but if she aims not in the right direction she will never attain this desirable end. Behold how indifferent men have, as a rule, been to higher art culture in this country. If they practiced music at all, it was done in a shallow and meaningless manner. Through the impulses given by foreign-born teachers, through the more thorough education of the last two generations, native talent began to develop, and many years must yet pass before we shall be a musical people in the full sense of the word. But unless we toil and train unceasingly, we shall never reach a high art standard. Let me say, then, to all young men and young women, study music; study it practically and theoretically; learn to appreciate pure art, and let us wait for the blessed results. America has pointed to many new ways; American women have greater educational advantages than have the mass of their sisters abroad; who knows but that America may yet give us a great female composer. Music should be made an elective, a fit substitute for any other study. There are college professors who claim that music is an easy study, and not an equivalent of others found in the curriculum. Let me invite you to try this study, take up music as an art and as a science, and in a year's time you will acknowledge that there is not a branch now taught in this university, metaphysics excepted, that presents more peculiar difficulties, that needs longer time for complete mastery, than the subjects of harmony, counterpoint and musical composition. Talent is what is required; gifts are the long poles that knock down the high-hanging fruits. By constant training, talent and gifts are developed. Let us, therefore, do our duty, letting the future take care of itself.

But whether we shall see the day when women become great composers, or not, this much is sure, that woman is eminently fitted for the work of teaching. With woman's progress came more serious views of the art, and, therefore, more serious views of the work of teaching it. Hitherto, most lady music teachers engaged in this work as a mere pastime, as a means to earn a little pin-money; women now enter our professional fields with the expectation of making the work of teaching a life calling. Women no longer regard marriage as the chief end of life; nay, they begin to view life with greater calmness and with a clearer mind than formerly; they are determined to be useful; hence they choose a calling; and I am glad to notice that they engage most seriously in their preparations for this work. It is this feature of my work here that interests me most intensely, and it is this feature *more* than any other that at times draws out my deepest sympathies. Music teaching is congenial to woman's nature, and those who will work hard are sure to meet with success. The standard of our profession is rising steadily, and if you would be a worthy member, you must work steadily and diligently; you must be wide awake. Ladies especially should devote themselves to singing, for not only will it prove a lucrative study, but it is the foundation of a thorough musical education, and, what is still more, it is conducive to bodily development. It gives us also more lovable and sympathetic voices, thereby increasing our social powers. We are too loud-voiced as yet, and need toning down. Remember what the poet praised in Annie Laurie:—

"Her voice was low and sweet."

If woman is not a composer, she has been closely connected with the production of great works. She has always exercised a powerful influence on composers' lives. Run over the works of Mozart, and thirty-three of them are dedicated to women, very few to men. Beethoven's name is thus connected with not less than thirty-five ladies, Schumann with thirty-six, Chopin with thirty-nine, and so forth. These ladies must all have been closely connected with the composers, and perhaps with the special works dedicated to them. If love or friendship were not the direct ties, there must have been esteem and admiration, for men do not dedicate their productions to any one or every one. A dedication is a mark of honor, a token of respect. Most composers were happy in love and chose wisely; a few only remained single or were illy matched. Bach was married twice, each time happily; yet the second marriage was the more congenial. He was a sturdy Christian, his character was well balanced, his wives were frugal, good managers and peaceable women. Händel was not married. He loved his mother most tenderly, and next to her he was wedded to his art. In England he enjoyed the friendship of the best ladies; most noteworthy among them were the Queens Anne and Caroline. Händel was not very sociable, nor was he domestic in his habits. He had a hot temper, and a wedded life would likely have proved to be stormy. It is said that two of his pupils loved him ardently, and both were ready to marry him. In one case the foolish remark of a mother broke off the prospective marriage. When the daughter expressed her willingness to marry Händel, the mother said, with indignation, "What! my daughter marry a fiddler!" Think of Händel as a fiddler! This remark wounded the great composer, and he would have nothing more to do with the family. After the mother's death, the father approached the composer again on the subject of matrimony, but Händel coldly replied that the time had passed for such an alliance. The lady, who loved ardently, fell into a decline and soon afterwards died. The other lady was one in high social standing. He could have married her on condition that he would forsake his profession, but the love for music was greater than that for woman, and the engagement came to naught. Beethoven loved a number of ladies and was eager to marry, but all his endeavors in this direction proved fruitless. He never found a fitting companion, and, indeed, it is a most unanswerable question as to what sort of a woman Beethoven's wife should have been. He remained chaste, as he wrote, says a writer. On my shelf stands a little volume entitled "Beethoven's Loves," and most interesting reading it is. He loved early and loved often, and there is reason to believe that he was quite susceptible to woman's charms. He imagined, for instance, that a certain lady, Amelia de Sebald, a great singer, loved him, because she looked at him intently, but when he proposed, he was promptly refused, "Because," as the lady said to a friend, "he was so ugly and half-cracked." Foolish Beethoven, he failed to realize that as a musician he was an object of admiration and curiosity, and that everybody looked at him when passing. The most noted among the ladies he loved was the Countess Guiccardi, to whom he dedicated his famous Moonlight Sonata. No doubt this love was genuine, and one can feel it in that matchless sonata, but he was doomed to disappointment, for he was not her equal in rank. She afterwards married a count, while Beethoven remained single. This lady exercised a decided influence upon our composer, and no doubt this love found its outlet in some of his matchless productions.

Haydn, the pure and good, loved a girl with all his heart, but she died while he spent some time in a monastery. He married unwisely, his wife being a regular shrew, a bigoted, ill-tempered, fault-finding woman, who made his life bitter. Yet he was blessed with the friendship of many noble-minded women, chief among whom was a Mrs. Genzinger. Doubtless these women inspired him in the production of his last great works, the Creation and the Seasons.

Mozart had some early love affairs, but he never loved seriously until he visited the Weber family in Manheim. Weber, who was the great composer's uncle, had two daughters, Aloyse and Constance. He fell in love with the former, and so deep was his affection, that he could scarcely wait for the time when he should see her again. Three months later he returned to the family, but the girl scarcely recognized him. She had fallen in love with a worthless actor, from whom she was finally separated. Mozart feigned indifference; he sang merry songs, and soon began to make love to the younger sister, to whom he was finally married. She proved to be a kind and loving wife, and no doubt made Mozart's life a happy one. He immortalized her in one of his operas, and it is beyond a doubt true that many of his best works were inspired by her.

Schubert never was married; it is even doubted whether he ever was seriously in love. In fact, he was not in a position to support a wife. Yet he had his sentimental friendships, and, had he married, his love would have been somewhat platonic in its character. Like Beethoven, he was unattractive in person. While spending some years on the estates of the rich and noble Esterhazy family, being engaged in giving music lessons to the Prince's daughters, he flirted for awhile with the chambermaid, and it is owing to her influence that he produced his beautiful divertissement, Op. 16. This number contains certain Hungarian melodies which this lady was fond of singing. Next he fell in love with the younger of the two Princesses, a mere child in years, who never knew of the secret affection of his heart. This girl was the secret influence that led him to write many of his best songs.

Schumann loved only once, but most intensely. He had a hard struggle to get the prize of his affections, for the girl's father was bitterly opposed to the match. Schumann had finally to invoke the aid of the law in order to secure his Clara. She was a famous player, and proved to be a most devoted wife, who exercised a powerful influence upon his mind and heart. Not less than one hundred and thirty-eight songs did he write to please her, and no doubt many of his best works were inspired by her. Early in life he was infatuated with a lady, a Miss Ernestine von Fricken, but it came to naught.

Mendelssohn was happily married; his wife's name was Cecilia. She was loving and true to the end. Mendelssohn had a deep love for his sister Fanny. She inspired him to write many of his great works. When she was about to die, May 14th, 1847, she said to him, "Depend upon it, by my next birthday you will be with me." He died four days before that date, on the 4th of November.

Chopin is the romanticist whom all ladies' love, and his own life was a continued romance. He was more of a woman than a man, hence it is easily understood how a love sprang up between him and the famous George Sand, who was more of a man than a woman. Early in life he felt an attachment for a Polish girl, whom he, however, forgot after he fell in love with George Sand. The poor girl was true to him till her end, and, as she could not administer to his happiness, she cared for Chopin's parents. It is difficult to say what was the attraction between him and the French lady with whom he lived for many years; neither can the story of their sad separation be told in this connection.

Weber was for a time warmly attached to an opera singer, Gretchen Lang, but, had he married her, it would have proved an unfortunate alliance. Happily, he met another musical lady, Carolina Brandt, whom he loved passionately. The first-named lady, however, caused a great deal of trouble, for she had gained a powerful influence over the composer. At last he met Miss Brandt for a second time; his former love was rekindled, and the two were married. She was a noble woman, true to her husband and his art. He counseled with her; she spurred him to continued activity; and while she saw much happiness in life, she also drank deeply of the cup of sorrow. She remained true to her ill-fated husband, who died in a foreign land.

But I cannot cease telling love stories without at least mentioning Wagner, the last of Germany's great musicians. He married early but unhappily. To his credit it must be said, however, that he never revealed anything that might lessen public esteem of his wife; but we know that she failed to enter into his art aspirations, and as the earlier life of Wagner was one of trouble and privation, her surroundings were such that, without a full appreciation of her husband's mission, she naturally became unhappy. She died in 1866. Four years later he married the second time. Liszt's daughter, Cossoma, had been married to Bülow the pianist, but the two were not congenial. She sought a divorce, and then married Wagner, with whom she lived happily till his death in 1883. She is a true, high-minded woman, and was fully worthy of a place by the side of so great a man. She understood him, exerted almost a magical influence over him; she inspired him in his work, and in every way made his life happy.

And now that I have shown woman's influence in musical art, let me urge you to follow and to imitate the illustrious women whom I have mentioned. Take it seriously with your art, for unless you are serious in your study of music, you will fail to be benefited by it. Study only the pure and the good, and aim to be worthy of so great an art. Study and teach with a singleness of purpose, always aiming to make mankind better and happier. Join every good enterprise calculated to advance our art; use it for the relief of the poor, for the enjoyment of your friends, for the benefit of your own souls. Never abuse it; ever be faithful in your devotions, remembering, that though your name may never be mentioned in a lecture or in a book, you should always feel a deep interest in woman's welfare and elevation. Bear in mind that music and woman are closely allied in the history of Christian civilization. Spread culture wherever you can and organize musical societies wherever there is an opening for them. Though your life as a teacher may be spent in a secluded spot, teach only the truth, bearing in mind that God loves the art; that He has given it to us for a wise and a noble purpose, and that you are engaged in a work which is honorable and praiseworthy, and that He will reward you and bless you according to your fidelity. These are among the pleasant duties that fall to your lot. With you rests the future welfare of our art; with you rests a part at least of the civilization of your own country and people. Sow good seeds and be hopeful of good fruit. Always develop the religious side of your work, for in this particular woman can do much good. Improve the music in church and Sabbath school, by lending your aid ungrudgingly, wherever it is needed, and thus you will have the realizing sense of having lived and labored for a good purpose.

With a quotation from an excellent German musical writer, I will close my article. "There is no living soul so capable of enjoying and correctly judging of a work of art, as a fairly cultivated woman, for her whole inner life is in itself a work of art. Even the highest kind of men have something formless and unfinished about their natures. The hasty demands of life do not stop to inquire whether it be Sabbath or not; they surprise men amid the worship of the beautiful, and scarcely give them time to refrain from profanation of the altar. But the life of woman, calm as a festival day, how full of harmony may it not, should it not be? When the storm-bells of passion have rung out, then pure ether remains behind, and in such minds the impression made by a work of art is correct and immediate, for they are prepared to receive it, themselves serene and pure, as bridal devotion."

HARMONY.

When I speak of theory, I do not use the term in that offensive sense which implies the impracticable as opposed to the sensible and useful. My object is not to belittle theory, but to present it to you in such a light that you may be induced to study it. Theory, in the common acceptation of the term, means an exposition of the general principles of an art or a science, and when viewing it in this light, it follows that musical theory really embraces the whole science of music. It touches upon acoustics, upon the laws of chords, upon the rules of composition, in fact, its field is immense. Many persons who endeavor to master this science without a teacher, soon find themselves in the predicament of inexperienced travelers, who start out alone on a trip over the prairies or over a mountain range. They seem to get along well, but presently they lose the trail; they find neither roads nor sign-posts; they miss their reckonings, and before they are aware of the fact, they are utterly lost. In dismay they retreat, and reaching home at last, they warn every one against making any attempts at exploring such a wild, rough country. Now, what is the real difficulty in the way of young students when exploring the fields of harmony? What is it that so quickly disheartens those in search of theoretical information? It is this; students are compelled to think and to work in another language, if it can indeed be said that we think in any language. The signs and sounds used in this science are different from those of the word language; pupils find it at first difficult to apply them, and in dismay they are heard to say that harmony is the most difficult study they ever attempted to master. This, however, is only an illusion. It is no more true than the assertion that music is all play and requires no brain-work. He who meets the study of harmony in a friendly spirit, with a calm frame of mind, he who takes time to study his problems, will eventually be forced to acknowledge that all things connected with the study of music are beautiful, and that the science of the art is just as attractive as the practice of it.

Theory is the science and the study of the laws requisite to combine tones so as to produce harmony and melody. It combines the study of harmony and musical composition; it is the art of inventing correct melodies, and of supplying them with good harmony. While the principles of acoustics underlie all musical art, in this study we deal more with principles of experience and observation than with natural science. The study of the principles of acoustics never leads to a musical art development. Students who dwell upon the single tone rarely ever get beyond it. Some of the most learned nations, as, for instance, the ancient Grecians, who studied the tone from its acoustic standpoint and not from its artistic, had no art music.

There are those who view harmony only as the science of laws necessary for the combination of chords; on the other hand, some demand that it should also explain the connection of the senses with the mind. The scholar who pursues the study from the first standpoint exclusively, loses much of its æsthetic beauty, and necessarily comes down to cold mathematical rules; hence Marx, who was a great authority, said that he would have nothing to do with purely mathematical harmony lessons. Those, on the other hand, who follow the second course, are often guilty of overshooting the mark, losing themselves in metaphysical speculations that lead to no good.

Harmony, as the grammar of music, teaches the rules according to which tones are combined into chords; but it is not its mission to prove the effect of these tone combinations upon the ear and the soul. Nothing is more difficult and deceptive than to speculate about our sensations and emotions. They play into each other; they are so mingled and mixed with each other that the most cautious observer could not positively define them, and show where and how they begin, as well as where and how they end. There is not in our hearts a single unmixed emotion, for one feeling springing up quickly is apt to cause many others to arise. In this play of sentiments, some of our emotions are intensified, others are weakened or wiped away altogether. If the emotions are so uncertain and so difficult to understand, why should we make it a part of harmony? Why should we try to lay down positive laws as to how they should be expressed, and that through the tone, the least tangible material artists are called upon to use? Yet there are theorists who extend the range of this study into such speculations, endeavoring to explore that mysterious domain of emotion in connection with chords and melodies. A study which in itself is so deep and difficult to master is deserving of the undivided attention of the best minds.

The study of harmony is old, though music as an art is young. The ancient Grecians studied out the mathematical proportions of intervals by the aid of the monochord, upon which they could lengthen and shorten a string. This result led them to imagine that they had discovered infallible principles and formulas, by means of which they could master and measure all combinations. This led them to the consideration and study of the single tone, and for this reason they were unable to build up an art such as we now have. The ancient Grecians sought in the tone proportions and intervals the key to the study of the soul, and thus music became to them the foundation of psychology. They sought in the art an explanation of those contradictions that manifest themselves in the human soul, hence ancient Grecian writers regarded music as the science of all sciences; it explained to them the heavens as well as the earth, the body as well as the spirit. In music they sought to find what was the true nature of the human soul, hence every Grecian scholar had to study the theory of the art, for, as has already been said, it was to them the foundation of all learning.

This Grecian idea of music made its influence felt among Christian writers. Only they sought to draw an analogy between religion and music, hence their peculiar explanations and very strange speculations. Let me quote a few of the principles pupils had to learn in those times. Many writers taught the lesson that the triad or threefold chord is a confirmation of the doctrine of the Trinity. The fourfold chord explained to them the four cardinal virtues. They speculated upon the tetrachord in connection with the life of Christ; one-half represented to them the Gospel of St. Matthew describing the humanity of Christ, while the other half showed the end of his life, the rending of the curtain in the temple, the darkening of the sun, etc. The tetrachord of the higher tones represented Christ's resurrection, while the highest tones indicated the ascension. The four tetrachords combined, in the opinion of some of the ancient theorists, represented the four Gospels, while the two modes, the authentic and plagal, were likened to a bridal pair. Arabo, an ancient writer, when speaking of these modes, said that they reach into each other like two wheels, and thus he alludes to the vision of Ezekiel. Manhettas, of Padua, compares music to a tree, the branches of which are arranged in beautiful proportions, its flowers are sweet chords, its fruit is harmony. Bernardus said, music of the universe is a grand whole, which at the bidding of God puts everything into motion, it moves heaven and earth. The octave is an emblem of justice, for the eighth tone was by the ancients called Justice. The fourth refers to the four seasons, the four points of the compass, the four Gospels, the four temperatures, and the four elements. Muris saw in music a picture of the church, and said that it was great as a unit, though divided into many parts. The same author compared the two tetrachords to Mary and Martha, while the two modes plagal and authentic represented love to God and love to our neighbor. The three tetrachords placed above each other, he said, typify the three steps in repentance, they represent also the three kinds of instrument used, wind, string and concussion. These three octaves also represent the Christian graces, Faith, Hope and Charity, and last, but not least, they represent the holy Trinity. Music, being written on four lines, is an emblem of the four Gospels. Seven tones are in the scale, said a writer, and so we have seven sacraments opening the heavens, while the seven tones open the portals of music.

As late as 1702 Andreas Werkmeister, in his theory of music, advanced many strange ideas, only a few of which I will here mention. Says he: "We read in Scripture that God built the world harmoniously. Hence, it is that Noah's ark had the best proportions imaginable, three hundred ells in length, fifty wide and thirty high. When carrying these proportions to the monochord, says the master, they give us the plain triad C. E. G." The tabernacle, the temple, and in fact all sacred buildings were erected on the strictest principles of harmony. Should this be accidental, asks our author? Everywhere we see harmony and order, and out of this all-wise system sprang music. This explains in a measure why music is so pleasing to man, for it is an exhibition of God's wisdom and order, and when these musical proportions reach the ear and through it the heart, they cannot fail to touch us. Hence, Luther said, "that he, who does not love music, has not a good heart, he is a rough block. Why do the people fail to like music," asks our great Reformer? Simply because their souls are in a disturbed condition, their nerves are not easily moved, their systems are not built according to the rules of that eternal harmony and order which underlies nature.

But this is enough of strange and idle speculations. After their unsoundness had been shown and understood, the subject of harmony separated into two divisions. The one followed up the metaphysical side of music and aimed to solve the secret workings of the art; the other depended upon physical principles exclusively and sought through them to lay the foundation for our present system of harmony. The first relied on uncertain speculations, the other depended upon exact facts.

The ancient Grecian ideas were slow to pass away. Thus, even Kepler, the astronomer, revived the ancient Pythagorean theory of a music of the spheres. All Christendom then thought the whole secret of music had been discovered. He also taught that our likes and dislikes for intervals must necessarily be more instinctive than intelligent. Leibnitz, on the other hand, was of the opinion that the soul unconsciously counts the vibrations of bodies. According to Euler, he is the best critic who can turn the unknown countings into known ones. Kant, Herder and Krause, however, are opposed to this theory. The latter day philosophers have decided that while Leibnitz's theory is true, it only solves the first riddle, the sensual influence of music. Helmholtz also advances an idea of this kind. After explaining the unconsciousness of the perceptions of form and law, he says: "We resemble the spirit which we comprehend." If we feel the spiritual powers that operated in the artist, powers which are far superior to our own conscious thinking, we must acknowledge that an immense amount of time, contemplation and labor is required to produce, as well as to comprehend, the same degree of order, connection, proportion and symmetry, which the artist establishes unconsciously through tact and taste, and which by our own tact and taste we can appreciate in an art-work. It is upon this fact that the appreciation of art and art-works depends. We recognize in the first the Genius, that divine spark of creative power, that goes beyond the lines of our own conscious thinking and reasoning, that distinguishes the artist from common mortals. Nevertheless, let us realize that the artist is but a man, as we are, and that we have the same powers of mind as he has, those very powers which have helped to produce the art-work; if it were not so we could not understand his language and its meaning. Herein lies the basis of the moral influence and the pleasant satisfaction which is produced by art-works.

Being a scientist, Helmholtz evidently lacks the courage or the ability to dive into the psychological and metaphysical relations of music. The same is true of all those that make acoustics a specialty. These higher investigations are left to those who study out the æsthetic side of our art. Our study, therefore, has nothing directly to do with the philosophical meaning and object of our art, yet in our lessons, we are often called upon to touch on this very deep and broad subject. The main study, then, before us is that of chord combinations and of a harmonic treatment of melodies.

The science of music, the study of harmony, is a progressive study. The ancients knew nothing of harmony such as we use. When they sang with several voices, they produced the same tune an octave lower or higher. The ancients, therefore, did not deal with chords such as we use. They knew only melody, hence their theory never goes beyond that of the modes (scales). Their musicians, and especially their theorists, were divided into two schools, the Pythagorean and Aristoxenian. The former depended upon mathematical calculations exclusively, the latter upon the ear. The Pythagorean proportions were accepted throughout the Middle Ages, and even up to 1590, as were many other Grecian theories and ideas. As we developed harmony in the modern sense, the Grecian ideas would not hold out, and thus musicians were compelled to step upon the purely empiric field to determine the laws upon which modern music was to be built, and upon the basis of which it could develop throughout coming centuries of progress. These rules once established, the art could and did develop. A real system of chords did not exist until 1720. All harmony prior to that time was written from a contrapuntal standpoint, four voices running by the side of each other, each carrying the melody. A true harmony is a system of laws upon which all chords that occur in music may be written. It must be acknowledged that the works of the last century are still the best authorities, though in many respects they are antiquated, and can no longer be used.

In former times, scores or full harmonic accompaniments were rarely ever fully written out. They gave the bass and added to it chord signatures, from which musicians played. This short-hand writing is called thorough bass. To enable a person to play from a thorough bass or figured bass, a complete knowledge of harmony is required. This study I desire to commend as absolutely necessary for a complete mastery of music. The time has come when no one will dare to pretend to teach the art who has not mastered this science, and in the estimation of musicians, no one, pupil nor teacher, amateur nor artist, should be without thorough training in it. And now that I have commended it, the question, no doubt, is asked: What are the advantages to be derived from this study? The study of harmony is for those who wish to understand and fully enjoy music, vocal or instrumental, as well as for composers. It increases, manifold, both the mental and the emotional pleasure of what one is hearing, if he knows the inner meaning of what is performed, and this harmony reveals. But those who do not understand harmony can only enjoy a surface gratification, even of the most common styles of music, and they are to a degree shut out from enjoying the grand creations of the great masters. The lamp of harmony makes light and clear to the mental vision the obscure passages, so that instead of a hazy mass of tone, one sees a clear field of beautiful emotional thought. The performer who does not know the science of harmony is much like a person reciting a poem in a language which he does not understand. No musical education is complete without a working knowledge of this important branch. It enables the performer to put both head and heart into his work, and that with a far greater intensity of expression. One cannot express that which he does not know. To thoroughly understand a passage of music is the best possible help to overcome both its technical and artistic difficulties. Gretry says, "Pearls do not float on the surface; they must be sought for in the deep, and that often with danger." The performance of an intelligent musician is always easily recognized. When hearing it, we are conscious that the artist has solved the problem, that he has been in the deep after the pearls.

Some of the direct and practical every-day uses of harmony are: It teaches the student to estimate music more at its real value, so that he will think the divine art something more than a mere fancy. It will help him to tell good from poor music. His taste will be on a solid foundation, and not an indefinable emotion. Music will be real to him, and not some ethereal thing dropped from the clouds. It gives ability to correct misprints found in every piece of music, thus saving the performer many a pitfall. It teaches scales and keys, an important bit of knowledge, too often neglected, for the performer should know in what key he is performing, and should recognize the modulations in his piece as he passes them. The more we understand a piece, the better we enjoy it. It fosters confidence and repose to know all about what one is playing. Harmony is an indispensable help in reading and playing scales, chords and arpeggios; it teaches how to modulate from one key into another, and how to make interludes. We all more or less play church music, and harmony fully prepares us for it. It is a great help in memorizing, for it classifies in groups what otherwise would be a hopeless mass of notes. It is easier to commit what is understood, and, to classify chords makes short work of a long subject, for music is made up of scales, chords, arpeggios, and these harmony teaches, so that we can recognize the common forms at a glance. To the teacher of music it is a necessity, for he must be able to explain, and to give reasons for his opinions and statements, and surely *he* should be able to talk about music in a common sense way. His opinions and judgments will be sought by friends and pupils because of his theoretical knowledge, his ready and correct answers, and thus he will increase his power, his reputation and popularity. A teacher of music cannot maintain a position in the profession without a working knowledge of his subject, for he must be able to teach it to his pupils, and here comes in the direct money value of his knowledge. Harmony is a great aid in helping us to accompany the voice in song. It enables one to transpose pieces to other and more desirable keys, and this is often indispensable to a singer or accompanist. Not the least of its advantages is the continual use one is obliged to make of harmony in the use of the pedals, and to use them correctly in a higher grade of music, the knowledge of harmony is indispensably necessary. In order that we may sing or play intelligently, whether as teacher or pupil, the study of harmony is needed. Whether you will become composers or not, it is a delight to any musician to note down his ideas. The skill to do this you acquire in the study of musical composition, and the knowledge of the forms and rules that underlie a tone poem, again enables you to better perform the works of the masters. Moreover no one can learn to improvise in correct style without a thorough knowledge of both harmony and composition. In fact the mastery of these branches makes you a skillful musician, a master in your art as player and as teacher. Of course, studying harmony and composition will not impart to you the gift of authorship, for that is inborn, but it enables you to develop and to use what gifts you may possess, and many students, after studying these branches, discovered greater talents than they supposed they possessed. At any rate you may accept it as a fact, that in these days of musical progress you cannot dispense, as teachers, with a knowledge of these two branches.

The rules of harmony and composition are deduced from the best works of the masters, and as the art advances, new laws must necessarily be established. A Wagner or a Liszt could not confine himself to those rules which we derived from the works of a Mozart, a Haydn, or a Bach, but the rules which these masters have laid down will be as binding upon the student of the future as they were binding upon these masters themselves. The modern composers have stepped over the boundaries of the past, and their works must be viewed in that light.

Practice must always precede theory. We do not lay down rules unless they have established their right to existence through practical demonstration in works of art. By far too many students are satisfied with mere practice, with mere technical production, but of intelligent musicians we make greater demands. A knowledge of theory is an indication of a higher education. It is not expected that you as teachers should be composers, but it is expected of you that you should be art teachers, and this implies a mastery of harmony and composition. If you lack the gifts of composition cultivate your powers as far as you can. By doing this, no one will dare to blame you for a lack of knowledge.

It is an old saying, that knowledge is power, and this is especially applicable to the study of harmony, for it gives power to the pianist. I hardly need to tell you that it is a comfort to the teacher to see students strive to acquire this power, hence there is no more important, and to me more interesting, class than the harmony class. A pianist without a thorough knowledge of harmony is, and always must be powerless. A little knowledge may be dangerous, but a little harmony helps a musician wonderfully. If you cannot study it for one or two years, study it as long as you can, get a little of it, for this is better than no knowledge at all. I am sure when you have acquired the little spoken of, you will desire more. When you once begin to enjoy the freedom which harmony affords you (for every pianist without this knowledge is handicapped), you are sure to cry for more liberty. A pianist cannot know too much, he cannot equip himself too well. The teacher without harmony is as a hoodwinked guide, he is helpless, he is sure to stumble and fall. He is shorn of power, hence he cannot impart it, he cannot educate pupils to that standard of freedom which alone affords true pleasure in art.

And now a few practical hints. It is absolutely necessary that you should advance slowly in these studies. Rapid work never amounts to much. The smaller and the more condensed the text-book is, the slower should our progress be, as viewed merely from the standard of pages to be read. As in geometry, in algebra, in logic, etc., the whole ground must be carefully gone over and thoroughly studied. It will not do to pick out certain lessons and neglect others; on the contrary, every lesson is of importance, every lesson must be mastered, else the results are defective. There are teachers who promise to take you over the entire field of harmony in a few lessons, but I frankly confess my inability to do this. A person may tell much in the course of a few weeks, but telling is not teaching.

But say some, "In the study of theory we enter too much into the mental and too little into the emotional nature of music, thereby losing its true enjoyment." This is as untrue and unsound as it would be to say that he who studies art, ceases to enjoy flowers or landscapes, or he who measures the stars and marks their course, will no longer enjoy the starry heavens in all their beauty. If the practical part of the art gives you so much pleasure, how much more delight would it afford you, were you to know its principles more fully. What if theory appeals preëminently to the mind, does it follow that there is no beauty in the study? Is there no beauty in mathematics, in geometry and trigonometry? Surely there is.

The rules of harmony are very simple and comparatively few. We have not many chords nor are there many inversions. We have only two, the major and minor modes, we have only the triad and fourfold chords, and their derivatives, and out of this simple material the grandest symphonies are built. Great intellect, of course, is needed to produce such works, but the intellect alone would accomplish nothing; the heart power, the inspiration is also needed. This is the power that leads man, as in a state of clairvoyance, to find those hidden paths, those mysteries of the art which the pure intellect, the reasoning faculties would never discover. Yet great as this power is, being divine in its origin, it must conform to law, to the rules of the beautiful. But say some pupils, these laws are oppressive, they hinder me in my work, they obstruct my path on every side, hence I am opposed to them. The same objections are raised by the evil doers against the common law of the country. Its authority obstructs their course on every side and for this reason they dislike it. The law does not impair or injure the rights of the good citizen; he is free under the law, for he chooses the good in preference to the evil. So he who has mastered the laws of harmony and composition feels not their restrictions; he is a free musician, for having studied the laws and forms, he knows and appreciates their force and value and cheerfully submits to them. He is a free man under the law. To rebel, therefore, against musical rules is an indication of evil inclinations, of improper musical conduct, and surely of ignorance. This opposition to the study of harmony should be the strongest reason why such students should at once commence to study it.

Have I succeeded in showing the advantages of this study? If so, do not you who mean to be thorough with your work, think you ought to devote the necessary time and labor to master it?

THE IMAGINATION.

The imagination is of such great value to the musician, not only in the capacity of composer, but in that of a player and singer, that it is a proper subject for our consideration. The imagination is that mental power which combines, creates and pictures; it enables us to produce new forms, new situations, and that without the aid of the senses. This, no doubt, is a defective definition, but it is almost impossible to define in one or two sentences such an abstract term, and it is especially difficult in view of the fact that this faculty is so varied in its relations and manifestations. When viewing it, however, in its relations to the arts alone, we have come close enough to its meaning to satisfy us. The imagination is that power which has created—using the term in a finite sense—all the great works in the domain of art, from the ancient times down to the present.

The imagination should be viewed in a twofold sense, once as a productive, and again as a reproductive faculty. The productive faculty is the higher of the two; it is the great power which distinguishes men of genius. The reproductive faculty is somewhat allied to memory, and it is exceedingly difficult to draw the line which divides them. The imagination is usually most vivid in youth, which is full of fancy pictures of the future. Young people often live in a fairyland; they dwell in air castles; they see everything in a halo of glory; the sun is golden, the flowers speak poetry, the rivulet sings, all nature speaks with a powerful voice to their imaginations. All events of youthful life are invested with a halo of imagination, and when we leave home and wander in strange lands, memory is aided by the imagination, and what seemed once very prosaic is now certain to be painted in poetic colors. Distance lends enchantment. It is the power of the imagination that draws men back to their old homes, even after many years of absence. The fancy pictures painted by youthful perceptions, and intensified by an ever active imagination, act as a magnet; they produce a longing that is almost irresistible. Alas! very frequently the reality proves that the imagination is guilty of exaggeration, is guilty of lying, and thus the spell is broken; the wanderer wonders how he could ever have experienced such foolish longings, and the realistic picture having taken the place of the idealistic, he turns away disenchanted and saddened. The same process occurs in life almost every day. Dreamy, imaginative youth sees a fairyland before it, but gradually and slowly the lesson is pressed upon the mind that the dreams of youth were mere fancy pictures, and that life is real, stern and often even cruel. Still, we love to turn back to youth as the ever-flowing fountain of joy and pleasure, and that simply for the reason that we cannot recall it, but we can bring before our minds the picture of our youth and our childhood home. But if we could see them as they really were, we would soon be disenchanted. Look at our own past. When reviewing life, we believe the past to have been happier than the present.

The older we become, the weaker is memory and the stronger becomes the imagination in drawing fancy pictures of youth and home. Imagination little by little wipes away all unpleasant recollections, and casts a perfect halo over the scenes that were pleasant.

The creative power creates that which had no existence ; the reproductive power brings before our minds scenes and situations which have already made an impression upon us, and it is this faculty which is of great aid to the pianist and singer, who are reproducing what the composer has created. Three qualities are required in order that the imagination may successfully perform its mission, namely, experience or observation, correct taste, and a good amount of enthusiasm. Experience and observation, because by it, we store our mind with pictures, scenes or situations ; good taste enables us to choose only that which is good and pure ; and enthusiasm, because without it the artist is unable to clothe his forms and visions with life, without it he fails to arouse observation and sentiment in others, without it his work will, in short, be lifeless. It is a fine question to decide which really is the art-work, the printed copy, or the performance of the same. It is a disputed question whether the musician in his performances should simply give the art-work as he conceives it to have come from the composer's mind, or whether he may be allowed to put upon it the impress of his own imagination.

Without wishing to enter into a discussion which is foreign to our subject, it may be said that the imagination is not the divine spark, yet it is no doubt one of the highest faculties of the human mind. The creative and the reproductive powers spring from the same source, they are much the same faculty, but of different degrees.

All intelligent persons are endowed with more or less imaginative powers. While only the few produce or create, all may reproduce situations and sentiments. Those who are permitted to open to us new scenes, to call forth new sentiments, are, as has been stated, our men of genius, they are the favored ones who may walk in and out at pleasure, among the gods on Parnassus Hill. But does not the inventor also produce that which is new ? Certainly ; but he does not work through the imagination. He employs reason, he starts out with certain tangible facts, he relies upon the laws of nature, he uses the unerring rules of mathematics and geometry, as well as the discoveries already made in the fields of science. The artist, however, fashions his work in a different workshop of the brain. Look at the Symphonies and Sonatas by Beethoven ! Where did the artist fashion these lovely productions if not in his imagination? All of you have read Shakespeare's "Midsummer Night's Dream ; " from whence than his fruitful imagination could such a production have sprung ? It may therefore be said, that the works of the useful arts are the products of reason, while those of the fine arts are the products of the imagination. They are truly created, as far as mortal man can create. Carl Maria von Weber said, "God allows man to create, so that through his creative activity he may show forth his divine origin."
The imagination first fashions, then produces. Next, memory retains and impresses upon the mind these productions. After this, and not until then, does reason discharge its functions, by sitting in judgment over the work of the imagination, applying the laws of harmony, composition and æsthetics. The study of these branches is therefore an absolute necessity, even to him who is gifted with the

most powerful imagination. He who lacks education, but has imagination, generally produces ill-shaped, defective works. Without education, without the rules of science, the most imaginative person is helpless, as helpless as he who has mastered all the laws of composition, but lacks the power of imagination. We must study the works of the masters in order to learn from them, as well as to awaken within us and to properly direct, the powers of our own imaginations. There are, however, some gifted with productive powers who abstain purposely from coming in contact with master minds, for fear their originality might be destroyed. Usually they are those who have but limited powers, and the children of their imagination are always hollow-eyed, hump-backed, bow-legged and whatnot else. Such originality surely is not creditable. Again, there are students who rebel against rules and laws, because they are restrictive, and in their estimation altogether too oppressive. The educated artist is as little fettered by the laws of his art as the law-abiding citizen is oppressed by the laws of his country. In order to make the operation of the imagination, in its relations to scientific musical laws, plain to you, let me say, that the imagination is to the artist what the sails are to the ship; they are the propelling power. His reason, applying the laws, is the rudder that steers the ship safely, the power that gives correct shape to his ideas. The imagination usually is set to work through sentiment, and when it is at work, the artist must be regarded as a sort of an involuntary actor. If the artist is gifted with great productive powers, if he is an educated man well drilled in the theory and practice of his art, if his emotions are pure and his aspirations noble, he will produce great works, but if any of these faculties be defective this defect is sure to be noticeable in his work. No matter how great the works are which the imagination has produced, this fact must always be borne in mind, that there is nothing perfect under the sun, nothing perfect can come from the human mind or hand.

It has been said that the useful arts are the product of reason and not of the imagination. Scientists often apply themselves so closely to their studies that the faculties of the imagination cease to operate freely. Dealing constantly with facts, they fail to cultivate the fancy, they neglect to give sway to the imagination. Having found it to be an untrustworthy faculty as regards their peculiar work, they have checked it whenever it showed signs of growing. This explains why scientists so often fail to grasp the true meaning of art, this explains why some of them have such a low view of it. From this it is plain, that scientists rarely ever become artists, while the artist would prove a miserable failure as a scientist. The one is exact to the minutest details, the other is a dreamer, he soars aloft, is at liberty to fashion the creatures of his imagination as he pleases. It is for this reason that mathematics and music are regarded antagonistic. Yet this need not be the case. Mozart, the great musician, whose imagination has created wondrous works, was exceedingly fond of solving mathematical problems, while the great Herschel, he who calculated the motion of the heavenly bodies with unerring certainty, started his life's career as a German band master.

The imagination always aims at something beyond the real, something without the world, and when it is at work, the artist dwells in an atmosphere foreign to real life. The affairs of this world then lose all interest to him; he is, as it were, spellbound, he is under art influences, and he looks at the pictures of his fancy as they appear in his imagination, just as men look at beautiful pictures. It is not surprising that at such an hour artists love to be alone, for they fear the intruder would disturb them and stop the work of their minds. Everything foreign to their mental and æsthetic existence is distasteful then. This spell is so powerful that men yield to it in the face of great privations; they deny themselves every creature comfort, in order to gratify their inclinations. The average man, however, laughs at all this; he calls the man thus under the influence of his imagination, a fool, a worthless fellow, lacking common sense, a man with a hobby, a man with one idea. Wagner said that a composer, when at work, is in a state of clairvoyance; the same should be true with regard to players, but to a less degree. When playing or singing good music we should be beyond the present, our imagination should be active, it should aid us in the performance of music. The musician must thus quickly turn from one picture of fancy to another; his whole self must be concentrated in what he sees or does; the world outside is, so to speak, dead to him. This concentration of self on one subject, this changing from one scene to another, explains the changeableness and moods of artists. Seeing an object of sorrow, they suffer intensely, while the next moment their tears may be changed into smiles; a pleasant object, like a sorrowful one, completely and quickly fills their souls and shapes their heart's emotions.

When I am about to perform music, I endeavor to concentrate my whole self upon what I am to play. If I am to perform a funeral march, I first strive to enter the house of mourning. There I see the dead one lying in his coffin, I see the floral offerings, and methinks I can smell the very tuberoses. I see before me the family of the deceased, with pain and sorrow depicted upon their faces, yes, I hear from time to time the moans and sobs which irresistibly escape their lips, breaking the monotonous and painful silence that pervades the death chamber. I hear the word of God read, I listen to the hymn of consolation, I see them close the coffin after the family have taken the last, sad glance, I see them carry the body out, I hear the creak of the hearse door, and a cold chill runs over me, as, in my imagination, I hear that terrible noise produced by placing the coffin within. I see the people standing on the pavement looking at each other with sorrowing faces, I hear the bells toll, I see the procession start, and thus I prepare myself to play a funeral march. When I hear that tender Aria from the Messiah, "He was despised and rejected," I see my Saviour's suffering face as he stands before Pilate, or as he is spat upon, mocked and struck by the rude hands of the soldiers. I see his forehead bleeding from the thorny crown, matting his hair, and staining his lovely face. A voice says "Ecce homo." The master's loving eyes look at me, and when I play the accompaniment, where the instrument moans and sobs, as it were, I often shed tears at the sorrowful sight before me. Then, when the song is ended, I feel a sense of contrition and sorrow, I hardly dare to speak aloud, I see my own waywardness that has brought all this suffering of sorrow and grief on this man. Oh! what a power is there in such a song, how it lifts us up and brings us nearer to God. Händel said, that when he wrote the Hallelujah chorus, he thought he saw the heavens open and the angels singing around the throne. So when I hear this strain, I stand on Calvary and I look up at the cross, and confess my own guilt, my lack of love.

When I hear a strain from the immortal Beethoven, I wander to that master's home, I see him dejected and suffering, I hear him complain of the hardness of this world, I hear him bemoan his deafness, I see him as a caged lion shut out from the world, and sadly I sit down by his side, and with awe and fear I listen to what he has to tell me. When I hear some of his strains I imagine him to be a Jupiter; then again his strains impress me as would the appearance of the ghost in Hamlet. Suffice it to say that my imagination is never idle, when playing this master's wonderful strains.

But listen to plain, simple "Home, Sweet Home." How natural it is for the mind to turn to the one spot dear to the heart. Oh! yes, I see the old homestead with the memorable apple tree before it; I see the flower-garden, so tenderly cared for by my father. I see the old rooms, with their quaint finish. Yonder sits father, while in the huge arm-chair rests dear, good mother, the crucifix by her side and the prayer book in hand. Alas, neither are living, neither of them shall I ever see again here on earth. And so I turn away from the spot linked only to memory, and come to my new home in free America, where all the home ties that bind men, bind me. Then I often think of those whose homes have been destroyed, of those that have no homes, of the outcasts, of the poor orphans, and my heart rises in gratitude because I am so richly blessed. And while thus my imagination is active, I also think of the truth, that our real home is in heaven above.

There is an air by Mozart, called "Non piu andrai." It occurs in the opera Figaro, in which a girlish-looking page, Cherubino, is caught in his tricks and wiles. He had been guilty of flirting with the ladies of the court, yes, even with the countess herself. At last he is discovered in the act, and his master takes him to account.

The page is a delicate boy of sixteen, with golden hair, and is clothed in silks and satins. The Count is a burly fellow and wears big boots and spurs, a sword, a big slouch hat, he has a long grizzly beard, a terrible voice and an awful look. He takes the boy to task, gives him a round scolding, tells him he has long enough turned the house upside down, has lived long enough in clover, that now he has to put on a military hat, wear a mustache, learn to smoke tobacco, go to war where cannons are fired and men are killed. All the while he shakes his finger at the page, who stands before him in great penitence, but as every now and then the Count steps forward in his excitement, as a soldier naturally would, the page becomes alarmed and steps back, and thus they are measuring the whole stage. The Count becomes at times sarcastic, talking about the sweet ringlets, and the fine sight Cherubino will cut when once in the army, but throughout the piece a commanding military tone is heard; here and there the effect is heightened by the sound of the bugle, while the whole has the character of a military march. All these scenes I see while listening to "None piu Adrai," and while hearing it I imagine myself sometimes to be the Count, sometimes I am poor Cherubino, and sometimes I am a spectator, and as I see the young scamp at last caught and frightened almost to death, I cannot help laughing at the ludicrous sight, and often do so while playing the accompaniment. At first reading the words of this song, they appear as nonsense, but when the whole picture is put together it is comical. Said a lady to me, "Why do you always smile when I sing this song?" "Oh," said I, "I laughed at what I saw, I laughed at poor Cherubino in his plight."

But let us turn from the opera and listen to America's sweetest song, "The Old Folks at Home." Though a negro song, it is worthy of a place in the portfolio of the best artist. I have seen slavery in its palmiest days, just before the war. I have lived in good old Virginia, where I saw some of the woes of the colored people, and when I used to sit upon the veranda of my southern home on a cool evening, and listened to the colored men singing "Hard Times Come Again no More," or "Old Kentucky Home," or "Old Folks at Home," I sighed and said, "O God, how long will all this last?" I have lived and moved among colored people, I know them and their sufferings, and I can understand them when they sing :—

"Way down the Swannee river,
   Far, far away,
Dere is where my heart is turning,
   Dere's wha' the old folks stay.
All up and down the creation,
   Sadly I roam,
Still longing for the old plantation
   And the old folks at home.

   All de world am sad an dreary,
     Ebrywhere I roam,
   Oh, darkies, how my heart grows weary,
     Far from the old folks at home.

"All around the farm I've wandered
   When I was young,
Then many happy days I squandered,
   Many a song I sung.
When I was playing with my brother,
   Happy was I;
Oh, take me to my kind old mother,
   Dere let me live and die.
     Refrain.

"One little hut among the bushes,
   One that I love,
Still sadly to my mem'ry rushes,
   No matter where I rove.
When will I see the bees a-humming,
   All around the comb,
When will I hear the banjo strumming,
   Down in my good old home.
   All de world am sad an dreary,
     Ebrywhere I roam,
   Oh, darkies, how my heart grows weary,
     Far from the old folks at home."

Plain though this song may be, it is full of tenderness; it displays Stephen Foster's loving heart and his vivid imagination. Southern planters claimed that this song was not second to "Uncle Tom's Cabin" in behalf of emancipation. Everybody in this broad land knew, and knows now, Foster's immortal melody, which is more than can be said of Mrs. Beecher Stowe's novel, great as its circulation was. This song always touched me deeply; it called forth my sympathies for the poor slaves, and it finally led me to go to old Virginia, to see and to study the institution for myself. Imagine, then, a quiet summer evening in Virginia; let us seat ourselves on the spacious veranda of a planter's mansion. Listen! from afar you hear the sweet melody appealing to your sympathy.

Among Mendelssohn's beautiful songs without words, there are several called Venetian Gondola Songs. Let us listen to one of these; but we must take a trip to sunny Italy. Let us go to Venice, with her palaces, her great churches, her watery streets, on which the gondolas or boats glide silently, carrying their living freight. They are long black boats, unsightly, but for all comfortable. The men who row them belong to an uneducated class, but, despite this fact, they, like all their countrymen, are singers, and often players of the mandolin and other instruments. Mendelssohn, who traveled in Italy, was no doubt impressed with the beauty of Venice, and in his fancy he produced these charming tone poems alluded to, calling them Gondola Songs. Thus, when I play one of them my mind goes to sunny Italy, and in my imagination I see Venice, with her streets of water and her beautiful blue sky. I hear the music of the boatmen, and whether my fancy-picture is correct or not it serves my purpose, it enables me to play and to enjoy the little tone poems to a higher degree. Listen to it, hear its passionate yet tender melody, and notice how, as the boat has passed away in the distance and the song is no longer heard, there is a spell left behind that holds you as in a dream; and after the little strain is ended, I sometimes sit spellbound and listen, as if I could still hear the gentle strain that has vanished so softly.

I have a little slumber song which I love dearly. Before I play it I often go to a quiet country home. There, on the rustic old porch, the mother has seated herself with her needlework; by her side stands a cradle, wherein lies her little treasure, about to take its afternoon nap. Oh, I can fairly feel the stillness of the day; I see the glorious sunlight as it falls on the thick vines that surround the porch, letting in enough light to throw the strangest and the most artistic forms of shadow upon the floor and wall. I hear the hum of the insects, I hear the distant voice of the ploughman, I hear the tinkle of the cow bell, and while the mother rocks the cradle she sings this sweet little air, called the slumber song. Listen to the accompaniment with its rocking, and then hear the sweet melody as it finally dies away, when the baby is asleep.

Only one more fancy picture I will bring before you and I shall pass on with my subject. Annie Laurie! What a charm there is connected with this tender love song. It may justly be called the world's love song, and, with his usual correct perceptions, Bayard Taylor, when speaking of the camp before Sebastopol, said,—

> "They sang of love and not of fame;
> Forgot was Britain's glory;
> Each heart recalled a different name,
> But all sang Annie Laurie."

When I hear this song I wander to the bonnie banks of Maxwelton, and there among the green grasses studded with the Scotch heather and the thistle, I see Douglas of Finnland, Annie Laurie's lover, wandering along casting shy glances at the windows of Annie's castle home. Alas, he never was permitted to lead to the altar the girl, whom he called the fairest that ever the sun shone on. She was given to another, and there is nothing left of their love here on earth except this song. Two hundred years have passed; thousands have died around the banks of Maxwelton; many monuments and graves have been obliterated, but Annie Laurie and Douglas of Finnland are still remembered, and their true love will reëcho in human hearts as long as the fires of love's passion burn.

From the foregoing you see that the true musician, when singing or playing, is out of the body; he roams in a land of fancy. This explains why musicians do not like to be disturbed by talking or walking while performing music, for not only does it indicate a lack of attention, but it destroys the spell. This also explains why, under certain circumstances, musicians are justified in refusing to play. Who would wish to perform any of the pieces given you before a talkative, noisy company? Having been at a funeral, having been with Beethoven, having seen the Saviour in his suffering, having tasted Mozart and listened to Mendelssohn, how could I now play a waltz, or how could I play any trifling composition? On the other hand, if I am in merry company, how could I attempt to play a dirge or a funeral march? Artists prefer to play before musicians, for there generally is sympathy and mutual appreciation, while it is often difficult to produce the same effect among the masses.

From the foregoing, you can also see the good that flows from pure music, if you will but rightly use that which is good. Oh, how often have I talked of these things, and how slow is the process of making lasting impressions, how slow is the work of awakening the imagination.

Let me beg you not to use poor music, not to abuse that which is good. Do not lower the art to the position of a mere plaything, to mere show-work. Seek the truth always and when you have found it, then prize it as a rich jewel. I would not have you understand that I have always such positive pictures before me as I have described; often we must be content with the awakening of pure sentiment, but pure sentiment in the course of time also leads to pure thoughts. The imagination of many pupils is too inactive, their emotions are too slow, they hear merely pretty sounds of music, they live yet in the state of infancy in artlife; had they the technique of a Liszt, they would produce merely sounds. But if the imagination is active, if sentiment is readily aroused, then simple music is just as much art music as the more difficult. Says Schumann, "If you listen at the doors of musicians, you may hear plain things well played." The average pupil, however, always aims at show first and at sentiment next. Let me ask you to reverse the order. Play a little thing well and you do more than by playing a most brilliant piece without sentiment.

And now by way of a close let me refer to a hymn tune written by Martin Luther. It always overpowers me, and I never play it without being deeply impressed. In my mind I turn to the reformer; I see him in distress; there are many who assail him, many who endeavor to undermine his work. He feels the terrible responsibility that is resting upon him, he feels his own weakness, he falls on his knees, in humility he prays to God for help. He pours out his inmost thoughts, he draws very near to his God, and with sobs and cries he says, "Save, Lord, bless and aid us, oh Lord, else all must go to ruin." All this I hear in this hymn tune, and the simple playing of it is to my heart a prayer, an act of worship. And thus you see how through music, even without words, we may sincerely pray.

By coming in contact with good music we are always elevated and refined, our imaginations are quickened, they are turned toward noble objects, our emotions are purified, love and sympathy are aroused; and let us not be unmindful of the fact that love and sympathy are virtues which religion teaches. To raise you to a higher sphere in art should be the object of a musical education; the power to play and sing are merely the means, and should never be regarded as the end.

Bear in mind that if you neglect the cultivation of the imagination, you neglect one of the very first elements necessary for the artist. Musicians should cultivate this faculty; they should not only study the music, but they should also learn to know its place in history; they should study the lives of the composers, all of which is calculated to give them keys to its fuller meaning; all this will enable the student to better understand an art-work. He who merely plays the tones of a sonata by Beethoven, he who fails to reproduce the inner meaning, fails in everything; his performance is as powerless and as meaningless as are the oft repeated prayers of mere religious formalists. Of course the imagination requires much culture and much care. It needs training from earliest childhood. Children have imaginations. The boy rides in cars made of chairs, or he builds houses with blocks, etc. The little girl plays with her dolls as if they were living children. A child's pleasures are largely dependent upon its imagination, and the same is true of grown people. Said an educator, "When a little child is asked in a school how many pints make a quart, it is often difficult for it to give quickly a correct answer. But let that little child in its imagination go with its pail to the store or the milk-wagon, and it instantly knows that two pints make a quart." It would seem that a power like this would receive the attention of educators; alas! many parents and teachers fail to comprehend the significance of this gift. They view it usually as a dangerous faculty, and no doubt such it can become by neglect or by false training. Our public schools aim too much at the cultivation of the reasoning powers and the development of memory, neglecting the imagination. Children are constantly called upon to imagine this or that, yet nothing is done to develop this faculty. There is no study in which it does not come into use. In professional life, others besides the artist need this power in order to be successful. The lawyer needs it, the editor needs it, and that minister of the gospel who can see the very heavens open before him, the minister who can soar to heights above, he is, all things being equal, also the most effective preacher. Yet it is only lately that the imagination receives any attention in our public schools. Many teachers, as well as parents, strive to exclude everything calculated to arouse this faculty; they strive to turn the child's mind too exclusively to practical things. This no doubt is the tendency of our age, and hence that of education.

The imagination is most active in youth; when riper years come, reason assumes control and men become critics, and cease to be poets. Still there are many instances on record showing that the imagination need not necessarily weaken with years. Xenophon wrote when 92 years of age. Æschylus wrote his best works in his 66th year. Sophocles wrote his Œdipus when 99 years of age. Michael Angelo painted his celebrated picture, "The Judgment," which displays the most wonderful flight of imagination, between his 60th and 70th year. So there are musicians who wrote their best works in advanced life. The imagination of these great men worked quickly, hence they were able to produce great works, and these are distinguished for their roundness and completeness, while slow working imaginations often produce mere patchwork. No faculty of the mind is more liable to go astray, and produce misery, than the imagination. It needs careful training, lest it descend into the fanciful and the incongruous. Of people who are afflicted in this manner we say that the wings of their imagination are too large for the tails of their judgment. They are people who imagine themselves sick or socially slighted on every occasion; people who imagine their enemies to be constantly endeavoring to do them harm. Of course they are miserable, and their sickly imagination is the cause of it. They constantly expect misery and want, and being in a state of torment, they make others miserable. Then there are those whose musical imagination is so vivid that they almost hear the grass grow while listening to Haydn's Creation. A certain musically inclined lady, living in London, went to one of Paganini's rehearsals, preceding a concert. Having failed to bring his instrument along, he borrowed one from a member of the orchestra, and, instead of playing, made merely a sort of a pizzicato, indicating the time in which he would play the piece. After the rehearsal this lady addressed Mr. Cook, the leader of the orchestra, saying, "Oh dear, Mr. Cook, what a wonderful man this Paganini is; I declare, that until this morning I absolutely knew nothing about music, I never knew what it is capable of." "Indeed," said Mr. Cook, "music is a great art, but allow me to say, that you are indebted to your imagination for this pleasure."

"How is this Mr. Cook?"

"Why, Paganini did not play at all, he did not even touch a bow."

"Extraordinary," replied she, "I am more than ever confirmed in my opinion of him, for if without playing he can affect people in this manner, how much more wonderful must be the sensation when he does play."

A certain great musician once was discussing musical subjects with Frederick the Great, and in the course of conversation they came to talk of the powers of the imagination. The musician boasted of his powers in that direction, saying, that he could imagine anything. In the meantime luncheon was served and Frederick, who was a little irritated because this mortal of a musician claimed to possess powers which his royal highness had not, turned to the musician, who looked with hungry eyes at the good things before him, and said, "Since you can do anything with your imagination, just imagine you have eaten a good meal." Nothing daunted, the musician kept on chatting cheerfully, as if nothing had happened. Taking pity on him, the king at last offered him some wine and confectionery, but the musician said sarcastically, "No, I thank your royal highness, I have partaken in my imagination of all the good things on the table, and dare eat no more, for fear of injuring my digestive organs." Perfectly surprised, the king said, "since you have such extraordinary powers of imagination, since you can do anything with it, allow me to suggest, that you mend your stockings with your imagination, for there are two big holes above your shoes." And with this he dismissed him. But I have said enough and will close by giving you a quotation from an educational journal, showing that this subject is attracting attention. "Great advantages," said the writer, "arise from cultivating the imagination. How shall we reach the people to benefit them if they have no imaginative culture? They are like oxen, they know only of food, of shelter, of warmth, they are out of our reach. The imagination furnishes us much of the happiness we enjoy; by cultivating it, we open new sources of pleasure and delight to mankind."

EXPRESSION

The external exhibition of our thoughts and emotions is termed expression. This exhibition may be accomplished in many ways, for instance, by words, looks, the voice, colors, musical sounds, etc. It is but natural that the thoughts we entertain, the sentiments we cherish, should eventually make an impression upon our faces. Hence we speak of the expression of the face, the expression of the eye; we say that the face of this person has a good expression, while that of another we abhor because it is bad. The Germans say that in the eye lies the heart, and for this reason we look into the faces, and especially into the eyes, of strangers, expecting there to find an exhibition of their characters. Shallow people look at the clothing or at mere outward beauty as an indication of character, and so shallow-minded people seek to establish character by means of outward appearances. It is to me one of the most interesting studies, as I pass along the streets, to analyze men's characters by looking at their faces, and while I realize the obligations of love toward all men, it is sometimes difficult for me to regard certain persons as human beings; their faces and manners are so repulsive and animal-like. A motionless face we fear, because it fails to give us a key to the character. Children are quick readers of faces, hence they turn with fear from those whose features are unsympathetic and stereotyped. Look at a child with a motionless face and it will turn from you, yes, it will show signs of fear and distrust, and if the little one is not taken away it will soon express its fear in cries. It is the expression of the face that draws or repels children. If, then, a person's character makes an indelible impression upon his face, it stands to reason the nobler a man's thoughts, and the purer his emotions, the better is his expression. There are faces out of which looks but goodness; one can almost imagine them to be surrounded by a halo of purity and gentleness. Others portray nothing but villainy, cunning, deceit, or vanity, or at best but ignorance and rudeness. As our faces are an exhibition of our thoughts and sentiments, so life itself is but an expression of our wills and actions.

But I mean to speak of expression in art, and more especially in music. Every art expression presupposes an art impression. Without pure art impressions, lofty and noble art expression is not possible. A genuine art expression is almost sure of making an art impression upon intelligent minds, no matter how feeble this impression may be. While, however, most people may be impressed through the arts, the power of producing such impressions is by no means very general even among intelligent people. All art must be measured by the amount of thought and sentiment it expresses; where these are lacking, art does not exist. Hence many play and sing brilliantly, yet they are not artists; their productions are not art works. The artist's inner nature must reveal itself in his art work, if it is expected to influence the souls of others. Mere brilliancy of tone and swiftness of execution, mere mixing of colors, mere jingling rhymes will not produce such results. The power to play and to sing with expression is therefore the ultimatum of every musician's work and education, and, so far as expression is concerned, all should be artists. An ounce of genuine art expression is worth more than a pound of technical skill or cold theoretical knowledge, simply because it speaks to men's souls, because it elevates them and affords pure and unalloyed pleasure. A player or singer whose powers of expression have not been developed, cultivated and refined, deserves not the name of musician.

If expression means an external exhibition of our thoughts and emotions, it stands to reason that, technical skill being equal, he who stands high in the scale of morality and intelligence, must surpass him who stands low in these respects. Good playing and singing, therefore, depend not only upon a musician's technique, but upon his intellectual and moral nature. Marx said that the practical musician is a seer, an interpreter of dreams. Schumann said that genius is only understood by genius, and Hoffmann expresses the same idea in these words, "the poet only understands the poet." Great men's ideas lie, not near the surface, like pebbles in a shallow stream, but they lie deep down, as the pearls at the bottom of the ocean. To reach these should be the student's object, and if he has found but one such pearl, he has done more for himself and his hearers than he who has sacks full of pebbles. The stock of pieces one finds in pupils' portfolios are like these pebbles, while one good piece is as a precious stone, more valuable than cart-loads of the other.

The power to receive art impressions, and to give expression to one's thoughts and sentiments through the medium of art, is not alike strong in all. That German philosopher was correct when he compared men's powers of musical perception to sounding lines, such as men use to measure the depth of rivers and seas. Some are exceedingly short, while others reach fathoms into the deep sea of art, yet there is no one that has reached the bottom of art. Many good people are capable of receiving art impressions, but it is exceedingly difficult for them to reproduce these impressions. Others lack culture, and it is about as unreasonable to expect them to be interested in art, and to be impressed with art ideas, as it is to expect the hard and uncultivated ground to produce lovely flowers; education is needed. Despite the fact that some persons know nothing about musical expression, they are often the loudest in their criticisms, and as a legitimate result, they indulge in a great deal of meaningless talk about correct expression. There are many critics who write for papers, musical and others, who readily detect a mistake made by the pianist or singer, but who fail to notice the grossest violations of the laws of correct expression.

Every composer aims to express his ideas and emotions in his art-work. The practical musician is expected to reproduce these, so that the audience may behold the beauty of the art-work. The player or singer is therefore the medium between the composer and the audience, and as such he must be conscientious toward both; by so doing he will necessarily be conscientious in the discharge of his own duty. Every player or singer should have a good technique, at any rate sufficient of it to overcome all the difficulties a piece of music presents. Next, he should be endowed with pure sentiment, in order that he may feel with the composer; and finally he should have a sound understanding of the best means to reproduce the composer's sentiments and thoughts. In the performance of a composition, the musician may merely reproduce the composer's ideas and feelings, or he may go a step further and put upon it the stamp of his own individuality, without, however, destroying the identity of the art-work itself. To do this effectively requires great skill and much native talent. The mere reproducer, say some, stands beneath the composer, while the artist who reveals himself in his performance stands by the side of the composer.

In the opinion of some, expression is possible only in large and showy compositions. This is a wrong idea. Expression is possible in the smaller forms as well as in the larger. There is power in the simplest thought, if it be good, just as the native lustre of a jewel is perceptible in the smallest fragment, just as magnetism is active in the smallest piece of iron.

Accept it as a truism, that you can never play with expression until you have overcome all the technical difficulties of a composition. You must be relieved of the thraldom of reading notes and watching expression marks, ere you will be free to yield to the spirit. Pupils should, therefore, not lay aside their old pieces as soon as they have learned to play the notes, for after this task has been accomplished there comes the second and greater task, that of catching and expressing the spirit. So in reality the student must study his pieces twice, and let me say that the second study is far more difficult and requires greater time than the first. Many teachers, and as a rule, most pupils, are contented with a mere correct performance, as judged from a technical standpoint; they neglect to aspire to a higher degree of artistic perfection—namely, that of playing with correct expression. Schumann said, that "Where the form is clear there the spirit also becomes clear," and Goethe puts the whole matter into a nutshell when he says: "Only what one understands, that one hears, and only what we understand that can we play readily."

PHRASES AND PERIODS.

Many musicians go to excess in their attempts at playing with expression. They disfigure any art-work, and, so to speak, turn the face of a saint into that of a clown. In the playing of such persons, one notices an undue swaying to and fro in the tempo; they use an excess of force, and go so abruptly from the piano to the forte that one's feelings are wounded. Of course, the true character of a composition is utterly ruined by such players. They use the pedal improperly; they phrase incorrectly or not at all; they fail to pronounce the melody well; in fact, their playing must be compared to an unintelligible scrawl. It is no wonder people fail to derive pleasure from such performances. Usually they wave their hands, move their bodies, turn their eyes, thinking to show great emotion, but all this is a mistake and should be avoided. Such sickly sentimentality has no affinity with art. The true artist is satisfied to let the art-work have its effect, and while speaking on this subject let me lay this down as an infallible truth, that a superior composition, well played, never fails utterly; it is sure to make some good impressions. Show-work may astonish for a time, but it will soon be denounced as such; true artistic performances, though unostentatious in themselves, are sure to find their way to the heart, their merit grows. Indulge, therefore, in no other.

To teach pupils, and especially young children, to play with expression is a very important part of a musical education. Doubtless most teachers are faithful in this particular; many I know, from observation, are not. There are those who claim that no special efforts should be made toward teaching children to play with expression. A teacher once said to me, "I aim at nothing but a correct technical performance with little ones." This teacher failed to comprehend the child's capacity. Had he better appreciated and understood children's hearts he would have pursued the opposite course. Let me add, that the early neglect of teaching children to play with expression has been the cause of pupils' absolute failure in later years. While the powers of expression may be developed and refined, they may also be neglected and weakened. The early development of expression need not lead to sentimentality; if a child should be inclined to go to excess the teacher can easily remedy the evil.

It is the observation of many thinking men that the heart power, the powers of sentiment, are too little developed among Americans. This does not imply that they are void of these gifts, but it does imply that our education is far too realistic and practical, and that by this course we are deprived of many of the more refined pleasures in life. This is the rock upon which the music teacher who is earnest in his work often founders. It is at times a slow and a most tedious process to till the ground which has been neglected for years; and it is at times painful to notice how anxious pupils are to learn to play with expression, but without immediate results. Pupils cannot always be impressed until after much instruction; and, as I have already said, where no impressions are made there no expression can be expected.

While some are readily impressed, others go away apparently empty-handed. Be patient, however, devoted ones, the light will sooner or later break in upon your minds; be faithful and your reward is certain.

Reading between the lines, and catching of the spirit requires much repeated hearing and playing. Sentiment originates within, but is very often aroused from without. The judicious teacher must use every means to arouse sentiment. Among these I would enumerate the reading of good books, especially of good poetry, looking at pretty pictures, the communing with nature, the hearing of good music, etc. All these agencies will help to develop sentiment, and if students were to hear some good music, only once a week, if they were willing to let its gentle rays fall upon their hearts, they would be happier and better for it, for it is sure to develop pure sentiment in them; it will make them more of feeling men and women, and as such they will be more useful and happy in life. Ah! music is not an idle play, it is not a mere empty pleasure, nor is it a love of display. There is a high and a noble aim we have in view, and that aim is to add to our culture and refinement. We wish to polish ourselves and others by listening to good music, we wish to arouse sentiment and cause it to overflow into life's actions, just as men dig down and bring to the surface a rich vein of water. The teacher, however, cannot give sentiment, no more than man can produce a vein of spring-water; he should however, develope it, and herein lies one of the great educational achievements.

All writers and musicians have acknowledged the superior and magic power of the human voice. The German writer, Schubert, said, "Song doubtless was the first article in the tone world, it is the axis around which everything in art revolves."

All instruments are imitations of the human voice. Song is the king who sits upon the throne, and before whom all instruments bow as slaves. The human voice is the first, the purest and the most perfect instrument in the world. To use this instrument properly and effectively, requires many natural gifts as well as true art-skill. To point out a few of these and to show how they should be used is the object of this paper.

Through its connection with the word, song is far more definite than instrumental music. While there is definiteness in the domain of thought, there is great uncertainty when we attempt to examine and to interpret our own sentiments or those of others. This is one of the main reasons why the masses, the musically uneducated, as a rule, do not enjoy instrumental music as much as songs. When launching out upon the vast sea of instrumental music, they are helpless, they find nothing to lead or to guide them in their interpretation of such music, while in listening to song, they have the words to guide them; they are the keys to the dark and hidden chambers of sentiment; they are comments upon music and explain situations. While the instrument and player are two separate beings, the one but a medium in the hand of the other, by which he expresses his sentiments, the singer and his instrument are closely united; they are one, indeed. This is the great advantage which the singer has over the instrumentalist, for through the medium of the voice all expression is direct and free. This is true only in speaking of a good and well trained voice. When Rossini said that the three requisites of a singer are voice, voice and voice, he was correct in one sense, for without it nothing can be done, without it there is no prospect, for teacher or pupil, of accomplishing anything. For all, it must be acknowledged that other powers beside that of voice are required to make a good singer. A person may have a good and well trained voice, he may have reached a high degree of vocal culture, and yet may utterly fail in an art performance. The singer must be a person of culture in order to appreciate points of beauty in a song, and to comprehend and see the situations as they are pictured in scenes and poems. The cold intellect, however, is not sufficient, for a mere recognition of points of beauty, the mere comprehension of situations will no more make a person a good singer, than the intellectual comprehension of Bible truths will make a person a Christian. Pure thought in itself is cold. Sentiment gives it life; it alone quickens. We must know the teachings of the Word, and we must love them and carry them out. Thought and sentiment are necessary in religion; so thought and sentiment are necessary for a singer's success, for without these the most perfect vocalization and technical training fail to move the soul within us. However, let us bear in mind that sentiment cannot discern, neither can it comprehend nor judge, nor hit upon the correct means to be employed to secure or to give proper expression, hence intellect and sentiment must combine, they must coöperate in the performance of an art-work. But these two factors need a third, namely, the imagination, that power which enables us, so to speak, to live ourselves in situations and conditions so that we become oblivious to the outer world. The singer, especially the one who expects to appear in opera, must be able to step out of himself; he must be able at any time to open and to enter the doors of grief or joy; he must possess the magic wand that transplants him into any situation desired. On the wings of the imagination he must soar to heights above, whither he draws his audience after him. If he possesses the powers of genius, if he has the intellect, the sentiment, the voice and the necessary cultivation, he cannot fail to attract; he will be a musical magnet, the power of which is irresistible to the human soul. The truest test of our musical faculties is the effect which they exercise upon others. If we awaken astonishment merely, we are far from being worthy of the title of artist, but if we silence the tongue, if we hold spellbound the ear and heart, if we call forth sighs and cause the tears to flow, with the charm of our performance, then we sing from the heart and to the heart, we speak with power of mind, we soar on the wings of the imagination, and we take with us on our upward flight whosoever is moved by us, and has the power to follow. In order to sing with expression, in addition to a good voice, therefore, three things are necessary, and these are a cultivated mind, depth of sentiment, and an active vivid imagination. He who combines these gifts is indeed highly favored. It is, therefore, not to be wondered that singers demand high salaries for their services, that they often become proud and are inclined to become jealous and quarrelsome. Yet the public and the press are too often to blame for these results, for both are guilty of flattering and indulging favorite public singers. Thus it happens that their modesty is often obscured, conceit becomes the ruling passion, making the possessor of the voice we love and admire an object disagreeable to us.

Song is linked to music and poetry. Song is merely a correct musical production of poetry. The singer, therefore, like the composer, should carefully study the words so that he may fully understand their meaning. In spite of the definiteness of the word, there may be various conceptions of one and the same poem. The various settings of one poem, as, for instance, Goethe's Erl King, proves this fact beyond a doubt.

Having fully entered into the spirit of the text, the singer should next study the melody and harmony, so that he may learn how the composer has treated the poem, and here let me say that it is best for the pupil to study first the melody and then the accompaniment. In his first studies let him confine himself to the study of the notes, and when these have been mastered he may also read between the lines, and put upon the music the stamp of his own conception and interpretation.

MAXIMS.

Waste neither words nor time.

Seriousness is the soil on which grows true artistic success.

The real happiness of a teacher lies in his love for his work.

Tune your hearts and tempers as well as your fiddles and pianos.

Music is the most subjective, the most intense and passionate of all arts.

The artist who loves himself better than his art is not worthy of that art.

Laziness is the cancer that eats out the life and prevents the success of many a talent.

Contact with the great may not make us great, but it makes us greater than we are.

Love your art, love the artist and the art-work, but beware lest you make idols of them.

Have respect for him who does well what he attempts, and does all that lies in his power.

If you do not put any heart power into your music, how do you expect people to feel it?

Never sink beneath professional dignity, nor rise above modesty and artistic simplicity.

A new and pleasing song or hymn tune is more contagious than the measles or smallpox.

Some men fly as high as eagles, but when they come down to you they are nothing but buzzards.

The musician needs character just as much as the theologian, the statesman, and business man.

Every one can hear the voice of nature, but he only hears music in it who has music in his heart.

Close observation is very apt to lead to success, on the part of the teacher as well as the pupil.

Many things are deserving of criticism, but not of condemnation. Condemnation is not criticism.

Egotism and conceit are two of the meanest rags hanging about the framework of the human character.

True art-culture passes only where it is understood. Common sense, shrewdness and wit pass anywhere.

The teacher who does not feel honored by the profession he follows, will probably not honor his profession.

Our affections for art should be very warm, but they should not be allowed to grow beyond our control.

Some people think everything is as defective and incomplete in art, as their own weak eyes behold it.

Coleridge said that some are like musical glasses; to produce their finest tones, you must keep them wet.

Only genius dares to set aside the old, only genius dares to overstep the conventional rules of the past.

As hot water hardens an egg, so constant and severe corrections and scolding harden a pupil's sensibilities.

If hollow heads were to hurt as badly as hollow teeth, many teachers would be better students than they are.

Music speaks from the heart and to the heart, it expresses emotions, but cannot describe scenes and situations.

What your pupil understands that he may remember. What he does not understand he is sure not to remember.

Fools pass criticism on everything that comes before them, wise men notice only that which is worthy of their attention.

Would you be successful in life, trust not in luck, but do your every day's duty well. So only will you achieve success.

Application and brain work; these are the only short cuts that lead to success in the study of music; there are no others.

As teacher, never discourage! Build up, impart new life wherever you can. Do not tear down and crush out aspirations.

The arts are like banks of roses placed by the side of life's weary course. How foolish not to rest thereon from time to time.

Never mind about your having no genius! Do what you can, do it as well as you can, and let the results take care of themselves.

As we grow morally better, we also view art more seriously, and so when the soul grows corrupt, we also corrupt art and abuse it.

Artists are as rare as diamonds. They must be polished before they show all their beauty. Life's cares usually do the polishing.

No progress is possible without a high aim, diligence and self-denial. This applies to progress in the arts as well as in morality.

Make your pupils think! That is worth more than stating a thousand facts. It is better than many lessons committed to memory.

Study music in order to beautify your own heart, and beautify your own heart in order to make this world more beautiful to others.

The way in which a correction is made has much to do with its effectiveness. Watch the tone of your voice and the look of your eye.

Love is the common ground on which art and religion meet. Without love, neither the one nor the other has any enduring powers.

When we think we usually cease to feel. Bear this in mind, ye learned musicians that come to concerts with scores under your arms.

"I know the subject of this lesson," said a teacher, with a good deal of self-satisfaction. That is well; but do you know the object?

There may not be as many bad pictures as there are bad songs, but the effect of a bad picture is far more serious than that of a bad song.

The musician who addresses the heart has the most hearers; he wields the greatest power; he is best loved and is longest remembered.

The improvisations of some organists are like much quartz with but very little gold therein. Improvisations of the masters are as solid gold.

The unjust critic does not love art. How can he love an art that comes from above, when he cherishes no love for his neighbor here below?

You may graft a tree and improve it after it has reached some growth; but the good artist springs up from the seed: you cannot graft him.

Music has no prototype in nature. It does not imitate objects, but it is a representation of life itself. It is totally independent of the other arts.

There are teachers and leaders of societies and choirs who are constantly in trouble, simply because they lack tact, because they know not how to govern.

Kings and emperors are rare, so are true artists. The former carry human crowns on their heads, the latter bear the divine stamp upon their hearts.

Encourage those who cultivate the beautiful, for their number is small when compared with the millions who are sadly in need of its benign influences.

"Some pianists ought to be very good people," says an old writer, "for their left hand never knows what their right one does—that is, upon the piano."

Oh, yes; your art enjoyments might be greater if only you yourself were greater. Your mind is too small a craft, is too easily filled, and draws too little water.

A music teacher may make light of his moral character, but he will sooner or later discover the fact that the public will not be indifferent to his every day life.

An artist is an artist, whether the rabble and the crowd recognize him as such or not. One ounce of inward self-consciousness is worth a pound of empty praise.

A workman's tool should always be in a condition for immediate use. So should the teacher's mind be kept sharp and active by study of art and literary works.

An hour lost is gone forever; but an hour ill applied is worse than gone forever, for it requires the labor of many hours to make good again what has been done wrong.

Very seldom does productiveness continue into old age. The youthful fiery mind is gradually cooled and tempered down to become mature, careful and critical.

We say men are accountable to God for the use of their means. Likewise teachers and editors are accountable for the use they make of their talents and of the arts.

Men have talked nicely about music, yet there is more sentiment in the child who sheds tears while singing a pretty song. Words come from the brain, tears from the heart.

All great minds are in the advance of their times. We ask not that music teachers be great men and women, but have a right to expect them to be at least up to the times.

To be worthy of praise and honor is more honorable than to be praised and honored. Strive first to be worthy of both, regardless whether you will be praised and honored or not.

Remember, dear fellow teacher, that if you are not advancing you are sure to slide back. What is not calculated to push you on is sure to be a load that hinders your progress.

The mere ability to play many pieces does not entitle a person to be called a musician. There is more needed than mere playing and singing in order to be worthy of such a distinction.

We generally dislike in music what is above our comprehension. When listening to a lecture, we are not apt to accuse ourselves of stupidity if we cannot understand what has been said.

First we build a house, and then we like to see it afford joy and comfort to its occupants. So composers write songs, first to please themselves, afterwards that others may take delight in them.

It is the teacher's duty to pour into his work all that is in him, all of his strength and love. If he withholds it, he is dishonest—and his dishonesty injures himself as well as his pupil.

Do your duty; be faithful; be generous and kind, and your hour is bound to come. Stand on the side of truth, and the world must come to you, for you have first come to God, who is the Truth.

There is much difference between teachers and musicians. Some give many things but not much of anything. Others give only a few things, but in these few things they bestow a great deal.

It would be foolish to throw away all ripe fruit that shows signs of decay, it is also unwise to criticise and to set aside wise men's minds, because they show mental weaknesses in certain directions.

The farmer must plow, sow, and cultivate his crops before he can expect to reap a harvest, yet many musical students expect to reap without preparatory work, and without the necessary hard toil.

See that you attempt only that for which you are fitted. Having found your field of usefulness, do your daily duty to the best of your ability, and realize that this is all of life. This road leads to success.

To trust one's own opinions and ways better than those of others, may, under certain circumstances, be an indication of individuality and strength of mental power; usually, however, it betokens conceit.

Opportunities rarely offer themselves twice; harvest and seed time come only once a year. Improve your opportunities faithfully; sow in time, so that you may also be permitted to gather in your harvest.

Many a man thinks he has a good case until he comes into the presence of a judge or a jury. Many a pupil thinks he has a good lesson until he comes into the presence of his teacher or before an audience.

To teach without much recognition, to labor contentedly for small wages, to work twelve and even more hours a day, hidden away in the school-room, requires a brave heart and a strong faith, say what you will.

Genius and talent are gifts, and it is foolish to boast of them. Show us your works and show us the gain you have made by the use of your gifts, and we will tell you whether or not you are deserving of honors.

Teach your pupils to think for themselves. Ideas do not grow in the skull as hair grows on top of it. There are many teachers who are mentally bald-headed, and, of course, they can only raise bald-headed pupils.

He who has no aspirations sees no shortcomings in himself. He who aims not to improve the world finds it, as a rule, good enough. This class of people take the world as it is, 'tis true, but they also leave it as it was.

He who works hardest values his efforts the most. Genius often comes easy by mental work, and hence is regarded but slightly. No matter how little he regards his own work, his art he always magnifies and adores.

All seeds do not spring up, and all your instructions are not productive of good results. It would be foolish for the farmer to fret himself because some seeds go to waste; and why should the teacher be less wise and reasonable?

It is better that as a teacher you should continue to long for improvement, without having your desires gratified, than that you should stand still, perfectly satisfied with yourself, feeling that self improvement is not needed.

Having eaten something unusually good, ladies look in the cook-book to learn how the article is prepared. A musical cook-book, a volume telling amateurs what pieces mean and how they are made, would have a good sale.

Everything good and pure must have its source in something better and purer, and so we may go backward and upward, when searching for the finality of the good and beautiful, until at last we find it concentrated in the Deity.

It is as great an error to treat some musicians with magnanimity as it is to treat others with severity. Some musicians are like dogs, they must see the whip; others are like spirited horses, the sight of the whip sets them wild.

Be a rational, thinking teacher, not a mere machine. Be a willing laborer, not a mere drudge. Be original, not a mere imitator. Be a leader, not a driver. Seek new and better paths, remembering that he who seeks shall find.

The emotions which are aroused by music in the hearts of some are much like those called forth by certain preachers in religious assemblies. They are mere nervous excitement. Neither true art nor religion have a part in them.

Most young people who make music their life's work seek self first, their own interests are dearer to them than the interests of art. It is proper to attend to our own affairs, but art should be of equal importance in the teacher's heart.

Talent is of great value to the student, but talent without work is as money that lies idle. It brings no interest and fails to be a means of support. Put your talents out on interest and endeavor to get the best per cent. for them you can.

Consider well, oh, critic, before you say bitter and unkind words. 'Tis easy to wound, but it requires years perhaps for the wound to heal. Always put yourself in the place of the artist whom you are about to criticise before you use severity.

Music expresses no definite ideas, but is a language eminently fitted for the expression of sentiment. What kind of music is that which neither awakens nor expresses sentiment? Music without sentiment is like religion without love!

Said a teacher, "This pupil is as hard as flint; you cannot get any fire into her playing." This may be your fault, dear teacher. Maybe there is no fine steel in your own make-up; or, perhaps, you are only soft iron, unfit to draw fire from a flint.

It is only a few years since the American pianist, Gottschalk, amused his audience by playing two tunes at the same time. If he were to come back to us, he would hardly dare to attempt such a thing again. Who brought about this change?

Measure not an artist by mere finger show or vocal flourishes. When listening to music, endeavor to feel the artist's pulse and try to see the lightning flashes of his brain power. These are the tests of artists, and they prefer to be tried by no other.

Cross words spoken with a smile, or pleasant words uttered with a frown, do not express the meaning they convey. The same is true of good music played by a trifler, or trifling music played by a learned musician. There is fitness in all things.

The scientist only makes new discoveries, he finds that which was hidden, but which already had an existence. The artist, however, produces new forms and ideas; in the finite sense of the word, he is a creator, and in this he stands near the Deity.

No matter how high we may rise in our art enjoyments, it is so ordained that we must return again to mother earth with all its thraldom and disappointments. Such pleasures are wisely allowed us only from time to time; it is our daily duty to live and toil.

There are few ideas in music, as in literature, that are entirely original. Our thoughts and sentiments play over into each other, like the shades of one and the same color. But, then, we admire these shades and praise him who produces them.

After the performance of a song, keep your mouth shut, so that other people may open theirs and speak in your favor. There are many singers who first do the singing, and then claim, also, the privilege of doing the talking—about themselves, of course.

There is One Being who has planned and made everything, and who rules and preserves everything. Why should not this rule apply to the arts? Truly God speaks through the arts as He speaks through nature, and its language is a call to come nearer to Him.

Do not fail to keep the old lessons bright, else you will be like the housekeeper who has but one clean room—the one she swept last. Go over the old work constantly, for reviewing makes perfect, perfection encourages, and encouragement leads to success.

Unless the pupil has a clear conception of the works of art he is to perform, there can be no clear expression. There is a twofold study, namely, that of the spirit and that of the technique. Many are satisfied with the latter, neglecting altogether the former.

He who is inspired in his work cannot be unhappy in it. If ever there is an occupation which is calculated to inspire men, it is that of teaching. He who enters his work without inspiration is a mere hireling, whose work will never be productive of great good.

You cannot carry a torch through a dense crowd without burning some one. You cannot drive your carriage over dirty roads without getting the wheels muddy. Neither can you edit a paper without meeting opposition and calling forth disapproval of some.

Let teachers in each lesson give one or two brief historic facts. Let these be stated in plain words, so that the pupil may understand and remember them. You will be surprised how much information can be imparted during a term or two by this simple method.

Keep calm, ye quiet workers who live in secluded places. Keep to the truth, do honest work, and let the results take care of themselves. It is better that you be worthy of honors than that you carry them unworthily. Keep calm, some day your work will be revealed.

There is no one so modest but that he likes to hear a word of praise and recognition. It is an error to withhold either for fear that the pupil will become vain. If it is your duty to point out shortcomings, it is also your duty to recognize merit. Be moderate in both.

A wonderful art is this of ours. It speaks to every heart, and that according to its own feelings. It addresses every intellect and teaches as much as the mind can understand. Yet neither head nor heart have ever exhausted the powers of music or reached its greatest depth.

Each teacher, like a mariner, is at liberty to take what course he chooses upon the vast sea of musical instruction. He has his chart, he has his instruments; let him use them judiciously. His speed and successful entry to the harbor will show what sort of an instructor he is.

The composer who minds public criticism, the opinion of the masses, tries to steer his ship according to the weather-vane. He will never go far in one direction, and in the end will be condemned by all for not making progress on the road of success. Mind your own affairs and go ahead.

Honor and reputation are two distinct things. Men may have honor but lack reputation, while many a man of reputation is devoid of honor. Honor grows in the garden of the heart; reputation grows in the commons of public opinion, and there it often appears as a worthless weed.

Some musicians seem to fail everywhere, hence they constantly complain of the hardness of fate and the treachery of the world. Let such remember that stones sink in water; corks and sticks, however float along. The world does not toss stones about; only windy foot-balls are kicked around.

Our peculiar mental construction often causes us to differ in our views concerning art, as well as in the enjoyment of the same. The one looks at it, as it were, through a green, the other through a red glass. Learn to see it without a glass, so that you may appreciate art in all its purity and beauty.

He only is entitled to criticise who fully comprehends the art work. Most critics merely search for faults and shortcomings, passing silently or perhaps ignorantly over all that is good, and this they call criticism. He who fails to realize the good in an art work has no right to point out its defects.

What if an architect cannot conceive the plan of a great cathedral or a palace? If he builds for us good comfortable houses we ought to respect him for what he does. What if a composer cannot conceive a great symphony: if he gives us good music for teachers' use, should we not honor him for what he has done?

It is an old saying, that all beginnings are difficult, but when applying this sentence to art, one may well add that both the beginning and the end are difficult. Our great pianists and singers have no easy task to keep up their professional standing. It is by no means easy for teachers to keep abreast of the times.

Some pupils are like those who take only a few bites of each dish. They taste many things and eat and drink until they have dyspepsia. So many pupils learn a little of this and a little of that piece they never digest anything well; their food does not nourish them; they cannot grow; they are musical dyspeptics.

There are too many mechanical teachers, men and women who merely assign lessons for the pupils to study, and hear recitations. There is not a spark of life or originality about their work. They go on to-day as they did yesterday, they use the same means with A which they apply to B. What can be expected from such teachers?

But recently, we noticed upon a concert bill the announcement that a certain singer had been heard by some of the crowned heads of Europe. It would have been more creditable to have boasted of having appeared before people that have something in their heads, than of having sung before people that have something on their heads.

Schopenhauer says that the amount of noise a man can support with equanimity is in inverse proportion to his mental capacity, and should be regarded as a measure of one's intellectual powers. He who habitually slams the doors instead of closing them gently is not only an ill-bred, but also a coarse-grained, feebly-endowed creature.

He who weeps over a pretty piece of music cannot be utterly depraved. Though his heart may be covered all over with rubbish, there will be found blooming in the little openings some gentle flowers, small and crippled, to be sure, but endowed with vigor enough to cause them to grow as soon as light and warmth are admitted.

Yes, yes; music is the art that best expresses emotion. That is good enough as far as it goes; but what are your emotions that music is to express? That is another question. And then comes still another. Do you know how to use an art as a means of expression? How many there are who display utter ignorance upon these points.

Stupidity and envy obscure many a man's good work. Stupidity we may pardon, but not envy. The first bears its own marks of recognition, the second is generally sly and deceitful. It is a mean man, who, seeing a greater light than himself, attempts to blow it out, or to put it under a bushel. Envy is a sure indication of inferiority, of a lack of culture.

The pupil who imagines that a superior teacher will carry him through without doing hard work himself is sure to be disappointed. Learn to stand upon your own feet, for you must walk over every foot of the road that leads to success. There are no stage coaches or bicycles that will take you there. If you covet success as a musician you must fight to attain it.

Many teachers regard work as a punishment, a task that causes them to moan and to fret. Why are you in the world? Surely not for the purpose of idling away your time. To work and to do something for the progress of mankind is a great privilege. If teaching is a task, quit it, and try something else. But if you are unwilling to do anything, then you hardly deserve to live.

Many persons are capable of receiving good art impressions, though they would utterly fail, were they to attempt to give expression to their impressions. Many newspaper critics, however, give expression to their views about art works, without having received any art impressions. They view art works as they would political speeches. Any one who listens, they say, can understand.

Seek always to see the bright side of your work, and be sure of this one fact, that there is a bright side. Do not look at the dark side of your professional labors. Look at its pleasures and not at its drudgery; look upward, not downward; look at your pupils with love, and not with a frown and an expression of despair. Thus alone will you do good, and be happy in your work.

Correct playing and singing is the work of years. It depends much upon mechanical accuracy, and this should by no means be neglected. But we would rather the pupil would make a few mistakes and let the light of his soul shine out of his playing, than that he perform a piece with a faultless technique and play without expression, without the voice of the heart being heard in it.

Those who have done much in life usually feel most keenly the littleness of their efforts and results. Those who have done but little usually are the conceited ones. They magnify their own importance, and one might let them alone in this particular, were it not for the fact that they are not satisfied with magnifying themselves. No, they must belittle others also. Contempt on such fellows!

Human nature is not always an agreeable subject for study, but all teachers must study it. Some natures are ugly, and some beautiful; some are as cold as winter, some warm as spring; some are prickly, as thistles, and others sweet, as violets; some are sly and venomous, as serpents, others are innocent, as doves. To adapt one's self to the different individuals is the real wear and tear of a teacher's work.

Only he who loves art for its own sake can endure hardships for it. Only the pure, unselfish love for art endures throughout life; it is like the waters of a spring, every day brings its own supply. He, however, who seeks only honors and riches in the domain of the arts, is a hireling; he flees when privations and difficulties stare him in the face, or having his desires, his love for the art soon wanes and dies out.

Critics should bear in mind the fact that there are other people endowed with just as good taste and correct judgment as they are. This will make them more considerate and truthful. Some critics seem to think that they alone have correct musical ears, while the rest of the people are not capable of forming a correct estimate of a performance. Such vanity often peeps out between the lines of newspaper criticisms.

A gardener was so absorbed in his cuttings that he failed to notice the arrival of a visitor. Upon seeing his friend, he said, "Pardon me, you see one must put his whole mind on these young things, if he would have them do well; and I cannot bear that one should die on my hands, for I should feel almost as if I had murdered it by neglect." Would that teachers could learn a lesson from this gardener and be as serious in their work.

It is the object of art to bring the beautiful down to man's heart and mind. There is but one source of the beautiful, hence all the arts are of one origin. In reality there is but one art, as there is but one virtue. Like the light from a great sun comes the benign influence of art. Men, however, separate its rays, claiming that one is brighter and more productive of good than another. The true artist loves art in its entirety and all its branches.

Some people's hearts and minds are like shriveled, yellow parchments. It is impossible to write intelligibly on them, much less possible is it to draw an artistic design on the rough surface. They must be smoothed out and bleached, before they can be beautified, and this preliminary educational process of smoothing out often requires a great deal of time and patience. Some hearts and minds, however, can never receive a smoothened surface on which to make pure art impressions.

The old Latin proverb says: "Repetition is the mother of study." If this is true of study in the literary fields, it is doubly true in the fields of musical culture. To keep bright what we have polished, to retain what we have earned and secured, requires as much and sometimes even more time and labor than it requires to gain additional skill and information. The fact that so many teachers forget this *repetitio* is the cause of their never having any well done work on hand, except it be the last piece.

The greatest artists and scholars best know the length of the road of learning; they remember the difficulties they have had to surmount. They are, as it were, standing upon a high mountain, from which they can survey the vast fields of learning yet unexplored. People who have progressed thus far in education, usually are modest. While they appreciate their own accomplishments, they are also aware of their shortcomings; they realize that a man necessarily leaves far more unlearned than he can master in a lifetime.

The reputation of many artists is but momentary. On the firmament of art, they appear as shooting stars. No matter how the sky may be studded with fiery orbs, the shooting star, for the time being, attracts everybody's attention! All cry, "See! See!" as it describes its fiery course on the sky. But notice how soon it is forgotten, never to be remembered! Yet by its side there shone all the while, the stars that gave their gentle light throughout ages, and whose course has been the object of study of many an astronomer.

"Every one who is worth anything must have enemies." These, or similar words, one often hears from the lips of those who have many enemies. The saying is only in so far true that those who are worth anything have enemies without offending people personally. There are many musicians who cannot live at peace with any one, simply because their manners are unendurable, and their tongues are unjust and unkind. Yet they always boast of the fact that they have enemies and regard it as an indication of personal worth. Such blindness!

Our Æolian harp was in the window, and the gentle evening breeze was playing upon the strings. Some children came by laughing and talking, but no sooner had they heard the soft tones of the instrument, than they stood silently and listened. A number of persons were talking in the room, when the sweet tones reached their ears. Though engaged in a lively conversation, they instantly became still and thoughtfully listened. Oh, Music! thou hast indeed great charms. Thy influence is more powerful and more general than that of any other art.

Warm sunlight is productive of growth in plant life, cold and chilling air destroys it. The growth of crops that required weeks of warm sunlight may be destroyed in a half-hour by icy rain. Compare your school-room or your lesson to the field, and see whether your conduct and your speech is like sunshine or like hail. Many teachers are like hail-storms in their intercourse with little ones. They are always severe and cold. Such teachers never raise good crops; they are not productive, but decidedly destructive. Severity may be needed, but it should be mingled with love.

Musical education, like all other mental progress, is of slow growth. Do what we will, the rosebud takes its own time to unfold. The same is true of the human mind. We may press the rosebud and force it to open, but the flower will not be as beautiful or as fragrant as it would have been had it unfolded in its own slow process. Neither will it be a healthy and enduring flower. Do not hasten the young mind, for this is a dangerous, unhealthy process. Too much work laid upon the pupil is often as injurious to the mind as too much water and heat for the plant. Give the child time for development.

The teacher should talk in his lessons; yes, he should be a good talker; but he should be far more than that—he should be a good teacher. Talking is not teaching. Beware of those who proffer to teach you all about harmony in a few days. They may tell you all about it, but they do not teach you all about it. There is a difference between telling and teaching. Some men may unduly lengthen the course of instruction in harmony, but no teacher can complete a course in a week or in a month. Yet there are teachers who claim to be able to do this very thing. A man may ride over a ten-acre field in a very short time, but it requires time to plough it well, and still longer to raise a good crop on it.

See to it that you well know what you wish to teach. Next endeavor to acquaint yourself with the best methods of teaching. Then study human nature, so that you may know how to control and how to stimulate to action those whom you are called upon to instruct. Be observing, so that you may realize whether your pupil is doing all he can do, and whether he is progressing as rapidly as he ought to. Last, but not least, keep the heart-fire burning within you, keep the love-light from going out; that is, love for pupil, love for art, love for truth, and love for mankind. By following these rules you are sure to succeed.

Those who devise methods usually claim that theirs are the only correct ones. There is more than one good method in teaching, and why should teachers become so wrathy when others differ from them in the way of doing things? The one-method idea does not serve in all cases. Neither human minds nor hearts can be pressed into one mould. There is great diversity in hearing and seeing, and also in appreciating. This world is full of diversity. No two trees, though of the same species, look alike. Different plants and animals require different treatment. Why should we deny this advantage to our pupils? Some teachers hang the coat of a method on all pupils' shoulders, whether it fits or not. Adapt the method to the child, do not endeavor to adapt the child to the method.

Do not only look at the world as it ought to be, but see it as it is. Of course, try to make it what you think it should be, but you will never succeed in doing this unless you know what the world really is. Have some object in view, have a definite plan with your pupils, and strive for that ideal you see before you. When you consider what your pupils ought to be, do not fail to study their real condition and see what they are. It is easy to find fault with pupils and with the world, but to make them both better, is quite another thing. There is no reward promised for the faultfinder, but there is a reward for him who corrects evils. This is the teacher's mission. By viewing your professional work from this standpoint, you will always find it interesting and honorable.

Are you cast down, fellow teacher? Give us your hand! Many times we have felt as if the world were, so to speak, boarded up, and our progress would be forever stopped! Many times we have felt as if we had lived in vain, and as if our work were but as dust. Yet, there comes again the night that is filled with music,

"And the cares that infest the day
Shall fold their tents like the Arabs,
And as silently steal away."

Bear up, fellow teachers, there is not a cloud but that is followed by sunshine, and while the cloud darkens your pathway, have faith in the sun and hope for its appearance.

www.ingramcontent.com/pod-product-compliance
Lightning Source LLC
Chambersburg PA
CBHW020904230426
43666CB00008B/1300